A MOST REMARKABLE MAN

The Life and Legacy of Daniel C. Jordan:
Musician, Philosopher, Psychologist, Educator

HARRY P. MASSOTH

ARCHWAY
PUBLISHING

Archway Publishing books may be ordered through booksellers or by contacting:

Archway Publishing
1663 Liberty Drive
Bloomington, IN 47403
www.archwaypublishing.com
844-669-3957

Edited by Harry P. Massoth

ISBN: 978-1-6657-2593-4 (sc)
ISBN: 978-1-6657-2594-1 (e)

Library of Congress Control Number: 2022911826

Print information available on the last page.

Archway Publishing rev. date: 10/19/2022

CREDITS AND ACKNOWLEDGMENTS

Articles from *World Order* magazine and the *Comprehensive Deepening Program* reprinted with permission of the copyright holder, the National Spiritual Assembly of the Bahá'í of the United States.

The chapter "Applying Knowledge of Human Development: New Dimensions in Parent and Teacher Education" appears in the book *Nutrition in Human Development* edited by Pattabi Raman and published in 1978 by Greylock Publishers. It is printed by permission of the publisher.

The book cover depicting the Anisa Tree of Life, based on the ANISA logo, was created by graphic artist in cooperation with the author. Anisa means "tree of life" and symbolically represents never-ending growth and fruition in the contexts of protection and shelter, and signifies the blending of the usable and fruitful past with a new sense of the future.

The exquisite portrait of Daniel Jordan was drawn in pencil by graphic artist Mindy Mendelsohn of Petaluma, California.

I am indebted to Keith Bookwalter whose e-document, "Who was Dr. Daniel C. Jordan? A Tribute," served as the template for chapter one of this book. His essay was not only inspirational but was chuck full of information.

I wish to thank David Langness, Mark Ochu, David Maytan, Judge Dorothy Nelson, and Arden Lee for sending me tributes and stories about Dan. I owe thanks also to Dr. Donald Streets for reading the preface and chapter one and making suggestions to improve the accuracy of the information on Dan Jordan's life.

Finally, I offer heartfelt thanks to Mindy Mendelsohn, Jacquie Richards and Linda Montgomery for their contributions of editing and proofreading the preface and chapter one of the manuscript.

Portrait of Dan Jordan

To Dan, his beloved wife Nancy
and their three daughters
Melissa, Sarah & Charlotte

CONTENTS

THEME AND VARIATION

(For Erma)

I

Fossile, fuchsia, mantis, man,
Fire and water, earth and air—
all things alter, even as I behold,
all things alter, the stranger said.
Alter, become a something more,
a something less. Are the reveling shadows
of a changing permanence. Are, are not
and same and other the stranger said.

II

I sense, he said, the lurking rush, the sly
transience flickering at the edge of things.
I've spied from the corner of my eye
upon the striptease of reality.
There is, there is, he said, an immanence
that turns to curiosa all I know;
that changes light to rainbow darkness
wherein God waylays us and empowers. (1)

Robert Hayden, *Collected Poems*

PREFACE

Just over one-hundred and seventy-five years have passed since the birth of the Bahá'í Revelation, the latest in a succession of messages from the Supreme Creator, God. It is assumed that most of the readers of this book will be familiar with at least the basic tenets of the Bahá'í Faith. The mere century and three quarters of its existence have witnessed its spread to the far corners of the world and, owing to the latest spate of inhuman persecutions of its followers in Iran since the revolution of 1979, it has regularly occupied an important place in the deliberations of international, national and local governmental and non-governmental fora concerned with the preservation of human rights, and has appeared in the headlines of the world's media. However, for those who hear of the Bahá'í Faith for the first time, know little about it and wish to learn of its history and teachings, there are many fine introductory books, some of which are listed in the bibliography. One can also access much information on the Bahá'í Faith through www.bahá'í.org and www.bahá'í.us.

It is important for the reader of this book to understand some of the background of the Bahá'í Faith in order to help the reader grasp the motivating impulse that drove Daniel Jordan to undertake the great task he envisioned—the goal of creating an educational system that might raise up a new race of men and empower them to address the great challenges of our age. Thus, I offer here a brief overview of the life and teachings of Bahá'u'lláh (1817-1892), the Prophet-Founder of the religion. The following section is an abridgment of the statement, *Bahá'u'lláh,* produced by the Bahá'í World Centre for the occasion of the centenary of the passing of Bahá'u'lláh.[1]

As the new millennium [dawns], the critical need of the human race is to find a unifying vision of the nature of man and society. For the past century humanity's response to this impulse has driven a succession of ideological upheavals that have convulsed our world and appear now to have exhausted themselves. The passion invested in the struggle, despite the disheartening results, testifies to the depth of the need. For, without a common conviction about the course and direction of human history, it is inconceivable that foundations can be laid for a global society to which the mass of humankind can commit themselves.

Such a vision unfolds in the writings of Bahá'u'lláh, the nineteenth-century prophetic figure whose growing influence is the most remarkable development of contemporary religious history. Born in Persia, November 12, 1817, Bahá'u'lláh began at age twenty-seven an undertaking that has gradually captured the imagination and loyalty of several million people from virtually every race, culture, class, and nation on earth. The phenomenon is one that has no reference points in the contemporary world, but is associated rather with climactic changes of direction in the collective past of the human race. For Bahá'u'lláh claimed to be no less than the Messenger of God to the age of human maturity, the Bearer of a Divine Revelation that fulfills the promises made in earlier religions, and that will generate the spiritual nerves and sinews for the unification of the peoples of the world.

If they were to do nothing else, the effects which Bahá'u'lláh's life and writings have already had should command the earnest attention of anyone who believes that human nature is fundamentally spiritual, and that the coming organization of our planet must be informed by this aspect of reality. The phenomenon lies open to general scrutiny. For the first time in history humanity has available a detailed and verifiable record of the birth of an independent religious system and of the life of its Founder. Equally accessible is the record of the response that the new faith has evoked, through the emergence of a global community which can already justly claim to represent a microcosm of the human race.

Bahá'u'lláh's writings cover an enormous range of subjects from social issues such as racial integration, the equality of the sexes, and disarmament, to those questions that affect the innermost life of the human soul. The original texts, many of them in His own hand, and others dictated and affirmed by their author, have been meticulously preserved. For several decades, a systematic program of translation and publication has made selections from Bahá'u'lláh's writings accessible to people everywhere, in over eight-hundred languages.

Central to Bahá'u'lláh's writings is an exposition of the great themes which have preoccupied religious thinkers throughout the ages: God, the role of Revelation in history, the relationship of the world's religious systems to one another, the meaning of faith, and the basis of moral authority in the organization of human society. Passages in these texts speak intimately of His own spiritual experience, of His response to the Divine Summons, and the dialogue with the "Spirit of God" which lay at the heart of His mission. Religious history has never before offered the inquirer the opportunities for so candid an encounter with the phenomenon of Divine Revelation.

Throughout the Near and Middle East, the nucleus of a community life was beginning to take shape among those who had accepted His message. For its guidance, Bahá'u'lláh had revealed a system of laws and institutions designed to give practical effect to the principles in His writings. Authority was vested in councils democratically elected by the whole community, provisions were made to exclude the possibility of a clerical elite arising, and principles of consultation and group decision making were established.

At the heart of this system was what Bahá'u'lláh termed a new Covenant between God and humankind. The distinguishing feature of humanity's coming of age is that, for the first time in history, the entire human race is consciously involved, however dimly, in its awareness of its own oneness and of the earth as a single homeland. This awakening opens up a new relationship between God and humankind. As the peoples of the world embrace the spiritual authority inherent in the guidance of the Revelation of God for this age, Bahá'u'lláh said, they will find in themselves a moral empowerment which human effort alone has proven incapable of generating. "A new race of men" will emerge as a result of this relationship, and the work of building a global civilization will begin. The mission of the Bahá'í community is to demonstrate the efficacy of this Covenant in healing the ills which divide the human race.

Bahá'u'lláh died at Bahjí, [a mansion near 'Akká, Israel,] on May 29, 1892, in His seventy-fifth year. At the time of His passing, the cause entrusted to Him forty years earlier in [the darkness of Tehran's pestilential dungeon,] the Black Pit, was poised to break free of the Islamic lands where it had taken shape, and to establish itself first in America and Europe and then throughout the world. In doing so, it would itself become a vindication of the promise of the new Covenant between God and humankind. For alone of all the world's independent religions, the Bahá'í Faith and its community of believers were to pass successfully through the critical first century of their existence with their unity firmly intact, undamaged by the age-old blight of schism and faction. Their experience offers compelling evidence for Bahá'u'lláh's assurance that the human race, in all its diversity, can learn to live and work as one people, in a common global homeland.

PART ONE
DAN JORDAN:
RENAISSANCE MAN

O Son of Bounty!

Out of the wastes of nothingness, with the clay of My command I made thee to appear, and have ordained for thy training every atom in existence and the essence of all created things ... And My purpose in all this was that thou mightiest attain My everlasting dominion and become worthy of My invisible bestowals ...

  Bahá'u'lláh, Prophet-Founder of the Bahá'í Faith, (1817-1892)

Son of man, bathe thyself in the ocean of matter; plunge into it where it is deepest and most violent; struggle in its current and drink of its waters. For it cradled you long ago in your preconscious existence; and it is that ocean that will raise you up to God.

  Teilhard de Chardin, Jesuit Priest,
  Paleoanthropologist, (1881-1955)

CHAPTER 1

---◆·●·◆---

WHO WAS DAN JORDAN?

When the great Italian astronomer and the father of modern science Galileo Galilei, around the year AD 1610, peered through his telescope and confirmed the Copernican heliocentric theory that the earth orbited the sun as opposed to the geocentric theory that the sun and all the stars orbited the earth, he set in motion a revolution that would reverberate through the ages. Building upon this theory, scientists such as Sir Isaac Newton and Albert Einstein would eventually lay the scientific foundation for humankind to put a man on the moon and send spaceships to the distant planets and stars in just a few more centuries. It is on the shoulders of giants such as these—Plato, Aristotle, Copernicus, da Vinci, Galileo, Newton, Darwin, Curie, Einstein, and a few others—that science progresses. We all benefit from the advances, discoveries, and social changes made by the giants that lived before we came along. We metaphorically stand on their shoulders because their genius, their tremendous achievements, and their hard work allowed us to progress to the point we stand today. These giants are sometimes referred to as polymaths or Renaissance men, due to their wide variety of talents, interests, and accomplishments. About fifty years ago I was privileged to meet such a man. His name was Daniel Jordan.

As I recall, it was in the spring of 1970. I was enrolled in a program at the University of South Carolina studying music education and early childhood development. I had also recently been invited to serve on a committee to help coordinate a two-day conference being sponsored by NABOHR, the North American Bahá'í Office for Human Rights, that was to be hosted by Benedict College—a local, predominately black school. The theme of the conference was "Education for a New Age."

On the opening day of the conference, I sat in the crowded auditorium in rapt attention as the President of Benedict College, Dr. Benjamin Payton, and the Dean of the School of Education of the University of Massachusetts, Amherst, Dr. Dwight Allen, welcomed the attendees and offered opening remarks. Then Dr. Daniel C. Jordan, Director of the Center for the Study of Human Potential at Amherst, gave the opening address on the theme of the conference, "Education for a New Dispensation." I sat enthralled as I listened to the charismatic Dr. Jordan paint a picture of the challenges and opportunities facing educators as the world prepared to enter the twenty-first century. Dr. Jordan presented the vision of a new educational model called Anisa, being developed by his staff at the Center for the Study of Human Potential, that they felt had extraordinary possibilities for meeting the needs of young children and young adults as they embarked upon the future. I was greatly inspired by this vision as I reflected on my own goals to pursue a career in education. Little did I realize at the time that I would have the privilege of getting to know and work with Dr. Jordan on several occasions within the next decade.

Just who was Dr. Daniel Jordan, this slight but intensely energetic man with such an extraordinary vision of the future?

Born June 2, 1932, in Alliance, Nebraska, the fifth of six children, Daniel Clyde Jordan, charmingly referred to by his Irish wife, Nancy, as Dan'l, and known as Dan to everyone else, was a child prodigy who at the age of nine was considerably on his own financially, paying, for example, for his own piano lessons. At the age of thirteen he began his musical studies on organ at the University of Nebraska. Already there were the makings of a life based on dependability, determination, and the accumulation of acts done for the right reasons. Dan's musical talents soon had him playing for social events all over town. He played for the Rotary and Kiwanis clubs, the Elks and Odd Fellows, the Eastern Star, and Job's Daughters, as well as his own Methodist Church and the Interreligious Council. Through these experiences he gained a great deal of knowledge and appreciation for the diverse innerworkings of his rather small community of around eight thousand people.

Dan's experiences around the community also led to his first crisis of faith. He tells how he was a very active and devoted Methodist and attended church regularly. On one of his outings, he visited his father who was carving tombstones as one of the many jobs he did to support his large family during the Depression. Dan happened to cross the tracks on the wrong side of town and came across an old wooden building that turned out to be the meeting hall of the African Methodist Episcopal Church and noticed that black people were holding a service there. Curious about what was going on at the church, he queried his father about this and asked him why those black people were not invited to attend their much more luxurious church. His father was quite embarrassed by Dan's inquiry and could not come up with a very good answer. Dan got to thinking about this and decided that religion with its teachings on brotherly love was not all that it was made out to be, and in his own words, "I threw the baby out with the bathwater." Much to his parents' chagrin, he decided to become an atheist at the young age of about sixteen and began reading challenging literature such as David

Hume's *A Treatise on Human Nature,* Thomas Paine's *Common Sense,* and Bertrand Russell's *Why I'm Not a Christian.*

Bertrand Russell (1882–1970), a British philosopher, had a profound effect on Dan's view of religion and life in general. Russell argued very persuasively through his writing and speeches that religion was merely a fallacy, and—notwithstanding any positive effects that religion might have on a person's emotional or psychological well-being—the concept of religion is, for the most part, detrimental to people. Bertrand Russell resolutely believed that religion and a religious point of view served to hinder knowledge and cultivate emotions of fear, anxiety, and dependency all of which were a hinderance to human growth and psychological health. He also held that religion was to blame for the war, coercion, tyranny, and misery that have weighed down the world.

Fortunately, Dan did not remain an atheist for very long. In 1950, at the age of eighteen, he matriculated to the University of Wyoming in Laramie where he continued his studies majoring in applied music and minoring in French. While at the university he was befriended by an elderly lady, Charlotte Gillen, who was studying international relations. Dan was struck by this "extraordinary woman" who soon had Dan stopping by her basement apartment in the evening to enjoy soup, hot chocolate, freshly baked cookies, and a dose of a book written by the Bahá'í Prophet Bahá'u'lláh titled *The Hidden Words.* Dan was so enchanted by the vivacity of Mrs. Gillen and the teachings of the Bahá'í Faith that he soon began to shed his atheistic beliefs and contemplate the possibility of converting to the Bahá'í Faith. However, he was cautioned by one of his professors to steer clear of that "offbeat religion" if he wanted to pursue his career in music. At the time, Dan decided to take this advice to heart.

Charlotte Gillen played another significant role in Dan's life. When he was a sophomore in college, she urged him to apply for a Rhodes Scholarship. He did so but was turned down. Mrs. Gillen pressed him to apply a second time. This time he was accepted and became the first American to be awarded a Rhodes Scholarship for music. At Oxford University in England, he earned both a bachelor and masters of arts degree in music composition, theory, and history, and he began his doctoral studies in musicology at the same institution.

While at Oxford Dan found that he was finally able to satisfy his unquenchable appetite for knowledge, as he could enroll in any class he wanted. In doing so, not only did he greatly extend the breadth of his knowledge, but he also met many fascinating people of all walks of life from around the world and representing many different faiths and points of view. This convinced him that no one culture or religion had a monopoly on the truth. He also began attending meetings hosted by a small group of Bahá'ís, which led to his enrollment in the Bahá'í Faith in 1954, and his spiritual life immediately began to affect everything he did. In 1956 his musical studies were interrupted when he was drafted into the US Army in which he served as a specialist in the Judge Advocate Generals Corps, stationed in Germany giving musical performances in Germany, Holland, France, and Austria. Recently married, Dan and his new wife, Nancy, often hosted meetings for GIs seeking counseling or fellowship. Dan served in the army from 1956 to 1958. During this time, due perhaps to his exposure to the precepts of the Bahá'í Faith as well as the courses he had taken at Oxford, Dan began to sense that there might be other important things to dedicate his life to than just music.

At this point Daniel Jordan made a critical decision that would change the course of his life. Turning down an offer to play Beethoven's *Emperor Concerto* with the Oslo Symphony Orchestra, which most likely would have set him on the tour circuit as a concert pianist, Jordan changed his career direction to human development and began collegiate studies again at the University of Chicago. In 1959 he completed the course work for his bachelor's degree but did not take the final exams because he already had two BAs. From

1959 to 1960 he earned a master's degree in human development - an interdisciplinary course of study that examined the development of the human organism from conception to death from biological, psychological, sociological, and anthropological perspectives. In 1964 he obtained a Ph.D. in human development with specialization in social anthropology and psychology. He went on to carry out a post-doctoral sequence in brain structure and brain chemistry and their relation to memory, emotion, and learning. During this time, he kept up his musical skills by playing piano for various Bahá'í events. Dan conceived a program where he would create musical analogies based on Classical themes to demonstrate various Bahá'í principles—a program that captivated the imagination of the audience. Over time this program was recorded as "Keys to Harmony" which was distributed widely among the Bahá'í.

Dan's doctoral dissertation, *An Experimental Approach to the Jungian Theory of Archetypes,* turned out to be unique in the annals of the field of psychology. Inspired originally by a dream Dan had of a shriek of bats attacking him, killing him, and then his being transfigured, like the mythical phoenix, into an ethereal being, Dan was later inspired by the work of the famous Swiss psychologist Carl Gustaf Jung to test his theory of archetypes one of which, the archetype of Unity or the Self, Dan believed the dream represented. To test the theory Dan created a 27-minute ballet in three scenes to which he wrote the musical score and scenario. The ballet, choreographed by his friend Dom Orejudos, was titled *Metamorphosis of the Owls.* In the ballet a parliament of eight owls kill a beautiful nightingale and carry it off to a cave where they engage in a ritualistic orgy. Seven of the owls leave the cave but one of the owls becomes enchanted with the dead nightingale. In its turn, the nightingale is resurrected and transforms the enchanted owl into a bird of paradise. When the other owls return to the cave they too are transformed, and the ballet resolves in joy, harmony and unity illuminated by a flood of light. To test his hypothesis that the ballet, designed as a psychoanalytic tool to differentiate between introverts and extroverts, was an archetypal stimulus, Dan created a series of circular designs, mandalas and non-mandalas, that the audience was to evaluate before and after the performance. Dan's hypothesis was that the ballet would affect people in such a way that they would change their attitude toward the designs such that they would select more mandalas over non-mandalas. His dissertation ultimately won Honorable Mention in the Creative Talent Awards sponsored by the American Institute of Research. In the process of developing his thesis Dan corresponded with Carl Jung on several occasions and had planned a meeting with him that was, unfortunately, thwarted as Jung passed away just prior to when the meeting was to take place. As it turned out, Dan's dissertation was one of the most elaborate and expensive projects ever carried out at the University of Chicago. The money was raised through ticket sales to the performances of the ballet with the proceeds being matched by a few anonymous donors.

In1965 Dr. Jordan became the Director of the Institute for Research in Human Behavior at Indiana State University in Terra Haute where his principal project was the Upward Bound Program for disadvantaged high school students. In 1968 he joined the faculty at the University of Massachusetts, Amherst, as the director of the Center for the Study of Aesthetics in Education, the director of the Tutorial Program for Minority Students, and the director of the Comprehensive Study of Compensatory Education in Massachusetts

It was from 1971 until 1977 that Dr. Jordan, with the invaluable collaboration of his long-time friend, former doctoral student, and administrative assistant Dr. Donald Streets, directed the Center for the Study of Human Potential at the University of Massachusetts. His principal endeavor at the Center was the ANISA Project in which he guided the conceptualization of a comprehensive educational system organized around a philosophical base—primarily the organismic or process philosophy of Alfred North Whitehead (1861-1947).

(The term "ANISA" has two meanings. It is an ancient Greek word meaning "the tree of life" and "symbolically representing never-ending growth and fruition in the context of protection and shelter, and signifies the blending of the usable and fruitful past with a new sense of the future." It is also an acronym that stands for American National Institute for Social Advancement, a non-profit organization the aim of which was to promote the ANISA Model of Education.) From this process philosophy foundation—a philosophy further supported by a review of the major concepts of the "nature of man" gleaned from some 2,500 years of philosophical literature--a coherent body of theory concerning development, teaching, curriculum, evaluation, and administration was generated. Dr. Jordan also guided the fielding of the ANISA Model of Education in Hampton, Maine; Suffield, Connecticut; Fall Rivers, Massachusetts; Kansas City, Missouri, and in southern Ohio.

In 1978 Dr. Jordan became the Chairperson of the Department of Education at the California American University in Escondido, California. In 1979, via the timely intervention of Dr. Donald Streets, Dr. Jordan joined the faculty of National University, San Diego, founded the University's School of Education and became its dean. The move was timely as the Department of Education at the University of Massachusetts was unable to support the ANISA Model's further development. Needing to strike out on their own, Streets and Jordan presented the ANISA Model to several prestigious universities around the country with the hope of implementing the ANISA-based school of education. The universities of renown turned a "deaf ear" to the proposal. The fledgling California American University was chosen but proved to be too small for the resources required. National University, newly founded, fastest growing, and one of the most innovative universities in California at this time, was contacted. Interest was expressed but hesitation followed. Dr. Streets intervened, reminded them that Jordan was a Rhodes Scholar and an upcoming figure in the field of education. The proposal was accepted and the ANISA-based School of Education was founded. During the same year Jordan was appointed to a "blue ribbon" National Task Force on Nutrition Education for Pregnant Women, Lactating Mothers, Infants, Children, and Adolescents which was jointly sponsored by the Department of Health, Education and Welfare, the U.S. Department of Agriculture, the White House, the National Institute of Health, and the National Association for Nutritional Education.

At the time of his passing in October of 1982 at the age of fifty Dr. Daniel Jordan was at the peak of his career. He had established at National University an accredited master's degree program, a university-based laboratory school for kindergarten through high school, and was on the verge of obtaining accreditation for a doctoral program. He had obtained a contract with the Association for the World University to develop their curriculum and was in the process of founding the International Center for Human Development the purpose of which was to serve as an international "think tank" for generating solutions to stubborn, national and world problems. All these programs were based on the concepts underlying the ANISA Model.

This chronology of Daniel Jordan's professional life needs to be supplemented with other miscellaneous notes of interest. During his undergraduate studies he was the recipient of several awards: Phi Sigma Iota Award for highest grade average in Modern Languages, Phi Mu Alpha Award for work in music, Phi Kappa Phi and Phi Beta Kappa Awards for highest grade average in graduating class, and the Theodore Presser Award for music. He was an authority on the work of Carl G. Jung and had a deep understanding and was an outstanding interpreter of the ideas and philosophy of Alfred North Whitehead. He gave courses, conducted seminars, and lectured extensively on both of these individuals and their ideas. In 1959-1960 Jordan worked as an orderly on the psychiatric ward at the University of Chicago's Medical Clinic and in 1975 he obtained a license to practice psychology. In addition to his extensive and varied consultant work, he was the guest lecturer to over seventy universities throughout the U.S. and other countries, and was the speaker or panelist on over two-hundred television and radio programs including popular talk shows over national networks such as The Dinah Shore Show and The Mike Douglas Show. In the area of the arts, in addition to being a virtuoso on the piano, Daniel Jordan had expertise in dance, drawing, musical composition, and film making. As already stated, as part of his doctoral work he wrote and directed a ballet for which he wrote the musical score and scenario.[1]

Dan's religious life and services were also deep and extensive. In 1962 he was elected to the national governing body of the Bahá'ís of the United States, called the National Spiritual Assembly, on which he served, often as chairperson or vice-chairman, for twenty years, until the time of his death. He was a frequent speaker at Bahá'í schools and workshops. One of the courses he developed was on the subject "Your True Self" that eventually became a pamphlet and booklet entitled *Becoming Your True Self* which can be found on the internet. He was also the project supervisor for the *Bahá'í Comprehensive Deepening Program* that was used throughout the country. Dan estimated that he devoted nearly forty hours a month to his religious activities. As a philosopher Dan was committed to the Bahá'í principle of the essential unity of religion and science. He was in full agreement with a statement made by the Universal House of Justice that if religious leadership was to arise to meet the needs of the soul and those of society, "such response must begin by acknowledging that religion and science are the two indispensable knowledge systems through which the potentialities of consciousness develop. Far from being in conflict with one another, these fundamental modes of the mind's exploration of reality are mutually dependent and have been most productive in those rare but happy periods of history when their complimentary nature has been recognized and they have been able to work together."[2] For Dan, "the insights and skills generated by scientific advance will have always to look for the guidance of spiritual and moral commitment to ensure their appropriate application; religious convictions, no matter how cherished they may be, must submit, willingly and gratefully, to impartial testing by scientific methods."[2] Dan practiced this concept both in his religious and academic work and it is reflected in all his writings.

ANISA: A Mission-driven Enterprise

It must be emphasized that the ANISA Educational project wasn't simply a novel idea that Dan Jordan came up with to build his own reputation as an innovative educator. Rather, he was responding to what was perceived by forward-looking social scientists as a crisis in education. As early as 1967 George A. Miller wrote an article entitled "Some Psychological Perspectives on the Year 2000" which pointed out that education would have to undergo a radical change if it were to shape the future in positive ways:

> If we are to remain true to our democratic heritage, one of the more obvious implications of the predicted increase in population is that our already crowded educational system will have to be vastly expanded and overhauled.

> Put together the increased number of students, the increased knowledge to be communicated, and the increased duration of the educational experience, and then try to imagine what kind of educational system we will need by the year 2000. Can anything short of an educational revolution meet our needs?[3]

To Miller's observation, Jordan raised a couple of questions of his own. "What would be the source of the needful change? Do we know enough to bring it about?" He goes on to point out that the truth of the matter is that we have an extraordinary amount of knowledge about the development of human beings, how they learn, and how they grow. Libraries are filled with books on education. But for a lack of a unifying principle it all remains undigested and therefore not very usable. He quotes the poet Edna St. Vincent-Millay who he feels put her finger on the problem:

> Upon this gifted age, in its dark hour Reigns from the sky a meteoric shower of facts; They lie unquestioned, uncombined. Wisdom enough to leach us of our ills Is daily spun, but there exists no loom To weave it into fabric.[4]

"The poet's pessimism notwithstanding," wrote Jordan, "there exists now an educational project that gives the promise of functioning as the loom on which may be woven the fabric of a new educational system—a system that may be able to make use of that 'meteoric shower of facts' by organizing them around the spiritual nature of man. This new educational model, or blueprint, now in the initial planning stages is called ANISA … The ANISA model rests on the premise that man was created to know and to love and out of various combinations of these two capacities spring all the potentialities which it is the obligation of an educational system to develop."[5]

Dr. Nancy McCormick Rambusch, founder of the American Montessori Society and fellow founder of the ANISA Model makes reference to Dr. Jordan in her doctoral dissertation as follows:[6]

> "The impulse behind the development of the ANISA Model came from within Daniel Jordan, its architect. It was a response to the broadest

assessment of existing cultural and moral conditions and existing education options within them, that he developed the model. As Dan himself wrote in an essay published in 1970:

> 'At the present time the world of humanity and the different cultures it represents are in the midst of the most extensive crisis ever known to man. The ways we have learned to feel, think, and act are no longer functional ...
>
> These crises are forcing humanity to seek a new culture, one that is universal and therefore functional for all men everywhere, one that can create a new race of men, new social institutions, and new physical environments.'[7]

There was no external pressure on Daniel Jordan to develop the ANISA Model. He was impelled by a personal sense of urgency to do this. The public problem which served as the basis for his action was his perception of the world as being in a state of collapse; his response was the formulation of an educational model which aspired to create 'a new race of men.'"

In another section of her dissertation Nancy Rambusch states:

"Dan Jordan was in a situation similar to that of Montessori before she left the University of Rome and struck out on her own to franchise her own educational model. The university setting represents a free market of inquiry. To work within a university setting is to invite criticism and evaluation. Dan Jordan was willing to do this, as Maria Montessori was not. He was the ANISA Model; the ANISA Model was he, in the sense that he was its ultimate interpreter as well as proximate 'manager.' The model was fully articulated in its essentials, prior to diffusion and it was fully realized in its essentials in the person of Dan Jordan. Dan was the 'center' of the center."

Dr. Rambusch also made a sadly parallel yet inspiring comparison between Daniel Jordan and Mahatma Gandhi:

"It [the ANISA Model] might also be considered, in its educational guise, as a social movement … Those drawn to participate in the ANISA Model came both because of the stunning intellectual clarity that informed it and because of the opportunity it offered them to work with Daniel Jordan, its propagator. A rare person and genuine innovator, Dan Jordan can be compared to Gandhi in his effect on those working close to him, as I perceived the relationship."

Just how was the ANISA Model developed?

Over a ten-year span, Jordan and his colleagues reviewed the most significant philosophic works as the basis for theory construction. As already stated, the organismic philosophy of Alfred North Whitehead generated, in their estimation, the best framework for analyzing and synthesizing knowledge about human growth and development, including the concept of purpose. In order to design a new educational system that is coherent and comprehensive (i.e., to be able to unite every aspect of human experience) required a philosophy that held promise for a new ideological base. Whitehead believed that "philosophy" is the endeavor to frame a coherent, logical, necessary system of general ideas in terms of which every element of our experience can be interpreted. His process philosophy, which is integrating and all-inclusive, nevertheless keeps any system open to new data with no claim that this system is final. Whitehead's system is a synthesis of both Eastern and Western streams of thought. However, it is not eclectic; the synthesis was seen as providing the basis for an educational model with cross-cultural implications.

Charles Hartshorne (1897-2000), currently the most outstanding process philosopher, makes the following observation on Whitehead's philosophy:

> "...one may say the basic principles of our knowledge and experience, physical, biological, sociological, aesthetic, religious—are in this philosophy given an intellectual integration such as only a thousand or ten-thousand years of further reflection and inquiry seem likely to exhaust or adequately evaluate."

Jordan in his review of the major philosophers, therefore, discovered an organizing principle for a science of education in specific form from the cosmology of Whitehead's book, *Process and Reality*. For Whitehead, the most pervasive characteristic of the universe is change. Change means process, and process presupposes potentiality. This for Jordan served as his first principle, the concept of process as the translation of potentiality into actuality.

It is interesting to note that this organismic concept had profound implications for the theory of evolution. The modern Darwinian theory of evolution is essentially materialistic holding that there is no objective or purpose in the evolutionary process. As one prominent Darwinian evolutionist puts it: the world is not at all the kind of world we would expect of one that was subject to the design of a creator. "On the contrary, if the universe were just electrons and selfish genes, meaningless tragedies like the crashing of [a] bus are exactly what we should expect, along with equally meaningless good fortune. Such a universe [ruled by evolution] would be neither good nor evil in intention. It would manifest no intention of any kind. In a universe of physical forces and genetic replication, some people are going to get hurt, other people are going to get lucky, and you won't find any rhyme or reason in it, nor any justice. The universe we observe has precisely what we should expect if there is, at bottom, no design, no purpose, no evil and no good, nothing but blind, pitiless indifference.,,.DNA neither knows nor cares. DNA just is and we dance to its music."[8] By contrast, the ANISA view of evolution based on the concept of "process presupposing potentiality" put design and purpose back into the picture thus sounding the death knell to the mechanistic philosophy originating from Newtonian physics and promulgated by Darwinian evolutionists. The ANISA definition of cosmic evolution offers a new paradigm of evolution that has a spiritual basis: i.e., "cosmic evolution can be described as the progressive advance into novelty, complexity of organization and actualization of enfolded possibilities, with matter (geogenesis), life (biogenesis), and mind (noogenesis or genesis of consciousness) as distinct thresholds or boundary conditions separating different ontological levels."[9] And where does man fit into this scheme of things? The ANISA Model agreed with Teilhard de Chardin's assessment that "[man] is not the center of the universe as was naively believed in the past, but something more beautiful. Man is the ascending arrow of the great biological synthesis."[10] Man is, in essence, evolution become conscious of itself—a perspective that puts man in charge of his own destiny.

Jordan viewed science as more than knowledge. A science of education could not be created until the massive information available about human growth, development, learning, and behavior could be organized into usable form. Jordan found such a principle in Whitehead's concept of process; this provided him with a basis for deriving a set of concepts that could be used to organize current knowledge about human development. This offered the possibility of translating it into a coherent body of theory that could serve as the substantive body of knowledge for professional educational practices. With such an empirical scientific footing, educational practice could be evaluated and continually refined. Analogous to medical practices, which are based on the biological sciences, education could then make more accurate predictions with a consequence of improved accountability. The end result of this would be the implementation of a genuine "science of education."

Jordan and his colleagues in establishing a coherent body of theory that addressed all aspects of education (i.e., human development, curriculum, pedagogy, administration, etc.) attempted to test every newly developed theoretical concept against relevant empirical studies available from the literature of the biological and behavioral sciences. Based on this broad and theoretical foundation, the beginning of a comprehensive and coherent model of education was generated.

An Untimely Death

It was around October 19, 1982, and I was contemplating the words I was going to use to introduce Dr. Jordan at the 2nd National Conference on Youth Violence to be held at the University of

Nevada, Reno. He had been a guest speaker at the 1st National Symposium the preceding year and his talk had been received with such enthusiasm that he was invited to be a keynote speaker at this year's event. I was also reminiscing over the fascinating talk he had given a few years earlier during a panel discussion with a Jewish Rabi, a Moslem, and a Christian at Reno's Center for Religion and Life on the topic "The Dawning Religious Renaissance."

I was suddenly interrupted by a phone call from a friend that sent a shockwave through my system. "Harry," she said in a tremulous voice, "did you know that Dan Jordan is dead?"

With those few words, my heart sank and my soul began to hurt tremendously. How could this be? Dan had recently turned fifty; he and his wife Nancy had three young children to look after; and the ANISA Project had at long last grown into a national movement. He had reached the pinnacle of his career and he and Donald Streets, along with a number of other dedicated colleagues, were on the verge of finally achieving some of their lifelong goals.

The next day, Edward Gargan of the *New York Times* wrote:

> A body found Saturday morning in a parking lot in Stamford, Conn., was identified last night as a dean from a California university who had been missing since he arrived in New York City Friday night, the police said.
>
> The dean, Dr. Daniel Jordan of the School of Education at National University in San Diego, had been stabbed to death with a sword, according to a federal source close to the investigation, and was identified by his wife, who had flown in from the couple's home in Escondido, Calif., Sunday night after her husband was reported missing.

The Federal Bureau of Investigation has formally entered the case.

Dr. Jordan's body was found at about 11A.M. Saturday face down at the rear of a parking lot in a commercial area of Stamford, according to Lieut. Joseph Falzetti of the Stamford police. He had been stabbed in the neck and his spinal column had been severed.

The dean arrived at La Guardia Airport from Minneapolis and was scheduled to speak to the Association for the World's Universities at the New York University Club on West 43rd Street the following morning, according to Lieutenant Falzetti.

Dr. Jordan, a Rhodes Scholar who received his doctorate from the University of Chicago, was appointed to dean three years ago. He was known for his work with the Anisa process, which stresses a "holistic approach to education," according to the university's president, Dr. David Chigos.

"It is an enormous loss to the university," said Dr. Chigos. "He was probably the most competent educator in my 30 years in education. He had this enormous capacity for work. He was a man with a mission."

In addition to his academic duties, Dr. Jordan was a high official of the Bahá'í Faith, a religion with more than 100,000 adherents in the United States and with roots in Iran, where Bahá'í has 400,000 members. –*New York Times,* October 21, 1982.[11]

Dan's murder was never solved despite being investigated by nearly 50 F.B.I. agents. With more than four decades now gone, we may never know the answer to that question. Dan's death remains a mystery.

We do know, though, that the Bahá'í world, the world of education and humanity itself suffered a profound loss with Dan's passing. A true visionary and genius, he left us an enormous legacy— but he had so much more to give, had he lived.

Dan's grave is in Stamford, Connecticut's Long Ridge Union Cemetery. His tombstone depicts the Tree of Life, and says "When the swords flash, go forward! When the shafts fly, press onward!" --Bahá'u'lláh

Dan Jordan's memorial service was held on December 13, 1982. Hundreds of his friends and colleagues were present. The spirit of the gathering was pensive, yet high as Dan was so dearly loved. One of the Bahá'í readings expressed the thoughts of many:

> *Wert thou to attain to but a dewdrop of the crystal waters of divine knowledge, thou wouldst readily realize that true life is not the life of the flesh but the life of the spirit. For the life of the flesh is common to both men and animals, whereas the life of the spirit is possessed only by the pure in heart who have quaffed from the ocean of faith and partaken of the fruit of certitude. This life knoweth no death, and this existence is crowned with immortality.*

One of Dan's friends, David Hoffman, a member of the Universal House of Justice, the Bahá'í International governing body, dedicated a poem to his memory.

O thou magnificent bird of the Western world, beloved Daniel. How endless your talents, your efforts, your vision, your light. Now gone from this wretched plane. How we yearn to trade our lives for you.

O thou magnificent bird of the Western world, beloved Daniel. You were so meek, so kind, and yet so powerful in your presence. You whose energies will ever be awe-inspiring. Now gone from this wretched plane. How we yearn to trade our lives for you.

O thou magnificent bird of the Western world, beloved Daniel. How tirelessly you labored, how diligently you struggled. How earnestly you endeavored and helped to raise us all to wondrous heights. Now gone from this wretched plane. How we yearn to trade our lives for you.

O thou magnificent bird of the Western world, beloved Daniel. What vile, contemptible soul has stained itself with your precious blood? What hateful viper dared stretch forth his hand to foist you from this earthly cage? Or was it but a mindless pawn in the hands of Fate or Destiny? Now gone from this wretched plane. How we yearn to trade our lives for you.

O thou magnificent bird of the Western world, beloved Daniel. Methinks I sense you already one of the eternal Concourse Awaiting the call of one and all who knew you well, or just a little. How many thousands of living souls must we touch to find another gem of similar quality? Now gone from this wretched plane. How we yearn to trade our lives for you.

O inhabitants of this gloomy globe. Grieve not for me For I am home though ever in your midst. Rather, raise up in His Name such a clamor that the skies will open And your nether world will find its connection to our heavenly palace. Go forth and teach. Raise up your voices. Remember me.

Yá Bahá-u'l-Abhá!

—*In memory of Dr. Daniel Jordan by David Hoffman*

Replanting Dan Jordan's Educational Legacy at Stanford

Do not allow your minds to dwell in the present, but with eyes of faith look into the future, for in truth the Spirit of God is working in your midst. –'Abdu'l-Bahá, *Paris Talks*

In February 2016 a group of Bahá'ís presented the archives that contain the life's work of educator, psychologist and philosopher Daniel C. Jordan, the creator of the ANISA Education Model, to the Stanford University Libraries.

Delivered personally by Dr. Jordan's widow Nancy Jordan and his education collaborator Donald Streets, the archives and materials contain more than a thousand documents, tapes, files and films spanning Jordan's remarkable career in education, philosophy, human development, music and psychology. The archives include Jordan's early work on the holistic, Bahá'í inspired

ANISA Education Project; his personal correspondence with major historical figures like the psychologist and writer Carl Jung and the inventor and thinker R. Buckminster Fuller; and his doctoral work at the University of Chicago in human development, social anthropology and psychology for which he wrote and directed a ballet accompanied by musical score and scenario,

"I couldn't be more pleased," Nancy Jordan, Dan's widow, said, "now that Dan's important work has found a permanent home here at Stanford."

It is interesting to note that Stanford has a long history of Bahá'í activity. During his trip to the United States, Stanford University hosted with the blessings of their president, David Star Jordan, a visit and a major address from 'Abdu'l-Bahá, son of Bahá'u'lláh, the prophet and founder of the Bahá'í Faith. Addressing the entire student body and faculty on October 8, 1912, 'Abdu'l-Bahá said:

> The greatest attainment in the world of humanity has ever been scientific in nature. It is the discovery of the reality of things. Inasmuch as I find myself in the home of science—for this is one of the great universities of the country and well-known abroad—I feel a keen sense of joy ...

> The highest praise is due to men who devote their energies to science, and the noblest center is the center wherein the sciences and arts are taught and studied. Science ever tends to the illumination of the world of humanity. It is the cause of eternal honor to man, and its sovereignty is far greater than the sovereignty of kings. The domain of kings has an ending; the king himself may be dethroned; but the sovereignty of science is everlasting and without end. Consider the philosophers of former times. Their rule and

dominion are still manifest in the world. The Greek and Roman kingdoms with all their grandeur passed away, the ancient sovereignties of the Orient are but memories, whereas the power and influence of Plato and Aristotle still continue. Even now in schools and universities of the world their names are revered and commemorated, but where do we hear the names of bygone kings extolled? They are forgotten and rest in the valley of oblivion. It is evident that the sovereignty of science is greater than the dominion of rulers. Kings have invaded countries and achieved conquest through the shedding of blood, but the scientist through his beneficent achievements invades the regions of ignorance, conquering the realm of minds and hearts. Therefore, his conquests are everlasting. May you attain everlasting progress in this center of education. May you become radiant lights flooding the dark regions and recesses of ignorance with illumination.

God has created man lofty and noble, made him a dominant factor in creation. He has specialized man with supreme bestowals, conferred upon him mind, perception, memory, abstraction and the powers of the senses. These Gifts of God to man were intended to make him the manifestation of divine virtues, a radiant light in the world of creation, and source of light and agency of constructiveness in the infinite fields of existence.[12]

In 2012, on the 100th anniversary of 'Abdu'l-Bahá's visit, the Stanford libraries established the first university-based collection of materials on the Bahá'í religion in the United States, beginning with the initial donation of the Jack H. Lee and Arden T. Lee Bahá'í Collection, one of the most extensive private libraries of materials related to the Faith. The collection includes thousands of books, letters, photographs and rare, out-of-print early Bahá'í publications.

"Don Streets and Nancy Jordan have been dear friends of my parents for nearly 60 years," said Shirin Lee Coleman, Jack and Arden Lee's daughter. "Dan and Nancy's entrusting of their personal treasures from Dan Jordan's life in the Jack H. Lee and Arden T. Lee Bahá'í Collection at Stanford is a full-circle expression of their mutual friendship and respect, especially when these treasures could have been gifted to any of the other academic institutions Dan Jordan was affiliated with, such as Oxford or the University of Chicago."

"The addition of Dr. Jordan's archives is a great addition to our Bahá'í collection and will provide resource for students, scholars, and researchers far into the future," said John Elits, curator for the library's' Islamic and Middle Eastern collection.

As 'Abdu'l-Bahá said about the great philosophers and immortal educators a little more than a hundred years ago, "Even now in schools and universities of the world their names are revered and commemorated."

Some Tributes to and Anecdotes about Dan

What follows are a few comments made by some of Dan Jordan's students, colleagues, and Bahá'í friends. They are not extensive, yet they serve as flashes of light in the darkness, illuminating briefly the various facets of one of God's very special souls as perceived by those who loved and admired him.

David Langness, a professional journalist, describes in detail two memorable meetings with Dan Jordan, "a most remarkable man."[13]

One of the truly wonderful things about being a Bahá'í: The people you meet.

As a young Bahá'í growing up in Arizona, I had the privilege and joy of meeting and getting to know some really remarkable individuals. Because the Bahá'í Faith is so diverse and so varied, with people from literally every culture and every walk of life, I met Navajos, Hopis and Apaches; I met physicians and construction workers; I met comedians and CEOs; I met black activists and Hispanic great-grandparents and Pacific Islanders; I met musicians and writers; I met Persians and Tongans and Kenyans and Alaskans and Russians; I met enthusiastic kids and accomplished adults and wise elders. Most of all, the friendly, warm Bahá'í I met showed me something I never encountered before—they were all serious, creative people trying to change the world.

For me, discovering the Bahá'í community and the remarkable people it contained was a revelation in and of itself—it opened my eyes to the enormous latitude of possibilities and pathways I could potentially choose from.

When I encountered the Bahá'í community and began to meet and get to know its incredibly diverse array of very different and yet very united people, I became intensely curious about their lives. When I met someone who interested me at a Bahá'í meeting, I developed the (probably quite annoying) habit of quizzing them about their life path. Like a budding but not very savvy teenage journalist, I asked them how they decided to do what they did; what experiences and inner convictions brought them to their spiritual path in life; and who they really wanted to be when they grew up. One of the most fascinating Bahá'ís I ever asked my questions to turned out to be a musician, educator and philosopher named Daniel Jordan.

I met Dan one night at a Bahá'í fireside—a casual introductory meeting where he spoke about the Bahá'í principles. A slight, intense man who wore black-rimmed glasses, Dan first played two classical pieces on the piano, where he had obviously developed a high level of expertise. At that time, I had no clue about classical music, but I could see how Dan's fluid and powerful playing emotionally affected the audience, so when they gave him a standing ovation, I stood up too.

Then Dan delivered an erudite, witty, insightful talk about Bahá'u'lláh's vision of a future state of human society. In his short, enthusiastic presentation, he laid out the blueprint of a unified, peaceful future world—a world where racial prejudice and hatred had disappeared; where swords had been beaten into ploughshares; where national borders had been erased; where women and men were finally equal; where science and religion agreed; where a universal auxiliary language allowed everyone on Earth to communicate with each other; where love and kindness and human creativity flourished. He asked us all to help bring that beautiful vision into reality. At the end he quoted a passage from Bahá'u'lláh:

This is the Day in which God's most excellent favors have been poured out upon men, the Day in which His most mighty grace hath been infused into all created things. It is incumbent upon all the peoples of the world to reconcile their differences, and, with perfect unity and peace, abide beneath the shadow of the Tree of His care and loving kindness.

I will never forget Dan's talk that night. It moved me tremendously and gave me a glimpse of what our world could potentially be. I had become a Bahá'í long before I met Dan, but in some mysterious way his talk gave me a new and deeper sense of what it meant to really incorporate the Bahá'í teachings into the center of my being. It goes without saying that when, after the fireside, I sat down with Dan, we talked, and I asked my questions, despite their obvious lack of sophistication, Dan answered them patiently and kindly. From that moment on, I resolved to try to live a Bahá'í life, as Dan obviously did.

Years later, I met Dan a second time when he was giving an overview of a new educational system called Anisa that he and his colleagues were developing at the University of Massachusetts.

Have you ever met anyone who focused and aligned all of their energies on a profoundly altruistic, humanitarian goal, who dedicated their entire life to the service of humanity?

It's an inspiring, life-altering event when you do. I've talked to people who met and spoke to Gandhi, Mother Teresa, Dr. Martin Luther King, Jr. and 'Abdu'l-Bahá and they all remembered how those remarkable human beings expanded their horizons, deeply touched their hearts and literally altered the course of their existence. Those people seem completely and fully alive, overflowing with the vitality of a heavenly spirit, radiant and bursting with energy and hope and love.

Because we rarely encounter such altruistic, soulful individuals, they have a profound impact on us when we meet them. Dan Jordan had that kind of impact on me.

I only met Dan a handful of times, and only had extended conversations with him twice. But somehow, his spirit truly inspired me. I think he generated such a powerful impact on others because he possessed that joyful, selfless ethic of service to humanity that characterizes the most developed, the most serious and the most spiritual people.

Don't misunderstand me, though—Dan wasn't a dour, severe person in any way. He had tremendous happiness and humor about life. Constantly smiling and laughing, his spirit seemed completely free, unconcerned about any difficulties and problems. Instead, Dan committed his whole being to the education of the human race. As a Bahá'í, Dan believed in the emergence of a new, universal global culture, which he felt he could best serve and help to bring about as an educator. This is what led him to develop the Anisa Education Model.

Initially conceptualized and constructed at the University of Massachusetts while Jorden worked there as a professor, the Anisa Model, inspired by the Bahá'í teachings and the philosophical work of Alfred North Whitehead, soon grew into a national movement that trained hundreds of educators.

Dan's deep spiritual life affected everything he did. A great deal of the inspiration of the Anisa Model came from the Bahá'í teachings. Dan Jordan and his colleague and collaborator Don Streets, both Bahá'ís, believed in the emergence of a new, universal global culture, and designed the Anisa Model to educate children and youth from all cultural backgrounds. For as Bahá'u'lláh urged, *"Forget your own selves, and turn your eyes toward your neighbor. Bend your energies to whatever may foster the education of man."*

Mark Ochu, a concert pianist who has performed throughout the United States and in many countries around the world, had this to say about Dan:[14]

I met Dan once at a National Convention where I played in Foundation Hall at the Bahá'í House of Worship. We shook hands and exchanged pleasantries. Unfortunately, I was unable to follow up with a more extended conversation. It was sometime later that I finally got a cassette tape of his "Keys to Harmony" that was so popular. In terms of Dan's influence, I've felt that we were kindred spirits, but I took a much different path mostly due to the fact that I simply didn't have his gifts. I focused more on how the Bahá'í Faith affected history and its connection with visual arts and architecture, although I did prepare a concert tour on the theme "Keys to Peace and Harmony" sometime after the International Year of Peace back in 1986-88.

Dan was a genius! His ability to improvise in various styles was remarkable. Then there was the ballet that he wrote that I heard excerpts from that captured this haunting worldly quality. Then there was also the "Comprehensive Deepening Program" that is exceptional in bringing the mysticism of the Faith into practical application.

Another musician, David Maytan, a professional trombonist and Bahá'í pioneer to Sweden for over 50 years, wrote this about Dan:[15]

As a teenager looking for a common-sense approach to life, I adopted the creator-creation paradigm. I realized I was an involuntary part of the created world but my free will had a difficult time perceiving how I might play a meaningful part in a sustainable future for our planet. General philosophy, religion and other sources presented a general paradigmatic description but nothing that helped me grasp my part in this great process. A good friend suggested that I read Daniel Jordan's pamphlet *Becoming Your True Self.* Thanks to this clear presentation I was able to perceive myself as part of creation given talents and capacities which should be developed in service to an ever-evolving civilization and the realization of God's plan for man. This one brochure has helped me create my focus in life. Besides Dan's "Keys to Harmony" program which relates music to human behavior, I really appreciate his writing on the human will as part of the creative process—the choice to participate in an ever-increasing appreciation for the creative powers of volition. Dan Jordan was truly a gift to human society and his writings will continue to influence generations to come. For my part, I am extremely grateful to him.

Judge Dorothy Nelson who served with Dan on the National Spiritual Assembly of the Bahá'ís of the United States for a number of years tells how he influenced her life:[16]

One of the highlights of my life was serving on the NSA with Daniel Jordan. Frankly I was in awe of him when he became a member. He was a Rhodes Scholar with two Master's Degrees and a Doctorate. He was a genius, erudite with indefatigable energy, innovative, altruistic with an extraordinary vision of the future. The NSA would meet three days each month. Each Saturday evening after dinner, Dan would play divine classical music of Beethoven, Chopin, Rachmaninoff, etc., and we would relax from 7:00 to 7:30 p.m. in joyous harmony.

At that time, I was a new dean at the University of Southern California Law School and he had been dean of the School of Education at National University. I latched on to him for ideas on how to be an innovative dean.

When I was a law student at U.C.L.A. I was greatly influenced by Roscoe Pound, the former dean of the Harvard Law School. Dean Pound emphasized that what was important was not the laws but the process by which justice was achieved. When I learned what Dan and his colleagues (Don Streets, in particular) were doing at the University of Massachusetts where Dan headed the Center for the Study of Human Potential, I became very excited. They were developing what they called the ANISA Model of Education. The model, inspired by the Bahá'í Teachings, was based on the framework of Alfred North Whitehead, an outstanding process philosopher. Whitehead's system is a synthesis of both Eastern and Western culture and emphasized the idea that process underlies the development of potentiality both cosmic and human. Dan, like Whitehead, bridged the cultures of art and science.

Dan's essay on "Becoming Your True Self" written in 1968, later became a Bahá'í pamphlet and the most sought after at our Bahá'í firesides. Close to two-hundred people would come to our house just to hear him speak and play the piano. Several who later became Bahá'í said the pamphlet was what led them to become Bahá'í.

Dan called upon religious leaders to uphold spiritual values that do not deny the truths of science. In his view, the technological order of society rested upon scientific knowledge, but the social and moral order needed to rest on spiritual values. This in turn would help unify mankind and allow technology to be used in constructive rather than destructive avenues of service. To Dan, promoting the unity of mankind was the fundamental purpose of religion.

So, this is what influenced me to adopt clinical education when some of my faculty said it would change us into a trade school. It was my desire to bring together scientists, educators, gerontologists, doctors, social workers, criminologists, etc., to associate with our faculty and students. We established the Western Center on Law and Poverty and the Senior Center on Law and Gerontology.

Needless to say, Dan had a profound influence on my life and career. For me as a law professor this can be summed up with one of my favorite quotes from Bahá'u'lláh, Prophet and Founder of the Bahá'í Faith: "It beseemeth you to fix your gaze under all conditions upon justice and fairness."

Mrs. Arden Thur Lee of Reno, Nevada, and a long-time friend of Dan and Nancy Jordan had this to say about the Jordans beginning with a statement of Bahá'u'lláh:[17]

> *Through the Teachings of this Day-Star of Truth every man will advance and develop until he attaineth the*

*station at which he can manifest all the potential forces
with which his inmost true self hath been endowed ...*

Rarely would we meet anyone in this life with more capacities than Dr. Daniel Jordan and he never stopped developing them. At the same time, he would share his accomplishments with anyone who asked. His vision took in all of existence and his expanded consciousness of spiritual reality was a magnet attracting seekers of knowledge and well-being.

His dear wife, Nancy, was always an integral part of his accomplishments. Dan came from a large family in Alliance, Nebraska, and there were no finances to support his further education after graduating from high school at the age of seventeen. At age twenty-one, while enrolled at the University of Wyoming, he became the first American to receive a Rhodes Scholarship to study music at Oxford University in England. He and Nancy decided that while he was studying, she would serve the Bahá'í Faith as a pioneer in Europe. I believe she went to Luxembourg and she and Dan had regular communication times. Dan would send a letter with one nylon stocking because to put them together would raise the postage; so she would get the second stocking in the next regular letter.

In 1962, Dan wrote, produced and directed "Metamorphosis of the Owls" for his doctorate at the University of Chicago. He wrote the music and the entire ballet as a psychological experiment to develop human potential and reach one's inner being. It was a moving experience.

In 1963, Dan became a member of the National Spiritual Assembly of the Bahá'í of the U.S.—a yearly elected governing body comprised of nine persons, usually ethnically diverse. He authored numerous essays, pamphlets, and articles, and participated in summer school programs and teaching activities, etc., from then until his passing in 1982. "Becoming Your True Self: How the Bahá'í Faith Releases Human Potential" was a booklet that touched my heart. A charismatic public speaker, he often gave enlightening programs at Bahá'í conferences and other meetings. One of the great programs was "Keys to Harmony" with him at the piano. I remember it from the Green Lake yearly institute in Wisconsin where more than 1,000 people came to hear him. Another program is "The Meaning of Deepening" in which he discussed many spiritual principles focusing on the theme "God's Purpose for Man." Thinking of these programs makes me realize how much he is missed.

Nancy was always working and when they lived in Chicago and could get a day off, my husband Jack and I were only 90 miles away in Shorewood, Wisconsin. Also in Shorewood lived the McKenty family. Beth and Dr. Jack were dear friends of the Jordans and the Lees. Those rare gatherings became more meaningful with time. Beth was Dan's "publicist." She is the one who arranged the rotogravure four-page picture display in the

Chicago Sunday Tribune Magazine of Jan. 6, 1963, of "Ballet in the Shadows of the Mind.," as well as the "Experiment in Ballet" in the National Observer of Nov. 5, 1962.

Whenever Dan and Nancy were together you would think they never had a problem in this world. If they were not together, it was the same feeling—we felt the love. Individually or together, their goal was to bring joy and meaning to every encounter—sharing some significant time on our eternal journey towards the Light. Their goal was to make this world a better place for all people and they had found the Source of love, guidance and assistance—the Messenger of the One Creator of us all for our time.

In the words of Lynn Laing, the news bureau director of the Vista Campus of National University: " ...I would say the best way to describe [Dan] is to say he was a genius. He also had a good sense of humor. He laughed often. He was well-liked and respected ... especially for his contributions to the university. To this comment about Dr. Jordan's genius, I would add a further dimension. He was a genius who was fully conscious of both his God-given giftedness and his responsibility to serve humankind, which such genius entails. On one occasion when he was speaking on some subject with his usual superb command of both concepts and pertinent data, he must have sensed my awe (or seen my jaw drop in wonder), for he stopped and commented to me, 'But I am not even bilingual and YOU are' in an unsuccessful attempt to reduce my amazement."[18]

The ANISA consultants, Gordan and Irene Hartley, attributed Dr. Jordan's power to attract and motivate people to his unique combination of genius and deep spirituality—his ability to "touch people at the very center of their being." They were also amazed at his knowledge and expertise in such a wide variety of activities that were of a very practical and technological nature: cooking, baking, carpentry, mechanics, construction, and others.[19]

The late Dr. Magdalene Carney, a close friend of Dan, wrote the following memo which was found appended to her dissertation,[20] "Dan, your ideal of excellence is a constant lure. With grateful heart and abiding affection for all you have done for me. Mag."

Dr, Pattabi Raman, in his dissertation[21] wrote the following acknowledgement:

"Words cannot do justice to the encouragement and constant guidance I received from Professor Daniel Jordan, Chairman of my Committee. His exemplary dedication to excellence in providing quality professional direction in all of his undertakings, a virtue on the wane in academic circles, has been one of the greatest sources of inspiration in this effort. His indefatigable energy, which met its ultimate test as he tried to read every sentence of the manuscript, and his constant emotional support during my periods of fatigue and depression will long be remembered and greatly appreciated."

Another doctoral student, Lawrence N. McCullough, expressed his "deep feeling of indebtedness and gratitude" to "Daniel C. Jordan for his professional interest and friendship extending over many years and for the inspiration of his broad vision of possibilities in education."[22]

In the acknowledgment section of his dissertation[23] Walter Leopold stated:

> "...I wish to acknowledge my indebtedness, gratitude and love for Dr. Daniel C. Jordan, who by his personal example taught me that a teacher is not only responsible for the intellectual growth of his students but must also be a physician of the soul."

Dr. George Bondra included the following words of acknowledgement in his doctoral dissertation:[24]

> "I wish to express my deepest thanks to Dr. Daniel C. Jordan, chairman of my dissertation committee, for his substantial contribution to the growth of knowledge and his devotion to putting that knowledge into practice as he did in working with me. To experience the universal in the particular, as I did in each step of this work with Dr. Jordan, is unique indeed—beyond any explicit verbal thanks."

In order to understand the profound and far-reaching effort that Jordan's work has brought about and will continue to bring about on the development of education as a new science (and art), I think that it is worthwhile quoting the following section from Dr. Bondra's dissertation, "The ANISA Model: A Scientific Paradigm for Education and Its Implications for a Theory of Evaluation:"

> "Since scientific models are the creation of an inventive mind, it will be helpful in understanding the ANISA Model to discuss some of the influences that have shaped the inventor's view of reality. Daniel C. Jordan, a Rhodes Scholar, epitomizes C.P. Snow's 'two cultures.' He has earned three degrees in music. He holds two degrees from the University of Chicago in an interdisciplinary course of study involving human development from sociological, psychological and anthropological perspectives. Post-doctoral study involved brain chemistry and its relationship to memory and learning. These influences contributed to his bridging the two cultures of art and science. He characterized Kuhn's

observation about men who have invented new paradigms; they are either very young or new in the field and not fully committed to the traditional rules permitting them to be freer to conceive of another set. Professor Jordan became aware of gaps between theory and practice in education. He believed that education was dominated more by practice than theory. There was no organized knowledge about human growth and development that could be optimally used for practice by teachers.

"His initial conceptual efforts began over eighteen years ago as Director for the Institute for Research at Indiana State University. Initially, Jordan observed that educators were more concerned with curriculum and not the nature of the child for whom it was designed. Very early on, therefore, Jordan selected his basic unit of study—man. Toward that end, he studied man's best thinking about the nature of man reviewing all the major philosophers from Parmenides to the process philosophers of today."

At this point, having examined some of the accolades showered upon Dan Jordan by some of his friends and colleagues, it is appropriate to look at a few remarks that professional educators made about the ANISA Model. The following statements reflect the views of educators who have observed the development of the ANISA Model or have sponsored and participated in its implementation.[25]

"We believe that Dr. Daniel C. Jordan and his colleagues have developed a philosophy and a theory of education which are unique and remarkable in their potential and promise. The Anisa Model provides a comprehensive synthesis of knowledge about human development, learning and teaching which has been notably absent in American education. I wish to firmly state that the community, the State Board, the administrative staff, and faculty have a commitment to try to develop and implement the Anisa Model of education because it provides for us, and we think ultimately for a large segment of the nation, the only truly comprehensive plan of education which we have seen."

Malcom D. Evans, Ph.D., *Superintendent of Schools, Suffield, Connecticut*

"My staff and I are delighted to participate in the implementation of the Anisa Model. The response to the training has been accepted with great enthusiasm. The Model has a sound scientific base, is extremely comprehensive, and creates a great deal of excitement among teachers."

Willard Hiller, *Principal of McGraw School, Hampden, Maine*

"Anisa has brought many changes in my thinking as well as changes in my approach to teaching.

"Ground rules have simplified the management of children. Our rooms are low-keyed usually, and quieter. Children are able to attend and are learning independently. They approach activities with purpose and are eager to work. We are teaching on a more individual basis and it seems to be a more efficient, exciting way to learn.

"The children are respectful and polite to one another, share willingly and resolve their differences in a friendly manner.

"They handle responsibilities well and appear to be ahead, academically, of the group last year."

Barbara Dowd, Teacher, Suffield Cooperative Nursery School

How did Daniel Jordan describe himself? As a specialist he considered himself to be an authority on human development. But during one of his lectures, he used a term which is more accurate. He referred to himself as an "integrative generalist" akin to such men as writer/biochemist Isaac Asimov, evolutionary biologist Edward O. Wilson, pianist/systems philosopher Ervin Laszlo, and Galileo's 20th century counterpart planetary scientist Carl Sagan (although Dan never would have compared himself to these individuals). And indeed, he was. But his knowledge and expertise were far too vast for anyone to refer to him only as an authority on human development. His friend, colleague and doctoral student Keith Bookwalter, reflecting on all Dan's accomplishments, paints a picture of him in the most glowing of terms:

> "Yes indeed, Dan was an authority on human development. He was also a psychologist (cognitive psychology was his area of specialization), an educator, philosopher, brain/mind expert, administrator, dean, staff developer, curriculum specialist, school plant design consultant, educational and religious leader, visionary, theorist, writer, author, pianist, artist, dancer, husband, father, friend and much, much more. He exerted himself day and night to keep his mind on the cutting edge of new developments in any and all fields which offered possibilities for

increasing the quality of human life, medicine, science, technology, parapsychology, psychiatry, brain research, social movements, government, and religion. Armed with this knowledge he not only moved the pre-paradigmatic field of education onto a scientific foundation, but he also chose for that foundation the leading-edge paradigm variously described as organismic, holistic, process-oriented, Whiteheadian—a new cosmology, a unified world view, a philosophy of reality which has already swept through the hard sciences and is bringing about radical changes in the human sciences and the traditional world religions. And beyond being a 'man of powerful ideas' Dr. Jordan was also the epitome of the 'man of action' who wanted to translate his new schemes of thought into viable, practical programs for the benefit of all people."[26]

In essence, it could be said without any reservation that Dan Jordan was a 20th century Renaissance man.

And now, looking back over the last forty years since Dan's passing, it can be seen that the activated participants in the ANISA Model have not failed to carry forward historical actuality towards the fulfillment of Daniel Jordan's dream of a new universal culture in which every person's potential faculties and talents will be brought forth into the sunlight of worship of God and the service of humanity. His fellow colleagues, his students, and those who have been attracted to the elegance of his scheme of thought and his call for a "new way" of educating the future generations of humankind have taken up his ideas and applied them each in his or her own sphere of life: in their classrooms; in the raising of their children; university research; professional associations; their writings; their school systems and communities; their way of thinking, feeling, and perceiving reality—their very way of living and being. No doubt the near future will see a resurgence in his process-based system of education and the distant future, when the fruits are in hand, will see Dr. Daniel C. Jordan being paid the homage he deserves as one of the most outstanding and far-sighted leaders the field of education has ever seen.

Dan Jordan's Writings

Now, some 40 years after Dan's tragic death in October of 1982, it has become apparent that he left us with a tremendous four-fold legacy. First and foremost was his family, his dear wife Nancy and their three children Melissa, Sarah, and Charlotte. Secondly, he left behind a large number of friends and colleagues whom he had met and worked with over a period of some twenty years. Then he left the legacy of his Bahá'í contributions many of which were essays published in *World Order* magazine distributed throughout the United States and the world which presented a wide variety of views as to how the teachings of Bahá'u'lláh were transforming the world. Finally, Dan left behind a considerable collection of ANISA materials which, as stated above, are now housed in a collection at the Stanford University library. In parts two and three of this book a sampling of Dan's *World Order* articles and ANISA essays are presented. It is remarkable that as one reads Dan Jordan's essays it becomes readily apparent that they are still as interesting and relevant today as they were when they were written nearly 50 years ago.

Chapter 2 offers an address that Dan gave at Howard University, Washington, D.C., in October 1966. The title of his talk was "The Dilemma of the Modern Intellectual" in which he focuses on the struggles that intellectuals have with the "question of how to move— how to exist, how to grow, how to become what potentially we can become—all through intellectual means alone." Dan points out that when dealing with the unknowns and ultimate unknowns of life—such as one's yet unactualized potentialities, the mystery of death, and the question of Deity—that man must eventually face, faith must be employed. He suggests that faith can be considered as an "organization of feelings about the basic unknowns which permeates one's emotional orientation to life in general." He goes on to offer the Bahá'í Faith as an attractive solution to the dilemma faced by intellectuals as it is a religion that is historically accessible and has many teachings that address the modern situation.[27]

Chapters 3 and 4, "Social Disadvantage—the Real Enemy in the War on Poverty"[28] and "Guardians of His Trust"[29] deal with issues that Dan addressed when he was Director of Indiana State University's Upward Bound Program and the Comprehensive Study of Compensatory Education in Massachusetts. In these essays he analyzes the "cycle of poverty" and offers the Bahá'í solution to the problem of poverty. While Dan pointed out that government had, during recent years, made some progress in addressing these issues, it is disheartening to recognize that during the last 50 years America has not by any means won the war on poverty. To give a couple of examples, the number of impoverished in 1970 was about 25 million, in 2017 it was 45 million with over 5 million living under "third world" conditions; in the early 1970's homelessness had almost disappeared whereas in 2019 some 554,000 adults were homeless and 1.6 million children were homeless. Dan was in total agreement with Bahá'u'lláh who had pointed out nearly 100 years ago that the real solutions to poverty lie in the spiritualization of the planet and when the "guardians of His trust"—the leaders and affluent among mankind—would assume their responsibility for looking after the poor and disadvantaged.

In 1968 Dan's most popular essay, "Becoming Your True Self," was published in *World Order* magazine and eventually distributed as a short monograph.[30] This essay, presented in Chapter 5, deals with the dynamics of personal and social transformation as set forth in the Bahá'í writings. According to Jordan, "personal transformation is a fundamental reason that people are attracted to the Faith, develop conviction as to its truth, and finally become Bahá'í ." In the essay, Jordan defines, from Bahá'í and psychological perspectives, the nature of human potential, faith and the release of human potential, anxiety and the unknown, and the spiritual and social matrices of transformation. It is interesting to note that, despite the brevity of this essay, it took Jordan nearly ten years to distill the ideas into a work that had real meaning for him and hopefully for others.

"In Search of the Supreme Talisman: A Bahá'í Perspective on Education," presented in Chapter 6, is another example of Jordan's clear thinking on social issues.[31] It deals with the crises in culture and education and demonstrates how his deep knowledge of psychology, sociology and anthropology can be brought to bear on contemporary issues. According to Jordan, "the crisis humanity presently faces can be simply stated: because true religion is dying out, the moral order is collapsing while science and technology, guided by a profusion of materialistic and secular philosophies, have been permitted to concentrate too many of their powers on more efficient ways of destroying man." He goes on to say: "Teetering on the edge of oblivion, what can man do to face this crisis of incomprehensible proportions? If the foregoing analysis is correct, we have only one hope—a renaissance of religion based on spiritual values that do not deny the truth of science but can direct the awesome power of modern technology into constructive channels of service to a mankind that is unified by the power of a new moral order derived from those values."

Jordan then proceeds to examine what it would take to bring about a rebirth of religion and the re-education of humanity. He emphasized his remarks by quoting Bahá'u'lláh as the supreme Educator of the new era:

> Man is the supreme Talisman. Lack of a proper
> education hath, however, deprived him of that which

he doth inherently possess ... Regard man as a mine rich in gems of inestimable value. Education can, alone, cause it to reveal its treasures, and enable mankind to benefit therefrom.

In a 1967 Ridvan Message, the Universal House of Justice, the supreme international governing body of the Bahá'í world, stressed the imperative need for Bahá'í to deepen in the Cause and clarified the nature of deepening. The main point they emphasized was that deepening "suggested a clearer apprehension of the purpose of God for man, and particularly of His immediate purpose as revealed and directed by Bahá'u'lláh, a purpose as far removed from current concepts of human well-being and happiness as possible." With this mandate the U.S. National Spiritual Assembly prepared materials for a "Comprehensive Deepening Program." Dan Jordan was appointed the Project Supervisor and with the help and diligent research of a large number of dedicated Bahá'í the program was eventually launched in 1973. Dan himself contributed a six-part monograph to the program entitled *The Meaning of Deepening: Gaining a Clearer Apprehension of the Purpose of God for Man.* Chapters 7, 8 and 9 are drawn from that monograph and cover the topics of the meaning of life, acquiring divine attributes, and obtaining a spiritual education.[32] Dan was cautious to point out that the perspectives presented were by no means the only ones, but "they provided the basis for an initial effort to implement a comprehensive deepening program organized around the theme of apprehending God's purpose for man."

Chapter 10, "Knowledge, Volition, and Action: The Steps to Spiritual Transformation," is also a part of the Comprehensive Deepening Program.[33] In this essay Dan was responding to Bahá'u'lláh's statement that *"the vitality of men's belief in God is dying out in every land ..."* Commenting on this he wrote that "one of the most striking evidences of the truth of this statement is the abdication of responsibility for one's life on the part of an ever-increasing number of people … The inevitable consequence is a yielding to the pressures of the old order and conformity with behavior patterns which hasten its downfall." The essay emphasizes that without knowledge, volition, and action, no spiritual transformation can occur, for as 'Abdu'l-Bahá declared:

> "The attainment of any object is conditional upon knowledge, volition and action. Unless these three conditions are forthcoming there is no execution or accomplishment."

While the essay is short, it is a *tour de force* that is meant to take away any excuses for not working to pursue the goal of attuning oneself to God's purpose for man.

Part Three of this book presents four articles that provide an overview of the ANISA Education Model. Of course, four essays can hardly scratch the surface of the vast amount of research, development, and testing that went into the construction of the model, but hopefully those really interested will find a way to access more of the materials via the Stanford collection.

In 1978 Jordan published an article (not included here) titled "RX for Piaget's Complaint: A Science of Education."[34] Jean Piaget (1896-1980) was a Swiss psychologist known for his work on child development. Piaget's 1936 theory of cognitive development and epistemological view are together called "genetic epistemology." He placed great importance on the education of children, and as Director of the International Bureau of Education, he declared in 1934 that "only education is capable of saving our societies from possible collapse whether violent or gradual." One of Piaget's major criticisms of education was that, despite all the knowledge available about human development, there was no bona fide "science of education" as there was, for example, in medicine where the physical sciences and biology lent themselves to a science of medicine. Dan

Jordan offered the ANISA Model as a prescription to this void and wrote that "we have ... developed a science of education, created the Anisa Model, and find that it holds enormous promise for the future."

Building on the issue raised by Piaget, Chapter 11, titled "Applying Knowledge of Human Development: New Dimensions in Parent and Teacher Education,"[35] Dr. Jordan offers an analysis of the breakdown of the family and school in present-day society, spells out the cost of institutional failure, propounds a conceptual base for organizing human development knowledge, and suggests a proposal for an institute to renew the family and the school. The article is quite pithy yet challenging and provides yet another glimpse of why Daniel Jordan was so committed to developing a new model of education.

"The Philosophy of the ANISA Model" is set forth in Chapter 12.[36] Jordan and co-author Raymond Shepard make the case that "contemporary education lacks a philosophy broad enough in scope to unify the vast knowledge we have about human growth and development and produce a body of theory that would enable us to provide solutions to the difficult and complex problems facing education as a social institution." They go on to point out that the inadequacy of contemporary educational philosophy becomes apparent when it is found that education has not adequately defined the nature of man—the organism for which it is trying to create a curriculum. The article then provides an historical perspective of how this situation came to be, and concludes by offering the Whiteheadian-based philosophy underlying the ANISA Model as a new paradigm for an updated philosophy of education.

Chapter 13, entitled "The ANISA Model," was written by Dan and co-authored by his collaborator Dr. Donald Streets.[37] It was published in *World Order* as early as 1972 and provides an extensive overview of the ANISA Model. The article presents the fundamental reasons that prompted the development of the ANISA Education

Model, outlines its philosophy centering on the spiritual nature of man, sets forth the concept of learning competence and the development of potential, and delineates nine categories of human potentialities that the model addresses. In essence, Jordan and Streets present a new vision of education as the transformation of man and a way to sustain it. "Every transformation of man," says Louis Mumford, "except that perhaps which produced Neolithic culture, has rested on a new metaphysical and ideological base; or rather, upon deeper stirrings and intuitions whose rationalized expression takes the form of a new picture of the cosmos and the nature of man."[38]

Chapter 14, "Being and Becoming: The ANISA Theory of Development," written by Michael Kalinowski and Dan, elaborates on some of the themes set forth in Chapter 13.[39] It begins by stating a challenging observation made by the evolutionary scientist Julian Huxley that man is "the only repository of cosmic self-awareness in the universe," an attribute that makes him "managing director of the biggest business of all, the business of evolution." The article goes on to define the ANISA concept of development, classifies the range of human potentialities, elaborates on the various sub-environments that man interacts with, explores the rhythm of development, and sets forth the educational implications of the theory of development.

In conclusion, it may seem unfortunate that Dan Jordan never wrote a book of his own that was published (he and Donald Streets did write an unpublished book titled *Releasing the Potentialities of the Child* which can be found on the internet) for, as we can see from the articles in this book, he certainly had the capacity to do so. His doctoral dissertation presenting a test for the Jungian theory of archetypes is in itself a fascinating book-length study. He also could have written a book on "Images of Man: 20th Century Philosophers and the Bahá'í Faith." But the fact is that Dan Jordan was driven by a greater dream—a dream to make educational knowledge more effective in the endeavor to transform the lives of people. He yearned to contribute to an ever-advancing civilization through promoting the idea of the spiritual nature of man as well as the unity of mankind. Dan guided the work of his doctoral students so that each dissertation would contribute to the development of the ANISA Model and not simply be a work that began with words and ended with words. Thus, his students were energized and inspired to work with him on this great project. Likewise, his service to and articles reflecting on aspects of the Bahá'í Faith manifested his desire to make the Revelation of Bahá'u'lláh relevant to the transformation of human potential into actuality. Daniel Jordan devoted his time and energy as well as his gifts of music, psychology, philosophy and education to making the world a better place. Tragically, he was taken from us before he could give all that he had to offer. But to quote the words of the poet Kahlil Gibran: "The light of stars that were extinguished ages ago still reaches us. So, it is with great men who died ... but still reach us with the radiations of their personality." May his example, his "radiations," be an inspiration to all of us.

Notes and References

Poem

1. Hayden, Robert. in Collected *Poems,* ed. Fredrick Gleysher, New York: W.W. Norton, 2013.

Preface

1. Bahá'u'lláh. Bahá'í Publications Australia, 1991.

Chapter 1

1. Most of the biographical information was taken from Daniel Jordan's "Curriculum Vitae," September 1979, as well as from some of his recorded talks. Major contributions were also made by Keith Bookwalter and David Langness.
2. Statement of the Universal House of Justice. "To the World's Religious Leaders," Haifa, Israel; April 2002
3. George A. Miller. "Some Psychological Perspectives on the Year 2000," *Daedalus:* Journal of the American Arts and Sciences (Summer 1967), p.889.
4. Edna St. Vincent-Millay. "Sonnet CXXVII," in *Collected Poems,* New York: Harper, 1956, p.697.
5. Daniel C. Jordan. "The ANISA Model," *World Order:* Spring 1972, p.22.
6. Dr. McCormick Rambusch, doctoral dissertation, pp. 186, 131, 118.
7. Daniel C. Jordan. "In Search of the Supreme Talisman," *World Order:* Fall 1970.
8. Richard Dawkins. *A River Out of Eden: A Darwinian View of Life.* London: Weidenfeld & Nicholson, 1995, pp.132-133.
9. S. Pattabi Raman. "Biological Dimensions of the Anisa Model," University of Mass., 1978, p.110.

10. Pierre Teilhard de Chardin. *The Phenomenon of Man,* trans. Bernard Wall (New York: Harper, 1959), p.36.

11. "Bahá'í Educator Slain in Connecticut," *New York Times,* Oct. 21, 1982. See also "Dr. Daniel Jordan slain in Connecticut," Bahá'í News, December, 1982.

12. 'Abdu'l-Bahá, *The Promulgation of Universal Peace: Table Talks Delivered by 'l-Bahá during His Visit to the United States and Canada in 1912.* Compiled by Howard MacNutt. 2nd ed. Wilmette, IL: Bahá'í Publishing Trust, 1982, pp.348-349, 352.

13. Personal communication with author.

14. Ibid.

15. Ibid.

16. Ibid.

17. Ibid.

18. Jim Orkerblom. Article in the San Diego Union newspaper, section B-1, Oct. 24, 1982.

19. Based on an interview with Keith Bookwalter.

20. Margret Magdalene Carney. "The Learning Competence Paradigm of the Anisa Model and the Preparation of Teachers," University of Mass., 1974.

21. S. Pattabi Raman. "Biological Dimensions of the Value Theory of the Anisa Education Model," University of Mass., 1978.

22. Laurance N. McCullough. "An Organic Approach to Educational Development," University of Mass., 1978.

23. Walter Daniel Leopold. "Creativity and Education: Some Theories and Procedures to Enhance the Development of Creativity Within a Classroom Setting," University of Mass., 1972.

24. George Bondra. "The Anisa Model: A Scientific Paradigm for Education and Its Implications for a Theory of Evaluation," University of Mass., 1980.

25. All these comments were taken from a brochure on the ANISA Model, circa 1975.

26. Keith Bookwalter. "Who Was Dr. Daniel C. Jordan? A Tribute," e-document, 2020.

27. Jordan, Daniel C. Dilemma of the Modern Intellectual. *World Order*: Spring 1967. Wilmette, Ill.

28. Jordan, Daniel C. Social Disadvantage—the Real Enemy in the War on Poverty. *World Order*: Fall 1966. Wilmette, Ill.

29. Jordan, Daniel C. Guardians of His Trust. *World Order*: Winter 1970-71. Wilmette, Ill.

30. Jordan, Daniel. C. Becoming Your True Self: *World Order*: Fall 1968. Wilmette, Ill.

31. Jordan, Daniel C. In Search of the Supreme Talisman. *World Order*: Fall 1970. Wilmette, Ill.

32. Jordan, Daniel C. *The Meaning of Deepening*. Wilmette, Ill., Bahá'í Publishing Trust. 1973, pp.7-46.

33. Jordan, Daniel C. Knowledge, Volition and Action. Comprehensive Deepening Program. Wilmette. Bahá'í Publishing Trust, 1973.

34. Jordan, Daniel C. Rx for Piaget's Complaint. Journal of Teachers Education, September-October 1979.

35. Jordan, Daniel C. Applying Knowledge of Human Development in *Nutrition in Human Development*, ed. Pattabi Raman, Greylock Publishers, 1978.

36. Jordan, Daniel C. and Raymond P. Shepard. The Philosophy of the ANISA Model. *World Order:* Fall 1972. Wilmette, Ill.

37. Jordan, Daniel C. and Donald T. Streets. The ANISA Model. *World Order*: Spring 1972. Wilmette, Ill.

38. Mumford, Louis. *The Transformation of Man,* New York: Collier Books, 1962, p.171.

39. Kalinowski, Michael and Daniel C. Jordan. Being and becoming. *World Order*: Summer 1973. Wilmette, Ill.

PART TWO
DAN JORDAN'S BAHÁ'Í WRITINGS

"God made religion and science to be the measure, as it were, of our understanding. Take heed that you do not neglect such a wonderful power. Weigh all things in this balance."

'Abdu'l-Bahá, Religious Philosopher, (1844-1921)

"Let no woman or man, think that anyone can search too far or be too well informed in the Book of God's Works or in the Book of God's Word. Instead, let everyone endlessly improve their understanding in both."

Francis Bacon, English Philosopher, (1561-1626)

CHAPTER 2

———•·•·•———

THE DILEMMA OF THE
MODERN INTELLECTUAL

By Daniel C. Jordan
published in *World Order:* Spring 1967

An Address by Daniel Jordan

*Daniel Jordan is Associate Professor of Psychology and
Education as well as Director of the Institute for Research
in Human Behavior at Indiana State University. He is
at present serving as Chairman of the National Spiritual
Assembly of the Bahá'ís of the United States.*

*One of a series of Centennial addresses sponsored
by the Andrew Rankin Memorial Chapel, Howard
University, Washington, D.C., October 30, 1966.*

One of the more sensible functions of an anniversary commemoration of the founding of an institution is the provision of an opportunity to consider anew its purpose and how that purpose can be understood in these present times of rapid social and technological change. During Howard's centennial year, the University's religious services at the Andrew Rankin Memorial Chapel provide a forum for the examination of some of the purposes of this unique educational institution as reflected in the overall centennial theme adopted by the Chapel: *Resources for Moral Readiness in a Changing Society*. Surely one of the purposes of the University is to discuss the many problems related to the achievement of moral readiness, and since a good percentage of us who are here have an image of ourselves as intellectuals, I wish to make some observations about the dilemma the modern intellectual faces when he confronts the issue of moral readiness in our changing society.

The dilemma can best be understood in terms of its historical development—a development which is so extensive and complex that in no way can I justify the cursory treatment that I'm going to give it this morning. I hope you will grant me this license.

The dilemma of the modern intellectual originated when, some millions of years ago, consciousness in man came into being. The more conscious he became, the more aware he was of himself as a creature distinct from his environment. The more aware he became, the more compelled he was to relate himself in one way or another to everything in that environment, including other human beings.

Men and animals ordinarily achieve the establishment of relationships in a very basic way through the various modes of sensory perception. But human beings want to know more than just what things exist in their environment; they want to know about the relationships among them.

In the process of trying to understand these relationships, man runs on to a very basic difficulty. How does he relate himself to unknown or unknowable things which he somehow intuitively suspects to exist?

There are, of course, a vast number of unknown and unknowable things about us, but I want to talk about two such basic unknowns which seem to have direct relevance to the question of moral readiness. How man relates himself to them determines, in part, the kind of power he can mobilize for moral readiness. One of these unknowns, which all men of all societies have sooner or later encountered, is that force behind the order in the universe—the force which down through the ages has been called by many different names—Allah, Jehovah, God, The Great Spirit.

The other concerns that unknown part of our own selves, the unexpressed potential, which I believe is that intangible reality analogously referred to in theological terms as the Kingdom of God within us.

The difficulty for many intellectuals in trying to deal with these two unknown forces stems from the fact that the intellect alone does not seem to provide a totally adequate means of relating the individual to them. This would probably be of little concern except for the fact that an inadequate orientation to these basic unknowns in our lives always precipitates a kind of free-floating anxiety, an existential anxiety—an objectless foreboding which frequently makes moral readiness impossible. In extreme cases it can lead an organism into a state of dysfunction, render it utterly incapable of assuming any responsibility for itself, and may progress to the point where the organism may even destroy itself.

Thus, having some reasonably consistent and satisfactory orientation to these two unknowns which assist in the preservation of the organism is for most a general mark of maturity and something well worth the effort to acquire.

To my mind, *the essence of moral readiness is the courage to become what you, potentially are in the face of a thousand forces which try to beat you down and away from that path of development.* Of course, intellectual supports are important and necessary when pursuing one's destiny, but they often are insufficient when it comes to coping with all of the obstacles which inevitably will be in the way.

The dilemma of the intellectual comes into sharp focus when he struggles with the question of how to move—how to exist, how to grow, how to become what potentially he can become—all through rational means alone.

The struggle persists because the intellectual tends to recognize as reality only those things which his mind can grasp and because the only acceptable approach to reality, as he defines it, is through intellectual activity. Yet, there is evidence that much of life's meaning comes from our relationship to these unknowns and therefore has an important non-rational dimension which cannot be ignored with impunity. This non-rational aspect of meaning cannot be crammed into the mold of logical propositions or mathematical formulae. The substance of it cannot be easily conveyed in words. This is why no society has ever been without art and religion, for these are the usual media through which much of the non-rational aspect of meaning in life is expressed and reflected.

Art and religion represent activities which draw upon some additional means of relating men to the two unknowns about which we have been speaking. The most important additional means, I believe, is faith.

To be sure, there are many, many definitions of the word *faith*, and no doubt not all would. agree with the definition which I wish to present, but for the moment, let us consider faith as an *organization of feelings about the two basic unknowns which permeates one's emotional orientation to life in general.*

When the same organization of feelings is shared by many people and the values stemming from those feelings become institutionalized, we then have a religion. Pointing out how vital religion is to man's development, 'Abdu'l-Bahá, the son of the founder of the Bahá'í Faith, stated that: "The greatest bestowal of God in the world. of humanity is religion; for assuredly the divine teachings of religion are above all sources of instruction and development to man. Religion confers upon man eternal life and guides his footsteps in the world of *morality*."

Now when an intellectual reaches the point of considering religion—of belonging to a community of persons who have a similar organization of feelings and values about ultimate things—he encounters yet another dilemma. Which religion (or which community) shall he belong to?

This dilemma is a real one, and a common destiny of many intellectuals is to remain on its horns forever. The discomfort of this position is usually made reasonably bearable by undertaking a course of self-study in comparative religion and philosophy. This often has the effect of confirming the intellectual's predisposition to remain on the fence and not become identified with any one religion, since there seems to be no way of sorting out the innumerable conflicts among them.

Yet, being on the fence and not making a decision about religion causes the intellectual to continue talking and talking until he ends up talking about nothing. He finds himself in the position of the philosopher, Husserl, who realized one day that he was spending all of his time sharpening his knife until there was no knife left. Consequently, it never fulfilled its function of cutting anything. The intellectual always runs into the danger of forever sharpening his wits, but never using them because he cannot become committed to anything except more wit sharpening-more talking.

Sharpening one's wit for its own sake is not entirely a bad thing, I suppose, but I can't help agreeing with E. M. Forster in his contention that it is far worse always to be preparing but never "called" than it is to be "called" even if one is unprepared. One of the direct consequences of always preparing for something but never actually doing it is that one begins to live entirely in the future and not at all in the present. This brings its own anxieties and discontents, and is a part of the pattern of maladjustment reflected in the lives of great number of human beings living in the Western world today.

The late Swiss psychiatrist, Carl Jung, was fond of saying that he never had a patient come to him over the age of 35 whose basic problem in the last analysis was not that of finding a religion to which he could become committed. It is psychologically difficult to become committed to anything of great import without making a decision about one's relationship to God and the unknown in himself–without developing legitimate ultimate concerns, to borrow a concept from Tillich. Lives without commitment are like fields which have been plowed but never planted or harvested. Characteristically, persons who never become committed to anything eventually develop symptoms of mental or emotional disturbance after they reach the middle of their lives. Part of this disturbance is nearly always reflected in a pathological fear of death. Jung pointed out that someone whose life has borne no fruit will never be ready for the harvest. It is as if man expects the harvest, death–itself an unknown–to reveal something about the two unknowns we have been discussing. If a whole life has been characterized by a postponing of decision about its relationship to those unknowns and a sea of words (philosophical knife sharpening) has been poured forth to rationalize the postponement, acute apprehension about death is understandable.

Bacon once said that a little philosophizing makes an atheist out of man, but that deep philosophy brings him back to God. As the wits-sharpening of the intellectual leads him into "deep philosophy" he tends to become dissatisfied with the sharpening of wits for its own sake and begins to concentrate his efforts on a search for a religion–a search for values about the unknown shared by others–which he can conscientiously uphold. Trying to make a sound decision through the intellect alone about which religion to embrace is the same dilemma in different guise still facing him.

Impressive numbers of intellectuals on campuses everywhere are actively avoiding this kind of decision making. But many others are earnestly struggling with the dilemma and when in the course of their search for an answer they hear of the Bahá'í faith, few can resist its magnetic power.

This Faith represents a new and powerful force in religion today. Its founder, Bahá'u'lláh, whose name translated into English means *The Glory of God*, diagnosed the ills of humanity and prescribed remedies for them in over a hundred volumes which comprise the sacred writings of the Faith. He predicted that the structure of the old order, based on out-worn principles and inadequate understandings of man's purpose, would collapse and that a new world order would be rolled out instead. The history of this Faith is filled with turmoil, violence, and unbelievable heroism. The extent to which it has spread throughout the world in just a little over 100 years is truly impressive.

Its greatest achievement, however, lies in its power to develop moral readiness in those who become committed to it. Because of this, and because of several other very appealing basic tenets, the Bahá'í Faith today is of particular interest to the intellectual who is facing the dilemma I have described.

In the first place, Bahá'u'lláh stresses the importance of arriving at commitment and faith through independent investigation of truth. In order to achieve independence of investigation, he warns that we have to put both love and hate out of our minds and hearts if objectivity is to be attained, and that we must free ourselves from subtle and unconscious needs to endorse what our forefathers have believed.

Secondly, the Faith clearly defines the position of science in our lives and indicates the need. for faith and religion to be balanced by reason and science. Bahá'u'lláh vividly expresses this need by likening science and religion to the two wings of a bird. If the wing of religion is strong and the wing of science weak, the bird will land in a bog of superstition; if the wing of religion is weak and that of science strong, then the bird will fall into the swamp of materialism. To keep the bird in flight, both wings must be equally strong.

Keeping the Faith from degenerating into superstition is an extremely important function, for a society that becomes superstitious will cease to progress. It will no longer be free to effect changes in its structure or in its collective actions, both of which are essential to the maintenance of an optimal level of adaptability. 'Abdu'l-Bahá noted that "the development and progress of a nation is according to the measure and degree of that nation's scientific attainment. Through this means, its greatness is continually increased and day by day the welfare and prosperity of its people are assured."

Down through the ages, man has shown a tendency to regard his own religion as a true faith, and the religion of others as superstition. This tendency was not checked in the past, partly because previous religious dispensations did not make in their scriptures a clear-cut definition of faith which would distinguish it from superstition. When presenting a talk on the Bahá'í faith in Germany some years ago, I began by asking anyone in the audience to define faith in such a way that it would be clearly distinguished from superstition. A protestant clergyman had come to the meeting and volunteered an explanation. Although he didn't offer a direct definition, he gave examples which he felt would clarify the difference between the two: "When a Christian believes in Christ as his saviour, that is an example of true faith; when a Buddhist believes in Buddha as his saviour, this is an example of superstition, since Buddha is not a saviour."

Although many of you may find this amusing or beyond belief, nonetheless an alarming number of people in the Western world would agree with that statement. It is alarming because lack of a clear definition of faith permits, and many times even encourages the formation of attitudes which are destructive of human relationships. In the Bahá'í Faith, the distinction is clear. Faith–the organization of feelings about God and man—may transcend reasoning, but not oppose it. In this dispensation, science cannot usurp all power and cast society into the throes of materialism nor can religion degenerate into institutionalized superstition. 'Abdu'l-Bahá emphasizes the role of science in keeping faith from becoming superstition when he says that "the man of science is perceiving and endowed with vision whereas he who is ignorant and neglectful of this development is blind."

To the intellectual, the Bahá'í view of the relationship between science and religion is a welcome one. It means that there is a faith in the world today which joins him in putting a premium on intellectual honesty.

Thirdly, the Bahá'í understanding of the role of religion in history makes good sense. To be a Bahá'í means to accept the cultural and spiritual validity of the great world religions at the time of each one's inception and development. The founders of the great religions—historical figures such as Muhammad, Jesus, Moses, Buddha, and Bahá'u'lláh, all of whom Bahá'ís would call Manifestations of God—articulated man's relationship to the great unknown, God, inspired commitment to a set of values based on that relationship and unified all men who would share them. On the basis of that unity, civilizations rose.

Thus, Bahá'u'lláh taught that the purpose of each Manifestation is to renew man's relationship to God in terms that enable him to respond successfully to the special exigencies characteristic of the period of history in which he appears. In other words, Bahá'ís uphold the principle of the relativity of religious truth. While accepting the world's religions as part of their own cultural heritage does not commit them to the outworn dogmas, doctrines, or rituals of past dispensations, it does commit the Bahá'ís to the principle of the oneness of religion as one of those values essential to progress and development in this age.

The fact that the Bahá'í Faith is of recent enough origin to have a good deal of historical information about its development available, also appeals to intellectuals. The original manuscripts of its sacred scripture are extant. This helps to insure the sacred writings against interpolation, substitution, and endless controversy over authenticity.

Many other basic teachings of the faith are not only appealing but already acceptable to the intellectual. The soundness of such principles as the oneness of mankind, progressive eradication of prejudice of all kinds as a prerequisite for world peace, universal compulsory education, the equality of the sexes, a universal auxiliary language to facilitate communication and understanding would be denied by few intellectuals.

But what makes the Bahá'í Faith an appealing religion for the intellectual to investigate is not necessarily what persuades him to embrace it. What is convincing is the subjective experience of feeling moral readiness—the courage to assume responsibilities for becoming what one can potentially become—growing within one's being. At that point, his dilemma disappears, deeds and not words become his adorning as Bahá'u'lláh promises, and he embarks upon a life's journey filled with high purpose and fruitful endeavor.

My friends, it has been a great honor for me to be with you on this occasion, and I am very grateful for the opportunity to extend to you, from this very platform from which 'Abdu'l-Bahá spoke on April 23, 1912, this invitation to investigate the Bahá'í Faith—a new religion for a new age, a powerful source of moral readiness for these challenging times, and a convincing response to the dilemma of the modern intellectual. That Howard should expose its students to diverse religious points of view through the Chapel series of addresses as one means of commemorating its centennial anniversary, is a testimony to its progressive spirit and a good omen for the next 100 years of its future.

CHAPTER 3

———◆●◆———

SOCIAL DISADVANTAGE THE REAL ENEMY IN THE WAR ON POVERTY

by Daniel Jordan
Published in *World Order*: Fall 1966

Daniel Jordan is Associate Professor of Psychology and Education, as well as Director of the Institute for Research in Human Behavior at Indiana State University. He is active in aiding disadvantaged students as a director of one of the Upward Bound Programs of the Office of Economic Opportunity.

In August of 1964, Congress passed the Economic Opportunity Act and two months later appropriated $800 million to help initiate an all-out war on poverty. During 1965, $1.5 billion were appropriated for poverty programs, and another $1.7 billion is expected for the current year.

These sums appear almost outrageously high until the enormity of the resources required to win the war is grasped. Thirty-five million people—9.3 million families with 12-15 million children, approximately one-fifth of the population—live in conditions of poverty or near poverty. In 1962, 5.4 million families had annual incomes below $2,000; some five million unrelated persons who lived alone or were without family ties had incomes below $1,500 and at least three million had incomes below $1,000.

Even if low income were to be regarded as the basic problem—the enemy in the war—the 1965 appropriation of $1.5 billion when divided among thirty-five million persons amounts to about $43 per capita each year. That is less than 83¢ per week per person. This tiny sum is not even enough to make any difference in the amount and quality of food each recipient could buy. If the $43 in cash were to be given to every poor person, the whole appropriation would simply evaporate without leaving a trace. Even if $1,000 could be given to each person directly it would probably have only a little immediate effect but no permanent consequence.

Seen in this light, the $1.5 billion appropriation is hardly significant. The only possible way that it may have significance is for it to be used in mobilizing special resources against the real enemy in the war—an enemy that has been difficult to identify because it has been and still is so well camouflaged.

Contradictory values in our own cultural heritage make it difficult to see through the camouflage and discern objectively the crucial factors that perpetuate poverty and which up to now have inhibited any effective action against it. On the one hand, millions of poverty-stricken families living in unsanitary urban slums and rural shacks cannot comfortably be ignored by a society which claims a Judaic-Christian conscience as part of its heritage. Yet, on the other hand, to do anything about it that will have significant results will cost several billions annually more than is currently being spent on the poverty program. That fact in itself is enough to cause considerable ambivalence, but the issue is confused even further by the traditional notion that there is something spiritually elevating about poverty and that we should therefore not be overly concerned about eradicating it. Many religious orders make vows of poverty a requirement of membership and Sunday school teachers teach that the poor are blessed. Though it may be difficult for some to understand, many have indeed found some blessing and spiritual upliftment in the kind of poverty that consists only of the lack of material things, so long as minimum shelter and food are available. Among such blessings are release from the burdens of maintaining and looking after material belongings, freedom from the many legal and economic worries that are associated with owning property and being pressured into accumulating more, and having time available to feast upon the fruits of man's religious, esthetic, and philosophical heritage. Those possessing intellectual and spiritual riches are the only ones who can, in fact, feel the blessings of poverty as narrowly defined above, and they are the only ones who have ever advocated poverty as a means of spiritual growth. When such persons have taken vows of poverty, they pledged to give up only material things. More than likely, the decision to take such a vow in the first place is predicated upon a certain intellectual and spiritual outlook that reflects a kind of non-material wealth which is not included in the vow as something to be given up.

Poverty more broadly defined as a cultural condition, however, is entirely different from a mere absence of material wealth. For those born into it, no riches of mind can be accumulated, little awareness of identity can grow, and there is almost no hope for the expression of individual potential. Instead, disease, sickness, insecurity, hunger, cold, and injustice prevail and there is little opportunity and no incentive to develop mind or spirit. An environment with these traits will also spawn a high rate of crime, delinquency, and mental illness. As a cultural condition, then, poverty bestows no blessings, and whatever spiritual elevation might be achieved by those whose lives are immersed in the culture of poverty will be largely in spite of it rather than because of it.

The camouflage is made up of many other beliefs which further impede action against poverty. There is, for instance, a general acceptance of the idea that the poor are inveterately lazy, without initiative, and, in the case of the non-white poor, innately inferior. From this premise it easily follows what the poor have is what they deserve. When beliefs of these kinds are coupled with the old conviction that as the nation grows economically, poverty will automatically disappear by itself in spite of the characteristics of the poor, a bulwark against remedial action is reinforced. In light of this background, it is not too difficult to understand why there has been no dramatically significant and nation-wide efforts made to reduce poverty before 1960.

During the ten or fifteen years prior to 1960, however, there was an increasing loss of faith in the general economic growth of the nation as the basic solution to the problem of poverty. Widespread unemployment among the poor, an alarmingly high average annual high school dropout rate, and the condition of poverty among 35,000,000 citizens, in spite of economic growth, have been disillusioning. Even the many good efforts to provide decent housing, place people on relief, create jobs, and distribute food have had, by themselves, few enduring effects. The disillusionment was good. It forced government agencies to collaborate with institutions of higher learning and private research organizations in a search for the critical factors of poverty and how they affect the personalities of the poor.

As a result of these joint efforts, much data has been collected and analyzed. Obviously, there are many different ways of interpreting the data. Each interpretation defines the problem differently and leads to the formulation of a different kind of attack. But no matter what or how vigorous any of the attacks are, if the real enemy is not identified, the war will be inevitably misdirected and ultimately lost.

One way of looking at the data has been particularly promising as a means of pinpointing the real enemy. Virtually, all of the basic factors which have been discovered to underlie the conditions of poverty can be traced to various kinds of disadvantages inherent in most of the social relationships which the poor are able to establish. Social disadvantage thus emerges as the real enemy in the war on poverty. The significant victory of the war will come when it is permanently removed.

Conviction that this in fact is the enemy has come largely from finally recognizing and accepting one glaring reality about poverty—that it perpetuates itself by a vicious circle that is sustained through social relationships. Seen in cultural terms, this is perfectly understandable. As used here, culture refers to ways of thinking, feeling, and acting which are transmitted from one generation to another through learning. People born into poverty learn to think, feel, and act in ways that adapt them to living in poverty, but they do not learn, and under ordinary circumstances cannot learn, how to think, feel and act in ways which insure survival in a non-poverty social and physical environment such as that characteristic of the middle class.

The process of cultural transmission from one generation to another is mediated by human beings through the social relationships they have. Since the rate and volume of cultural transmission is greater during the early years of life, the social relationships of these years are the most crucial. If his primary relationships are with middle-class people, a child will have a middle-class culture transmitted to him, and he will adapt to this kind of environment with facility. Similarly, the relationships that a child born into poverty will have are going to be with other poor people who will transmit to him ways of thinking and behaving that will, to be sure, adapt him to a poverty environment, but which will also vastly increase the probability of his failing in school. This, in turn, will very likely doom him to a life of poverty which he will then transmit to his own children, thereby completing the vicious circle. To win the war on poverty means, therefore, to break into the circularity of poverty.

Social disadvantage—the real enemy—lies, then, in the fact that one who is born into poverty cannot have social relationships with those who can transmit to him what will enable him to leave a poverty environment and still survive. When compared with others who can have such relationships, he is clearly disadvantaged socially. From this disadvantage springs nearly every other kind of disadvantage that might be mentioned.

The full force of this disadvantage is hard to grasp without an understanding of the nature of learning and the socialization process. A few concrete examples will help to demonstrate its magnitude.

Since attaining success in school is, generally speaking, the quickest way to break out of poverty, much of the deleterious power of social disadvantage can be understood in terms of the ways in which it precludes the possibility of a person's developing the skills and abilities on which success in school depends. The socially disadvantaged young person is almost always educationally disadvantaged. He became that way because he lacked, when he was growing up, the many important experiences that the non-disadvantaged person had to prepare him for achievement in school.

Paramount among these experiences that are lacking among the poor are those which in middle class society are mediated through relationships with family members. Ordinarily, the disadvantaged young person experiences little or no family conversation which would stimulate him to ask questions, provide him with answers, extend his vocabulary, encourage him to explain and defend his point of view, and most basic of all, give him practice in listening to whole sentences which express meanings that acquaint him with the powers and pleasures of abstraction—the basis of intellectual activity. He will also have no example set by others who are significant to him of persons who read and thereby convey to him the value of reading and writing. No one will read to him, and he will have no chance to learn to speak standard English. There will be few play materials available to him to stimulate his imagination and develop hand and eye coordination. Without these experiences and many others like them, young people have no opportunity to develop aspirations to participate and succeed in learning activities that will equip them for survival outside the sub-culture of poverty; their judgments about time, number, and other basic concepts are apt to be poor; they are likely to have underdeveloped powers of auditory and visual discrimination; chances are that they will have little self-understanding, confusion about their worth, low self-esteem, and no sense of a personal future.

As lengthy as it might appear, this is nonetheless only a partial list of ways of thinking and acting that are not transmitted to the children of the poor because they do not have social relationships with people who can transmit them. It is long enough, however, to demonstrate concretely the magnitude of the disadvantage. Its ramifications are even more staggering when viewed in the light of extensive data recently examined by Dr. Bloom, Professor of Education at the University of Chicago. This data suggests that around 50% of a person's intelligence measured at the age of 17 is already determined by the age of 4, and another 30% of the development of intelligence takes place between the ages of 4 and 8. For all practical purposes, social disadvantage guarantees deprivation of basic experiences which are crucial to the development of intelligence. Moreover, the debilitating effects of this kind of deprivation are in many cases relatively permanent and in all cases extremely difficult to reverse.

From an acceptance of social disadvantage as the real enemy, it logically follows that the strategy for waging the war on poverty should be developed around two basic campaigns: one to remove social disadvantage so that oncoming generations will not perpetuate the culture of poverty, and the other to reverse the effects of deprivation among the millions who are already its victims.

One may well ask at this point, whether or not the generals waging this war—the three branches of the federal government and all of the public and private agencies collaborating with them—have agreed that social disadvantage is, in fact, the enemy. The answer to that question, as yet not fully answered, could turn out to be the best part of the story.

The 1954 Supreme Court decision concerning school desegregation paved the way for legislation which may be considered the monarch of all the laws passed to help in the struggle against poverty—the Civil Rights Act of 1964. Without its provisions which strike at the basis of legalized institutionalization of social disadvantage, no war on poverty could conceivably be carried out. It struck powerfully at the heart of the enemy. Following in the wake of that victory came the Economic Opportunity Act which created the Office of Economic Opportunity. This office has vigorously assumed responsibility for inaugurating a number of programs to break into the vicious circle of poverty and reverse the effects of deprivation. Under its auspices Community Action Agencies have come into being throughout the nation. They carry out, often in collaboration with other public and private agencies, such programs as Headstart (for pre-school children of the poor), Upward Bound (for disadvantaged high school students to prepare them for college), legal services programs of various kinds, and Foster Grandparent programs. In the Job Corps, youth are trained so they can become employable. VISTA (Volunteers to Service in America) is the nation's domestic Peace Corps. The Department of Labor sponsors the Neighborhood Youth Corps which provides work and recreation for young people who would otherwise quite likely become a social liability. Rural loans for farmers in need are available from the Department of Agriculture, and small business loans are available from the Small Business Administration to help maintain small businesses which are useful to the economy and will provide jobs for those needing employment. The Department of Health, Education and Welfare administers a full spectrum of educational programs to reduce poverty. The Higher Education Act and the Elementary and Secondary Education Act, both passed in 1965, provide millions of dollars for a direct attack on poverty through education on all levels. The Manpower and Development and Training Act authorizes the Department of Labor to implement research and training programs designed not only to remove poverty but also to utilize human resources valuable to our economy.

What has happened so far is very encouraging. There is, however, another kind of social disadvantage which is less obvious, but an enemy, nonetheless. This is the disadvantage of the-non-poor when they try to administer programs for the poor—a kind of social disadvantage in reverse. Information about the feelings and behavior of the poor is obviously essential to the success of any program that is supposed to eradicate poverty. Yet, many who are working in the programs have had no meaningful relationships with people who are poor and therefore have never had experience with the ways of thinking, feeling and acting characteristic of the poor. Social disadvantage clearly works both ways and can make the planning and execution of poverty programs extremely trying and difficult.

Very few affluent people can see this latter kind of social disadvantage as a disadvantage because they are usually completely unaware of its effects. Yet, in some ways it is even more insidious than the former kind because it is institutionalized and therefore easily ignored and extremely resistant to change. In its role of educator of the poor, the public school is one obvious example of institutionalized disadvantage in reverse. The faculty and administrative personnel of almost all public schools are disadvantaged when it comes to understanding and educating the poor, and it has caused them to fail in that job. This failure, responsibility for which in all fairness must be shared by other institutions, is tangibly evident in the one million annual dropouts, the 7-9 million functionally illiterate adults, and another 10-12 million under-educated Americans. It is a failure costing the taxpaying citizen billions of dollars annually to support welfare programs, penal institutions, courts, mental hospitals, and police forces on municipal, state, and national levels. Around $20 billion are spent each year on job creation, relief, food distribution, and special housing programs, all of which are over and above the special programs that have been recently initiated as a part of the war on poverty. It is a bad enough disadvantage for the affluent to have to bear this financial burden, but the disadvantage is further increased because these funds are used in a way that does not eradicate poverty but in fact helps to perpetuate it. In essence, the money goes to help keep the poor alive and since it is not used to remove social disadvantage, it has the effect of enabling the poverty culture to be transmitted from one generation to another.

Unfortunately, not much has been done about removing social disadvantage in reverse. Although a great deal of research has yielded very useful information about poverty and its effect on human beings, it is frequently unknown or not applied by poverty program administrators, particularly on the local level. In any case, knowing things about other people from reports on research is one thing; feeling comfortable and being effective in cooperating with them is another. Having the former doesn't necessarily guarantee the latter. One clause in the Economic Opportunity Act reflects an understanding of this problem. It provides for a close working relationship between the poor and the non-poor in carrying out poverty programs. This provision, found in Title II of the Act, requires that the Community Action Programs be "developed, conducted and administered with maximum feasible participation of residents of the areas and members of the groups" being served. On theoretical grounds alone, it could have been predicted that this "maximum feasible participation" clause would cause a great deal of controversy. In effect, it calls on people of two different cultures, who don't know each others' ways of feeling and acting, to cooperate in a massive revolution of major aspects of our society.

Implementing the provision has, in fact, been extremely difficult in many cases, and has almost always proved controversial. Yet, understood in terms of the harm that lack of close communication and joint efforts without a democratic spirit can do, this provision is of profound importance in the long-range success of the whole anti-poverty effort. Without it, the war against poverty could easily turn into a war against the poor.

In spite of the controversies over the stipulation of maximum participation and the loud cries of the critics against other aspects of the poverty program, the prospects are good; some would say even thrilling. Besides bringing hope and restoring dignity to the lives of millions, the government will have its investment in each participant of poverty background returned many times over as each one successfully enters or rejoins the labor force. Not only will he not be using public funds by being on welfare or not adding to the crime rate, but he will be paying annual income tax at a rate which will undoubtedly amount to a good deal more than the cost of the services he received while participating in one or more of the programs. It is also certain that public education will never be the same in this country because of the new approaches in education being developed to assist in the war on poverty. These new developments and related research findings will be of benefit to everyone. But more than all that, in recognizing social disadvantage for what it is, the nation acknowledged the spiritual nature of man and assumed a moral obligation long ignored. The effect this can ultimately have on all men everywhere stirs the imagination. It could well be the harbinger of a 20th century renaissance.

CHAPTER 4

---•◆•---

GUARDIANS OF HIS TRUST

A BAHÁ'Í SOLUTION
TO THE PROBLEM OF POVERTY

By Daniel C. Jordan
Published In *World Order:* Winter 1970-71

THE CAUSES OF POVERTY are institutionalized. Any serious attempt to do anything about poverty on a widespread scale will meet resistance from the most prestigious of the world's religious institutions; economic institutions; business and industrial organizations, legal systems; civic, educational, recreational, and medical organizations; and government itself. Therefore, a permanent and effective solution to the problem of poverty will ultimately require, in Bahá'í terms, a *"rolling up of the old world order"* and *"spreading out a new one in its stead"*——one which will be free of the values which sustain the cycle of poverty. This is not to say that nothing can be done at the present time to alleviate the conditions of the poor. The Bahá'í teachings concerning poverty provide a spiritual perspective on the issue. The spiritual principles involved can be applied with guaranteed efficacy, even though, in ultimate terms, the permanent solution may require the establishment of a new world order.

Trying to deal with the problems of poverty through purely economic means can only result in failure. The institutionalized values which perpetuate the poverty cycle through successive generations, while having a bearing upon the economy, are not primarily economic in nature. 'Abdu'l-Bahá, son of the Founder of the Bahá'í Faith, stated that *"When we see poverty allowed to reach a condition of starvation, it is a sure sign that somewhere we shall find tyranny."*[1] Thus, until the causes of tyranny are dealt with, the problems of poverty cannot be solved. Over one hundred years ago, Bahá'u'lláh addressed all the kings of the earth collectively in a message known as the "Tablet of the Kings." In this message, He speaks to the issue of tyranny and injustice as it relates to the economy and the condition of the poor:

> *O kings of the earth! We see you increasing every year your expenditures, and laying the burden thereof on your subjects. This, verily, is wholly and grossly unjust ... Do not rob them to rear palaces for yourselves; nay rather choose for them that which ye choose for yourselves.*[2]

> *Tread ye the path of justice, for this, verily, is the straight path. Compose your differences, and reduce your armaments, that the burden of your expenditures*

---

[1] In J. E. Esslemont, *Bahá'u'lláh and the New Era* (Wilmette, Ill.: Bahá'í Publishing Trust, 1970), p. 149.

[2] In Shoghi Effendi, *The Promised Day Is Come* (Wilmette, Ill.: Bahá'í Publishing Committee, 1941), p. 26.

may be lightened, and that your minds and hearts may
be tranquilized. Heal the dissensions that divide you,
and ye will no longer be in need of any armaments
except what the protection of your cities and territories
demandeth. Fear ye God and take heed not to outstrip
the bounds of moderation, and be numbered among
the extravagant. We have learned that you are
increasing your outlay every year, and are laying the
burden thereof on your subjects. This, verily, is more
than they can bear, and is a grievous injustice.[3]

In that same Tablet, Bahá'u'lláh places the responsibility of
caring for the poor on those who occupy positions of power:

Know ye that the poor are the trust of God in your
midst. Watch that ye betray not His trust, that ye
deal not unjustly with them and that ye walk not in
the ways of the treacherous. Ye will most certainly be
called upon to answer for His trust on the day when
the Balance of Justice shall be set, the day when unto
every one shall be rendered his due, when the doing of
all men, be they rich or poor, shall be weighed.[4]

Although Bahá'u'lláh wrote these words over one hundred years
ago, societies the world over still expend vast sums on armaments while
funds for alleviating their own domestic conditions of poverty are in
short supply. If all the military budgets of the world were totaled up,
they would amount to a financial resource of staggering magnitude.
These budgets stand as a colossus of tragedy—a monument to our
collective ignorance and an agonizing manifestation of the extent to

---

[3] Ibid., p. 21.
[4] Ibid., p. 22.

which injustice and prejudice operate as determinants of economic policies. The basic injustice to which Bahá'u'lláh refers time and again is the exploitation by those who are in positions of power of those whom they govern, largely through excessive taxation and the misuse of public funds. This misuse reflects a set of priorities which is morally and spiritually reprehensible. No social system can tolerate indefinitely the kinds of pressures which build up when such priorities serve as the basis of governmental policy. Bahá'u'lláh Himself predicted the consequences of ignoring His counsel concerning these inverted priorities when He warned the monarchs that their kingdoms would be thrown into confusion, their empires would pass from their hands, commotion would seize all the people, and abasement would hasten after them as long as they remained heedless.[5] From the middle of the nineteenth century to the present time, we have been witnessing the commotion and confusion that have arisen in the wake of the efforts of the oppressed and the poor to secure their rights.

Another manifestation of the kind of injustice associated with poverty in the United States and a number of other countries is reflected in the disproportionate number of non-whites and members of ethnic minorities who are poor. In this country alone there are over thirty-five million people living in poverty as defined by the Office of Economic Opportunity. About half of them are nonwhite. For the most part they consist of American Indians living both on and off the reservation; Negroes who have migrated recently from the rural south to the industrial centers of the north; Spanish-speaking people with a rural background living in the west and middle-west, and Puerto Ricans who have moved to several northern metropolitan areas; and, to a lesser extent, European immigrants with a rural background. It is obvious that the problem of poverty cannot be dealt with successfully so long as ethnic prejudices prevail

---

[5] Bahá'u'lláh, "Tablet to Napoleon III," in *The Promised Day Is Come,* p. 29.

because these prejudices severely reduce the number of opportunities available for gaining economic security and destroy incentives for work.

The expenditure of so much of the public treasury on armaments and the perpetuation of the vicious cycle of poverty through prejudice and discrimination is bad enough. But the true picture is even bleaker. A significant percentage of the vast sums spent on trying to deal with the problem of poverty actually makes the situation worse. A number of researchers have demonstrated that behavior which guarantees a low economic status in the future is socialized in early childhood and that no program of intervention will be effective unless it involves the socialization or re-socialization of children from welfare families. Since welfare monies are not used in any way to assist in the resocialization of children, society's present way of dealing with poverty does not eliminate it, but, in fact, institutionalizes it. This has the consequence of creating a permanent "welfare class."[6] We are thus confronted with a doubly demoralizing situation: not enough funds to do anything significant with the problem, and available money used in a way which effectively perpetuates the problem rather than solves it.

Responsibilities of the Powerful and Affluent—the Guardians of His Trust

BAHÁ'U'LLÁH has placed special obligations upon those who occupy positions of power in the government and upon the affluent in working out a permanent solution to the problem of poverty. In His communications to the heads of states, Bahá'u'lláh identifies the poor as the *"trust of God"* and cautions the rulers to establish justice if they are to avoid betraying His trust. In *The Hidden*

---

[6] Robert D. Hess, "Educability and Rehabilitation: The Future of the Welfare Class," *Journal of Marriage and the Family,* 26 (Nov. 1964), 422-9.

Words Bahá'u'lláh extends this responsibility to the affluent: *"O YE RICH ONES ON EARTH! The poor in your midst are My trust; guard ye My trust, and be not intent only on your own ease."*[7] Thus, both the powerful and the affluent are guardians of His trust. Throughout His Writings, Bahá'u'lláh assigns a number of specific responsibilities to these "guardians." In addition to the ones already mentioned, Bahá'u'lláh calls for the abolition of both chattel slavery and industrial slavery. He insists on the reduction of the extremes of wealth and poverty through legislative means and the voluntary efforts of those with ample incomes to assist the poor. Bahá'u'lláh's teaching on inheritance establishes a new pattern for distributing the estates of the deceased which makes the massive accumulation of wealth within particular families very difficult, yet does not deprive such families of a high standard of living. Bahá'u'lláh also advocated the adoption of a graduated income tax so that the tax burden would not exacerbate the economic condition of the poor. Capital must not exploit labor. When 'Abdu'l-Bahá was in Dublin, New Hampshire, in 1912, he told one of his audiences that *"According to the divine law, employees should not be paid merely by wages. Nay, rather they should be partners in every work."*[8] In the "Tablet of Ishráqát," Bahá'u'lláh says:

> *The fifth Ishráq (Effulgence) is the knowledge by governments of the condition of the governed, and the conferring of ranks according to desert and merit. Regard to this matter is strictly enjoined upon every chief and ruler, that haply traitors may not usurp the positions of trustworthy men nor spoilers occupy the seats of guardians.*[9]

---

[7] Bahá'u'lláh, *The Hidden Words of Bahá'u'lláh* (Wilmette, Ill.: Bahá'í Publishing Trust, 1963), p. 41.

[8] In *Bahá'u'lláh and the New Era,* pp. 152-3.

[9] Ibid., p. 147.

While Bahá'u'lláh does not forbid the charging of interest on money, He cautions that it is a matter that must be conducted with moderation and justice and indicates that in order to keep the poor from being exploited, the maximum rate of interest allowable will have to be determined by the government. In essence these last three responsibilities entail the obligation of the affluent and government leaders to establish and maintain legitimate incentives for the poor to work and to accumulate as much wealth as their efforts will bring them.

The guardians of His trust also have a responsibility for providing the poor with the kind of education which will guarantee their employability. Thousands of Americans who have worked in anti-poverty programs sponsored by the Office of Economic Opportunity have been disillusioned by their discovery that providing an economic opportunity––a job opportunity or the opportunity to train for a job––is not enough to help someone out of the cycle of poverty. Being offered a job and accepting it is one thing. Being able to perform on the job responsibly enough to keep it is another. Developing a marketable skill and having an employment opportunity which requires that skill solves only half the problem. Being reliable in showing up for work, being on time, working at a reasonable rate, and being motivated to do quality work represents the other half of the problem. Educational programs having the objective of intervening successfully in the cycle of poverty must equip the person not only with a marketable skill but must also help him to develop a set of attitudes and commitments which will enable him to keep a job once he has the opportunity to take one. Characteristics which guarantee job tenure, such as reliability, trustworthiness, and promptness, do not have survival value in a poverty culture. That is why a welfare system which provides only subsistence but does nothing about the problem of helping to socialize or re-socialize children who are born into very low-income families, simply ends up financing the transmission from one generation to the next of attitudes and behaviors that are not compatible with reliable performance on the job. It is for this reason that Bahá'í education is concerned with character development as much as it is with the development of good scientists, artists, technicians, and craftsmen. Modern psychology has demonstrated the fact that the roots of character development lie in the experiences of early childhood. That is why 'Abdu'l-Bahá stresses the importance of early childhood education:

> *As to thy question concerning training children: It is incumbent upon thee to nurture them from the breast of the love of God, to urge them towards spiritual matters to turn unto God, and to acquire good manners, best characteristics and praiseworthy virtues and qualities in the world of humanity, and to study sciences with the utmost diligence; so that they may become spiritual, heavenly, and attracted to the fragrances of sanctity from their childhood and be reared in a religious, spiritual and heavenly training.*[10]

Furthermore, if parents are unable to provide an appropriate education for their children, then it becomes the responsibility of the Bahá'í community.

Responsibilities of His Trust—the Poor and Needy

STRIVING TO FIND ways of eradicating poverty is not only the responsibility of the affluent. Bahá'u'lláh assigns a number of responsibilities to the poor, so that they may be worthy of being His trust. He forbids begging and makes it incumbent upon everyone

---

[10] 'Abdu'l-Bahá, *Tablets of 'Abdu'l-Bahá Abbas,* (Chicago: Bahá'í Publishing Society, 1909-16) I, 87.

to engage in some occupation. The poor are not permitted to sit by passively and receive the attention and bestowals of the wealthy. Bahá'u'lláh says:

> *"Please God, the poor may exert themselves and strive to earn the means of livelihood. This is a duty which, in this most great Revelation, hath been prescribed unto every one, and is accounted in the sight of God as a goodly deed. Whoso observeth this duty, the help of the invisible One shall most certainly aid him.*[11]

In His message to the rulers and the people of Persia, 'Abdu'l-Bahá exhorts the poor and the downtrodden to make efforts on their own behalf: *"Open your mind's eye, see your great and present need. Rise up and struggle, seek education, seek enlightenment."*[12] Furthermore, it is important for the poor to strive to become educated because ignorance invites the very oppression, exploitation, and injustice which perpetuates poverty. In that same message, 'Abdu'l-Bahá makes the point that the uneducated lack the vocabulary to explain what they need and cannot adequately plead their case in court, even when the chance is given.[13]

Spiritual Values and the Abolition of Poverty

IT IS REMARKABLE that in the one hundred years since Bahá'u'lláh promulgated these teachings about poverty, some progress has been made by the United States in applying every one of them. Many legislators have been making efforts to end war, reduce

---

[11] Bahá'u'lláh and 'Abdu'l-Bahá, *Bahá'í World Faith*, 2nd ed. (Wilmette, Ill.: Bahá'í Publishing Trust, 1956), p. 131.

[12] 'Abdu'l-Bahá, *Secret of Divine Civilization* (Wilmette, Ill.: Bahá'í Publishing Trust, 1957), p. 91.

[13] Ibid., p. 18.

armaments, cut military expenditures, and turn those funds into domestic programs for the eradication of poverty. Vast segments of the entire population have been outraged by the extravagance of the military budget, particularly when compared with the resources put into efforts to reduce poverty. As recently as the 1950's, very little money outside of minimal welfare assistance was allocated by state and federal governments to finance programs designed to abolish poverty. The last decade and a half has witnessed the passage of legislation which provided for the establishment of an Office of Economic Opportunity––an agency officially charged with the responsibility for designing permanent solutions to the problem of poverty. The Elementary and Secondary Education Act of 1965 and the Higher Education Act of 1965 both provided billions of dollars to finance educational programs for disadvantaged children from low-income families––special programs which are designed to prevent the poverty culture from being transmitted from one generation to the next. The Manpower Development Training Act also provided means for establishing training programs for the poor so that their employability might be increased and job tenure secured.

Yet, we can never achieve ultimate success in arriving at a permanent solution to the problem of poverty until there is a shift from material to spiritual values as the basis of our economic policies. So long as material values dominate our lives, avarice, greed, and a compulsion to exploit the poor, rather than assist them, will ever be present. Bahá'u'lláh taught that true religion is the only instrument capable of inducing man to make that shift from material to spiritual values as the dominating force in his life. Although it is important that special laws be made in order to reduce the extremes of riches and want, nonetheless, 'Abdu'l-Bahá says that *"The rich must give of their abundance; they must soften their hearts and cultivate a compassionate intelligence, taking thought for those sad ones who are suffering from lack of the very necessaries of life.*"[14] In a letter to the Central Organization for a Durable Peace, written in 1919, 'Abdu'l-Bahá emphasized the voluntary nature of assuming responsibility for the welfare of others:

> *Among the teachings of Bahá'u'lláh is voluntary sharing of one's property with others among mankind. This voluntary sharing is greater than (legally imposed) equality, and consists in this, that one should not prefer oneself to others, but rather should sacrifice one's life and property for others. But this should not be introduced by coercion so that it becomes a law which man is compelled to follow. Nay, rather, man should voluntarily and of his own choice sacrifice his property and life for others, and spend willingly for the poor, just as is done in Persia among the Bahá'ís.*[15]

Furthermore, 'Abdu'l-Bahá affirms that:

> *Wealth is praiseworthy in the highest degree, if it is acquired by an individual's own efforts and the grace of God, in commerce, agriculture, art and industry, and if it be expended for philanthropic purposes. Above all, if a judicious and resourceful individual should initiate measures which would universally enrich the masses of the people, there could be no undertaking greater than this, and it would rank in the sight of God as the supreme achievement, for such a benefactor*

---

[14] In *Bahá'u'lláh and the New Era,* p. 149.

[15] Ibid., p. 150.

would supply the needs and insure the comfort and well-being of a great multitude.[16]

And again:

Is there any greater blessing conceivable for a man, than that he should become the cause of the education, the development, the prosperity and honor of his fellow-creatures? No, by the Lord God! The highest righteousness of all is for blessed souls to take hold of the hands of the helpless and deliver them out of their ignorance and abasement and poverty, and with pure motives, and only for the sake of God, to arise and energetically devote themselves to the service of the masses, forgetting their own worldly advantage and working only to serve the general good.[17]

Not only is it of benefit to the poor to receive assistance from the wealthy, but it is good for the rich to understand the nature of true wealth and to give to the poor in a spirit consistent with that understanding. Bahá'u'lláh states: *"The essence of wealth is love for Me. Whoso loveth Me is the possessor of all things, and he that loveth Me not is, indeed, of the poor and needy."*[18] Repeatedly, Bahá'u'lláh cites the debilitating and destructive force of being heedless of the needs of others and teaches that to be happy, stable human beings we have to assist in meeting the needs of others. Excessive wealth not used in spiritually correct ways will bring despair and tragedy upon its possessor precisely because it prohibits him from becoming and remaining aware of the nature of true wealth. Contemporary life is

---

[16] *The Secret of Divine Civilization*, p. 24.

[17] Ibid., p. 103.

[18] *Bahá'í World Faith*, p. 141.

full of examples of the wealthy whose existence is an utter misery because they are heedless of their spiritual and moral obligations. They squander and waste their fortunes, eventually facing both spiritual and material bankruptcy. Bahá'u'lláh makes the point in unequivocal terms:

O CHILDREN OF DUST!

Tell the rich of the midnight sighing of the poor, lest heedlessness lead them into the path of destruction, and deprive them of the Tree of Wealth. To give and to be generous are attributes of Mine; well is it with him that adorneth himself with My virtues.[19]

As the spiritualization of the planet takes place, new institutions which will deal with the problem of poverty from a spiritual point of view will be raised up, and the guardians of His trust will more and more assume their responsibility for looking after that trust. When this happens, Bahá'u'lláh's promise to the poor that "the Lord of wealth" will visit them will come true.

O SON OF BEING!

If poverty overtake thee, be not sad; for in time the Lord of wealth shall visit thee. Fear not abasement, for glory shall one day rest on thee.[20]

DANIEL C. JORDAN has become a cherished and reliable contributor to our pages. One of his articles for WORLD ORDER ("Becoming Your True Self," Fall 1968) has been reprinted in

---

[19] *The Hidden Words,* p. 39.

[20] Ibid., p. 16.

pamphlet form. Dr. Jordan is Professor of Education in the Center for Aesthetics at the School of Education, University of Massachusetts, and has served as consultant on educational and social programs at all levels of government. He is a member of the National Spiritual Assembly of the Bahá'ís of the United States.

CHAPTER 5

---•◆•---

BECOMING YOUR TRUE SELF

How the Bahá'í Faith Releases Human Potential

By Daniel C. Jordan
Published in *World Order*: Fall 1968

OVER A HUNDRED YEARS ago, the Founder of the Bahá'í Faith, Bahá'u'lláh, made the staggering claim that His Revelation would be the chief instrument by which the unification of mankind would take place and through which world order and world peace would ultimately be established.

Few will disagree that to progress from the present state of world turmoil and conflict to world peace and unity, social institutions and the human beings making them up will have to undergo a radical transformation. Whoever is truly interested in world peace will therefore have to have an interest in how that transformation can be brought about. The Bahá'í Faith having spread throughout the world in such a short time and having demonstrated its power to transform the lives of so many human beings, there has developed much interest in the nature of the actual process by which the Faith does enable a human being who embraces it to become transformed into his true self.

It would be wise to confess at the outset that it is not possible to discover or understand all of the forces latent within so vast a revelation which nurture and direct the transformation process; but there is much in the Bahá'í Writings that sheds a great deal of light on the way in which the Faith transforms the lives of its adherents by releasing the human potential.

The interest in how human potential is released is personal rather than academic, for millions everywhere are longing to become, as Bahá'u'lláh expresses it, fully noble, rather than remain imprisoned and abased.

Of course, Bahá'u'lláh's teachings concerning the transformation process are stimulating to the mind, but knowledge of them has also a practical purpose for, as we shall see, conscious knowledge of what is happening to oneself during that process helps to consolidate the gains and enables one to identify and accept, often through painful experiences that may at first appear needless or cruel, opportunities for further growth.

Personal transformation is a fundamental reason that people are attracted to the Faith, develop conviction as to its truth, and finally become Bahá'ís. The reason is simple. People who come in contact with the Faith and feel themselves being transformed by it have an experience that is self-validating. No one can take that experience away from them and no intellectual argument can make it appear insignificant or unreal. Feeling oneself becoming the best of what one can potentially be constitutes the highest joy. It promotes a sense of self-worth, obviates the need for expressing hostility, and guarantees a compassionate social conscience——all prerequisites of world unity and peace.

The Nature of Human Potential

BUT WHAT IS THE "BEST" of what one can potentially be? Bahá'u'lláh teaches that the highest expression of the self is servitude. The degree to which this highest station of servitude can be achieved is commensurate with the degree to which the basic powers or capacities of the human being can be released. The process of becoming one's true self, then, is synonymous with that process of developing basic capacities and dedicating them to the service of humanity. The daily decisions and actions which reflect this "becoming" are essentially religious in nature, for Bahá'u'lláh equates work of all kinds performed in a spirit of service––in the spirit of that highest station of man––with worship. The person who begins to see the religious nature of "becoming" will not only recognize a profound new dimension in work and worship, but will also see religion in a new light. He will begin to understand that when the force which continually enables one to grow disappears from any religion, it is time for it to be renewed, for religion devoid of that force is little more than empty rituals, meaningless dogmas, and social conventions which block the expression of the human spirit and impede social progress.

Service to mankind is given quality by the depth and character of the capacities of the human being rendering it. What are these capacities? Bahá'u'lláh identifies them in His statement of the animating purpose behind man's creation: to know and to love God. Here the two basic powers or capacities of *knowing* and *loving* are clearly specified and linked to our purpose––our reason for being. Thus, for a Bahá'í *becoming one's true self means the development of one's knowing and loving capacities in service to mankind.*

This understanding gives substance to the notion of spirituality. A spiritual person is one who knows and loves God and who is committed to the struggle of developing those knowing and loving capacities for service to humanity. By definition, then, being closed-minded about something, refusing to look at new evidence—blocking the knowing capacity, or reacting to others in unloving ways—are all signs of spiritual immaturity or spiritual sickness.

All other virtues can be understood as expressions of different combinations of these basic capacities of loving and knowing as they are applied in different situations. The loving capacity includes not only the ability to love but also the ability to be loved—to attract love. We cannot have lovers without loved ones. If we do not know how to be loved or cannot accept it, then we frustrate others who are struggling to develop their capacity to love. Not accepting someone's love is very frequently experienced as rejection and does untold amounts of damage, particularly in young children.

The knowing capacity also includes a knowledge of how to learn and how to teach. Teaching and learning are reciprocal aspects of the knowing capacity.

No teacher is a good teacher who cannot learn from his pupils, and no good pupil fails to question his teacher so that both teacher and pupil learn.

Each capacity supports and facilitates the development of the other. In order to know, for instance, we must love learning; if we are to love, we must know how to love and how to be loved.

These two capacities constitute the basic nature of human potential. From a Bahá'í point of view, true education refers to a drawing out or a development of potential to the fullest extent possible. Unfortunately, much of contemporary education is concerned only with a presentation of information rather than a drawing out of potential. For this reason, schools are primarily a place where facts and ideas are dispensed by the teacher and stored by the pupil. Consequently, diplomas and degrees do no more than certify that certain kinds and amounts of information were dispensed and that the recipient of the diploma was able to demonstrate at various points during the course of his formal education that he had stored the information long enough for it to be retrieved and written down on an examination. Such degrees or diplomas say nothing about the loving or feeling capacity of the student and therefore say very little about character——a word which refers to a person's ability to apply his knowledge constructively and express his love for humanity.

Furthermore, it has been demonstrated that if the loving capacity is blocked in any way, there will be learning problems and the development of the knowing capacity will be impaired. That is why a school system based on the narrow "dispensing-of-information" view of education can never adequately serve the needs of society. True education should foster development towards the achievement of the highest station——servitude——and must therefore be concerned with the whole person and his character rather than just a small part of him.

Faith and the Release of Human Potential

IT IS ONE THING to describe the nature of human potential and another to be able to release it. The Bahá'í Faith does both. The nature of human potential has already been briefly discussed. Let us now explore the ways in which the Faith initiates and sustains the transformation process by releasing human potential.

The basic source of the power for transformation is the Writings of Bahá'u'lláh. Exposure to His Writings nurtures the development of faith——the first prerequisite for transformation. Basically, faith refers to an attitude towards the unknown or unknowable which ultimately enables one to approach it in a way that something more of it becomes known. It thus represents a special interplay of the two basic capacities of knowing and loving. In essence, faith means a loving of the unknown or unknowable——an attraction to whatever is unknown and a capacity to approach it. Since, as Bahá'u'lláh affirms, God is unknowable, it takes faith to become attracted and related to Him.

We all have a kind of cosmic hunger, a need to be related to all things including the infinitude of the Universe. This is a natural by-product of consciousness. Since we experience ourselves as beings distinct from all other things in the universe, we feel compelled to find out how we stand in relationship to every other thing, and this includes being related to those unknown or unknowable things which also exist in the universe. The ultimate unknowable mystery of the universe is called by many names: 'Alláh, Jehovah, God, Supreme Being. Now, because man has the capacity for faith——a particular attitude toward the unknown——he has, down through history, responded to the Founders of the world's great religions Who came to manifest the attributes of that unknowable mystery in the universe——God——and satisfy our cosmic hunger. Thus, faith is one important expression of our purpose, which is to know and to love God.

It is interesting to note that, if our basic capacities are knowing and loving, and if we are created in the image of God, then knowing and loving must be among the attributes of God. In *The Hidden Words,* Bahá'u'lláh indicates that this is so. He says, *O Son of Man! Veiled in My immemorial being and in the ancient eternity of My essence, I knew My love for thee; therefore I created thee, have engraved on thee Mine image and revealed to thee My beauty.*[21]

Further, if God is unknowable and if we are created in His image, then we may expect something in ourselves also to be unknown. This unknown is the as yet unexpressed potential within us——latent capacities for knowing and loving. In a very dramatic way, Bahá'u'lláh points to that vast unknown in ourselves when he quotes in the *Seven Valleys* the verse of a well-known Persian poet: "Dost thou reckon thyself only a puny form / When within thee the

---

[21] Bahá'u'lláh, *The Hidden Words* (Wilmette, Ill.: Bahá'í Publishing Trust, 1954), p. 4. Emphasis mine.

universe is folded?"[22] In another verse, Bahá'u'lláh says, *Ye are My treasury, for in you I have treasured the pearls of My mysteries and the gems of My knowledge.*[23]

None of us knows his capacity for love or how much he can learn. Just as we had to have faith before we could learn about the attributes of God, so must we have faith before we can know something of ourselves. We must love––be attracted to, have a particular attitude towards––that unknown in our own selves if it is to become released. If we relate satisfactorily to the unknown in ourselves, we will be able to relate to the unknown in others. In other words, we have to accept others not only for what they presently are but also for what they can become; otherwise, we impede their process of transformation and keep them from becoming their own true selves.

This is why a person who has given up on himself, who has stopped becoming and has therefore betrayed his potential, will find all his relationships with other human beings disturbed, unsatisfying, and even painful. To accept and relate to another human being just as he is at a particular moment in time precludes the development of anything more than a superficial relationship. To achieve deeply meaningful relationships with other human beings, we have also to accept the unknown possibilities within them, for that acceptance constitutes one important source of their courage to become. In more personal terms, if you do not accept the unknown possibilities in yourself, you will not be able to establish anything more than superficial relationships with other human beings, and you will not be able to help them to develop their potential nor yourself to develop your own.

---

[22] Bahá'u'lláh, *The Seven Valleys and the Four Valleys* (Wilmette, Ill.: Bahá'í Publishing Trust, 1952), p. 34.

[23] Bahá'u'lláh, *The Hidden Words*, p. 20.

Since a human being's potential is an extremely important part of his reality—in fact, the basis of his future growth—it must be accepted by others and play a part in human relationships before he can feel *totally* accepted. Total acceptance on the part of others constitutes a special kind of trust that is very difficult to betray. It is one very important source of benevolent pressure to become and one of the most significant criteria of real love and friendship. This kind of pressure reciprocated between two human beings will spiritualize any relationship, but has particular significance for marriage. It forms the spiritual basis of Bahá'í marriage.

The necessity for reciprocity in this kind of relationship is clearly expressed by Bahá'u'lláh in *The Hidden Words*. He states, *O Son of Being! Love Me, that I may love thee. If thou lovest Me not, My love can in no wise reach thee. Know this, O servant.*[24] In this verse, God commands, through His Manifestation, that we love Him and accept Him in spite of the fact that He is unknowable. Being attracted to the unknowable is the essence of faith. If there is no faith, no attraction to that primary mystery—God, then we become alienated from the mystery in our own selves and cut off from the power to grow and develop. The statement quoted above starts with *O Son of Being* and ends with *know this, O servant*. Thus, in that very short verse, the two basic capacities of loving and knowing are again emphasized in the context of being and serving. It connects the process of being or becoming with that highest station of servitude.

Anxiety and the Unknown

FACING ANY UNKNOWN is not easy. The prospect of it, particularly when facing the unknown in ourselves, is always accompanied by anxiety. An extrinsic unknown is nearly always perceived as a potential threat to our security for it brings up a question that

---

[24] Ibid., p. 4.

represents an intrinsic unknown––do we, or do we not have what it will take to deal successfully with that extrinsic unknown?

Anxiety has all of the qualities of a fear reaction, except that it usually has no clear-cut object. Both fear reactions and anxiety reactions are characterized by a rapid energizing of the system which prepares it to deal with an emergency situation. One can handle the fear reaction more easily, since the threatening object is identifiable and can be removed or avoided. In the case of anxiety, the system goes into a state of preparedness for an emergency when it is not clear what the emergency is. Without any object, it is difficult to know what action to take and the system is never quite certain when to declare the emergency over. *Anxiety may thus be seen as energy without a goal.*

The only successful way to deal with anxiety is to treat that energy as a gift and find a concrete goal for it which will serve the more basic goal or purpose of developing capacities for loving and knowing. Determining what that goal should be in specific terms is perhaps the most universally creative act of man. It entails assuming a risk and stepping into the unknown, bearing the burden of doubt, yet always hopeful of discovering some new capacity or some new limitation (which is also part of one's reality). Being attracted to that unknown in ourselves is *faith*; being able to utilize the energy from anxiety by formulating a goal and taking steps toward it is *courage*. Thus faith, doubt, anxiety, and courage are all basic aspects of the process of transformation––the release of potential. If there were no unknowns, there would be no doubt or anxiety; and with no doubt or anxiety there would be no need for faith and courage.

The Spiritual Matrix of Transformation

THE POWER of the Bahá'í Faith to transform human beings by releasing their potential stems directly from the fact that it keeps doubt and anxiety from reaching unmanageable proportions and provides an incentive and motivation to deal with them constructively through faith and courage. Bahá'u'lláh himself indicated that the primary source of the power for transformation comes from an acceptance of His Word—the Word of God. His Writings are often referred to as "the creative word" precisely because human beings have felt themselves being created anew as they have become more and more exposed to it. Bahá'u'lláh clearly affirms that if you want to become transformed, you must *immerse yourselves in the ocean of my words.*

Immersion into that ocean begins the process of transformation by creating an awareness in us of the essential nature and purpose behind our creation. Nobody can read Bahá'u'lláh without feeling his own loving and knowing capacities being awakened and developed.

As we continually explore the Writings, we begin to see ourselves differently and to see the environment differently. As we begin to see ourselves and the environment differently, we begin to feel differently about things. As we begin to feel differently, we begin to feel differently about things. As we begin to feel differently, we begin to behave differently. Behaving differently is the tangible manifestation of one's having embarked upon the adventure of becoming what he potentially can become.

The Writings therefore serve as that intervening force which enables us to become free from all of those attachments and fears which keep us imprisoned and unable to take that risky but creative step into the unknown. We know that human beings are often changed by intense experiences of one kind or another. Immersion in the ocean of Bahá'u'lláh's Words is not just reading; it is an experience for the whole man which can become intense enough to free him from ties to the status quo and to set him forth on the pursuit of his destiny. As we are freed from crippling attachments to what other people think of us, we are less likely to be manipulated by them—imprisoned by them—and develop instead a source of intrinsic motivation.

The Writings also reduce general anxiety and doubt to manageable proportions by making sense out of human history and the world's present state of perpetual crisis. This means that we need not pretend the crises do not exist or refuse to face them. Thus, understanding something of the problems which face us not only reduces anxiety but attracts courage.

A further source of courage stems from Bahá'u'lláh's indication, in general terms, of what kinds of goals are legitimate and in keeping with the purpose of our creation. That gives us some guidance in taking that creative step of defining a goal which can be achieved by utilizing energy from anxiety. We have an option here. We can either take that creative step of defining a goal and facilitate the transformation process or we can refuse to do that, in any conscious way, and hope that the anxiety will finally go away by itself. Obviously, persons who have a great deal of guidance in what kind of goals to establish will be more apt to make conscious decisions in regard to defining goals. In the absence of such a definition, energy from anxiety is likely to be expressed in aggressive and hostile acts towards other human beings, whose reactions to the attack will very likely further impede growth and development not only in themselves but in the persons to whom they are reacting.

Thus, the Writings stimulate our knowing and loving capacities in a unique way which we may call faith and courage. That, in turn, serves to guarantee a continued growth and development of those two basic capacities. In other words, knowing and loving used in the right way through faith and courage will increase the knowing and loving capacity––will release human potential.

The Social Matrix of Transformation

BUT THIS IS NOT ALL of the picture. Bahá'u'lláh has made provisions for the formation of communities whose institutions may safeguard and promote the transformation of humanity. The Bahá'í Community becomes, then, the social matrix of transformation.

Because of Bahá'u'lláh's affirmation of the principle of the oneness of mankind, all Bahá'í Communities are composed of human beings from diverse linguistic, racial, national, and religious backgrounds. This diversity in the Bahá'í Community represents to every member many unknowns—or, in less euphemistic terms, the Bahá'í Community is made up of human beings many of whom one would not ordinarily be attracted to or choose to be one's friends. It is well known that we tend to choose for our friends others who think the same as we do, who feel the same way about other things as we do, who have similar tastes, and who like doing similar things. Within such a homogeneous group, one's transformation can easily come to a halt, for a set repertoire of responses is developed and there is no stimulus to develop new ones. That is why one of the most precious attributes of a Bahá'í Community is its diversity.

When one joins a Bahá'í Community he joins a family of extremely diverse human beings with whom he will have to work and establish meaningful relationships. The first thing he finds out, is that his old repertoire of responses is no longer adequate. So many different human beings represent a great many unknowns and trying to relate to those unknowns creates energy (anxiety), which sets that reciprocal process of knowing and loving through faith and courage in motion. *Defining a legitimate goal which will constructively utilize the energy from that anxiety will call forth a new repertoire of responses. Each new response is a bit of one's latent capacity made manifest—a release of human potential.* Another way of saying it is that the Bahá'í Community offers more opportunities for knowing and loving under growth-fostering circumstance than can be found anywhere else.

Typically, a Bahá'í moves through a pattern of spiritual evolution starting with tolerance for the diversity of his fellow community members. As knowledge is added, that tolerance grows into understanding. When love is added, understanding blossoms into appreciation. This appreciation for diversity is the spiritual and social opposite of ethnocentrism. The journey from ethnocentrism, through the stages of toleration and understanding, to a state of appreciation always entails many anxieties and doubts. We are often put in the position of not quite knowing what to do or if we do know what to do, we do not feel like doing it. These are tests which are prerequisite to our transformation. 'Abdu'l-Bahá, Bahá'u'lláh's son, states unequivocally that without tests there is no spiritual development.

Here we come to a very critical issue. Tests can many times destroy an individual. 'Abdu'l-Bahá explains that if we turn away from God for the solution, the test may indeed destroy us. If we turn to God for the solution and if we have the loving support of other members in the Community, we can pass the test successfully. Thus, the Bahá'í Community, because of its diversity, provides many of those tests which are essential to our spiritual development. At the same time, guidance from Bahá'í institutions and the commitment of the members of the community to accept each other for what they can become provides the courage to turn those tests into vehicles for spiritual development––for the release of human potential.

In brief, that is the spiritual meaning of adversity. Bahá'u'lláh states, *My calamity is My providence, outwardly it is fire and vengeance, but inwardly it is light and mercy. Hasten thereunto that thou mayest become an eternal light and an immortal spirit. This is My command unto thee, do thou observe it.*[25]

Thus, for a Bahá'í happiness is not a life free from anxiety or tension. That is the Bahá'í definition of boredom. Happiness for a Bahá'í is having tests and knowing how to summon the courage to pass them in such a way that his knowing and loving capacities are further developed in service to humanity. Living in the community

---

[25] Ibid., p. 15.

provides the tests which become the opportunities to acquire experience in translating abstract principles into concrete realities, and this gives faith a foundation of conscious knowledge. It is this ever-expanding conscious knowledge of how to apply the principles of the Faith in real situations that consolidates the gains in spiritual development and provides the base for continued growth.

Prejudice—A Block in the Path

UNIFICATION OF ALL peoples of the earth cannot take place if individual human beings are not united within themselves. Bahá'u'lláh indicated that He could find no human being who was inwardly and outwardly united. If one's knowing and loving capacities are in conflict, then one is not inwardly or outwardly united. The consequence is that one's words and deeds will not be in harmony.

The conflict of these capacities is reflected outwardly on another level. Science, for instance, may be regarded as an expression of man's knowing capacity and religion as an expression of his loving capacity. Bahá'u'lláh taught that science and religion must go hand in hand, or the conflict will cause destruction. Today we see how knowledge of nuclear energy without love creates a constant threat to our survival.

In a very basic sense, the word prejudice refers to conflicts in the way these two capacities are expressed. A prejudice is a belief (a kind of knowing) in something that is not true coupled with an emotional confirmation (a kind of loving). In other words, a prejudice is an emotional attraction or commitment to falsehood or error. Actions based on that commitment are nearly always damaging to the person who is the victim of the action as well as to the one who is carrying it out.

On a personal level, prejudice represents a definite blockage in the expression of human potential because the loving capacity has been used to impede the knowing capacity. In a fundamental sense, almost all neuroses and psychoses can be understood in terms of this kind of conflict. The goal of therapy therefore always has to be a removal of the blockage towards becoming one's true self by enabling the person's loving capacity to support his knowing powers and vice versa.

On the social level, prejudice in action results in massive injustices ranging from discrimination and segregation to open violence and hostility organized in the form of wars. In like manner, this represents a definite blockage in the expression of society's potential.

Every barrier to the unification of mankind is sustained by a prejudice——by widespread culturally determined emotional commitments to a falsehood. For this reason, Bahá'ís see the process of unification of mankind as being synonymous with the progressive eradication of prejudice. Before the barriers to unification can be torn down, the prejudices which support them must be abolished.

Why is prejudice so difficult to eradicate? One reason is that human beings often are unaware that they have a prejudice. Fundamentally, this is what bigotry is——being ignorant of one's ignorance while making bold and confident assertions of the rightness and truth of one's position. Bigoted persons are in a tragic position because they always avoid exposing themselves to any situation which would confront them with the fact that they may possibly have a prejudice. How would a person know whether or not he did have a commitment to an error in the form of a prejudice if he were never exposed to the experience which would reveal it? In concrete personal terms, how would you know that you had a prejudice against somebody who spoke another language or had a skin color different from your own, if you never had the opportunity to be with such a person——an experience which would help to reveal the error?

This is precisely why the Bahá'í Community is so essential to the progressive eradication of prejudice. It provides an opportunity at every turn for everyone to have the kinds of experiences which will let him know where his prejudices are. It is for this reason that the struggle for world unity takes place more within the Bahá'í Community than outside it. Outside the community, people can insulate themselves from those experiences which will reveal their prejudices to them while continuing to hear only those experiences which enable their perceptions to remain distorted and their commitment to falsehood strong.

For a Bahá'í, discovering a prejudice in himself is always a test, and the moment he recognizes it he knows that he must struggle to eradicate it, not only because it will make him be unjust to other people if he does not, but also because his own spiritual development absolutely depends upon it.

What happens to a person with a blocked potential——a person who for whatever reason has not been able to find out how to become his true self? If he is a passive or introverted kind of person, he will escape into a fantasy world, withdraw into a world of drugs and alcohol, and will probably eventually become so dysfunctional that he may have to be institutionalized. If the person is action-oriented and extroverted, he will be hostile and aggressive and may eventually have to be institutionalized for committing crimes. The point here is simple: the person who is in the process of becoming, whose loving and knowing capacities are being continually developed, does not want to escape responsibility into a world of fantasy, nor does he want to fight, hurt, or kill. It is impossible for human beings who feel their human potential being released to engage in a war of any kind. Under such circumstances there is absolutely no motivation for hostile action. It is for this reason that Bahá'u'lláh claims that His Faith and the Bahá'í Community will be that agency through which world peace will be ultimately established.

The Image of God and the Kingdom of God on Earth

THAT UNKNOWN in ourselves which the unexpressed potential represents has been referred to as the image of God. Becoming our true self means relating to that unknown in such a way that more and more of it becomes expressed. This always involves finding a goal for the energy from the anxiety that comes from facing that unknown.

This entire process has a social counterpart. What the image of God is to the individual human being the Kingdom of God on earth is to human society. That kingdom represents what society can potentially become just as the image of God represents what the individual can become. When there is transformation of individuals on a massive scale through the release of human potential––when the latent capacities for loving and knowing are organized and expressed on a social level as the progressive eradication of prejudice––we advance towards the establishment of the Kingdom of God on earth.

Bahá'u'lláh's Revelation did not deal only with the transformation of the individual in a vacuum, for this would be extremely difficult if not impossible. He also provided a blueprint for building a new world order. That building process is directed and guided by Bahá'í institutions in a way that will enable society to become its true self–– the Kingdom of God on earth. The response to anxieties and tests on an individual basis also has a social counterpart. Social institutions have their tests too; and their development depends on whether or not they can take that creative step into the unknown and form new kinds of legislation sustained by new kinds of judicial supports.

Bahá'ís accept the Kingdom of God on earth as a reality ultimately attainable, not through a passive waiting for it to happen to us in an instant by some miracle, but through dedicated efforts over a long period of time to become what we can become in the face of many trials and tribulations. Those who make these dedicated efforts feel themselves to play an active part in the greatest miracle of all––conscious acceptance of the responsibility to become knowing and loving servants of mankind for the glorification of God.

Thus, as greater and greater numbers of human beings find a way in the Bahá'í Faith to become their own true selves––to reflect the image of God in their lives, society will also be in the process of becoming its true self––the Kingdom of God on Earth.

If the travelers seek after the goal of the Intended One, this station apperteineth to the self––but that self which is "The Self of God standing within Him with laws."

On this plane, the self is not rejected but beloved; it is well-pleasing and not to be shunned. Although at the beginning, this plane is the realm of conflict, yet it endeth in attainment to the throne of splendor ... This is the plane of the self which is well-pleasing unto God. Refer to the verse: "Oh, thou soul which art at rest,/Return to thy Lord, well-pleased, and pleasing Him: ... Enter thou among My servants,/And enter thou My paradise."[26]

O My servants! Could ye apprehend with what wonders of My munificence and bounty I have willed to entrust your souls, ye would, of a truth, rid yourselves of attachment to all created things, and would gain a true knowledge of your own selves––a knowledge which is the same as the comprehension of Mine own Being. Ye would find yourselves independent of all else but Me, and would perceive, with your inner and outer eye, and as manifest as the revelation of My effulgent Name, the seas of My loving-kindness and bounty moving within you.[27]

---

[26] Bahá'u'lláh, *The Seven Valleys and the Four Valleys*, p. 47.

[27] Bahá'u'lláh, *Gleanings from the Writings of Bahá'u'lláh* (Wilmette, Ill.: Bahá'í Publishing Trust, 1952), pp. 326-7.

CHAPTER 6

---◆●◆---

IN SEARCH OF THE SUPREME
TALISMAN
A BAHÁ'Í PERSPECTIVE
ON EDUCATION

By **Daniel C. Jordan**
Published in ***World Order*: Fall 1970**

CULTURE IS THE UBIQUITOUS EDUCATOR of man. Over long periods of time human groups have accumulated vast bodies of experience which have been distilled into particular patterns of thinking, feeling, and acting. These patterns constitute the culture of any given group and are reflected in its basic institutions, such as family, school, or economic system. Functioning as mediators of educative experience, these institutions transmit from generation to generation the culture which sustains them.

It is possible to accomplish the transmission of culture to the oncoming generation only because man is a creature with extraordinary capacity for learning. It is the process of learning in all its multifarious forms to which education in its broadest sense refers. Since man is endowed with few instincts, he has to rely almost entirely on what he learns––his culture––for survival. Thus, the kind of education available to man at any given point in time has direct implications for both the probability and quality of his survival.

The Crisis in Culture and Education

THE RELATIONSHIP of man to his environment is not static. It is dynamic and therefore always changing. His interaction with the environment changes it, and those changes have reactive effects on him. If patterns of thinking, feeling, and acting––man's culture–– are not modified to reflect a constructive accommodation to those changes, the culture may easily become nonprogressive, eventually maladaptive, and ultimately genocidal.

For instance, we have succeeded in polluting the air and our water resources to such an extent that we now face ecological problems serious enough that our survival may depend on their solution. This is a good example of how culturally sustained patterns of behavior, when continued beyond a certain point, become dysfunctional and even dangerous. Whenever this happens, the culture enters a period of crisis. In the past, if new ways of thinking, feeling, and acting could not be found and accepted by the majority of people comprising the society facing such a crisis, the culture died out along with the people who clung to it; or a neighboring group that was more progressive absorbed it and, in the process changed it. Such crises in themselves are usually educative experiences and may be regarded as extracultural in the sense that they force a search for new patterns of acting that are outside of those sanctioned by the culture that has become maladaptive.

At the present time the world of humanity and the different cultures it represents are in the midst of the most extensive crises ever known to man. The ways we have learned to feel, think, and act in relationship to both our physical and social environments are no longer functional. Instead of bringing us peace and tranquility, they cause us to be destructive of each other through internecine riots and wars; of our own selves through drugs, alcohol, and a variety of psychological disorders; and of our physical environment through pollution, uncontrolled erosion, and ruthless exploitation of natural resources.

These crises are forcing humanity to seek a new culture––one that is universal and therefore functional for all men everywhere; one that can create a new race of men, new social institutions, and new physical environments. To survive these crises, we must learn new ways of thinking, feeling, and acting. Man must be re-educated.

But what will the re-education of mankind consist of? What new patterns of thinking, feeling, and acting have a reasonable hope of success in delivering us from these crises? No answer can be fully appreciated without understanding how a shift in values has brought us to our present condition.

Changes in Value Priorities—An Analytical Perspective on the Crises

WE ARE TAUGHT by our culture how to feel about everything in our environment––ideas, events, people, and objects. It is the culturally sanctioned pattern of positive and negative feelings about these things which constitutes the value system of any society. Every value system can be understood in terms of three subsystems organized around the way man defines his relationship to three different types of environments: physical, social, and supernatural.[28] The function of these value systems is to bring some kind of order and structure into those relationships. A certain kind of balance must be maintained among the subsystems if the whole society is to have an order that is functional, adaptive, and progressive. Understanding the changes in relationships which have occurred over the last century and a half among these three subsystems not only sheds light on the present crises but also establishes the indispensable nature of the Bahá'í perspective on education.

Values organized around man's relationship to the physical environment.––Man's struggle to relate himself to the physical environment in ways that increase the probability of his survival has led to a progressively more detailed knowledge of the nature of matter. The accumulation of this knowledge and its application to the environment gave rise to a subsystem of scientific values which now supports a technological order of vast proportions. This order has been so effective in giving man extensive control over the physical environment that few people would even consider questioning its "rightness".

Values organized around man's relationship to the social environment.––The experience and wisdom man has accumulated concerning how to live with others and function in groups are formally expressed through patterns of law and government and informally expressed through custom and tradition. Both expressions are sanctioned by a system of social values which sustains the moral order. The stability of community life depends upon members of the community sharing the social values which support the moral order. When the moral order disintegrates, there is no basis for community life.

---

[28] 'Abdu'l-Bahá uses similar categories to classify types of education: ". . . education is of three kinds: material, human, and spiritual." See *Some Answered Questions* (Wilmette, Ill.: Bahá'í Publishing Trust, 1964), p. 9.

Values organized around man's relationship to ultimate unknowns.––Man's capacity for consciousness has impelled him to strive continually for an understanding of his relationship to everything which exists, including the unknown in himself and the mysteries underlying the infinitude and order of the universe. From time to time, down through history, prophets and visionaries have appeared and articulated man's relationship to these unknowns. The events transpiring in the wake of their appearances have generated subsystems of spiritual values which sustain the religious orders of the communities in which they appeared.

Type Of Environment	Related Value System	Type of Order Sustained by the Value System
physical	scientific	technological
human beings	social	moral
supernatural (ultimate unknowns)	spiritual	religious

The scientific, social, and spiritual values that maintain respectively the technological, moral, and religious orders of society are all interrelated. Changes in one have effects on the others. The three subsystems and the values they represent are not held to be equally important or significant. Different societies at different times accorded them different priorities depending upon their past history and the exigencies they happened to be facing at any given moment. Whatever the priorities were or are, the values that are dominant determine the goals of a society and how its resources will be used–– in effect, its destiny.

For most of man's history, spiritual values have generally been dominant over social values, which in turn have usually been considered more important than values which related man to his physical environment. However, when science, as a method of discovering and verifying truths about our physical environment, began to develop, conflicts among the subsystems of values also developed and the dominant position of spiritual values was challenged. Since that time, scientific values have been accorded an increasingly more powerful position in the total value system. It is partly for this reason that we have seen in the last 150 years the emergence of a portentous secularism accompanied by a de-emphasis of spiritual values and a disintegration of the religious order.[29] The major institutions which stood as the bulwarks of the religious order have either crumbled or joined the rising tide of secularism and in both cases have lost their potency.

Any chronicle of the outstanding events of the nineteenth and twentieth centuries would disclose the collapse of the most prestigious and seemingly invulnerable ecclesiastical institutions and religious systems of the world. This includes, for instance, the dissolution of the caliphate and the consequent secularization of Turkey; the crumbling of the Shí'ih hierarchy in Persia and the rapid decline of its fortunes; the evaporation of the temporal sovereignty of the Pope; the disintegration of the Holy Roman Empire; and the accelerating fragmentation of Christianity in general. That traditional religions are dying out in almost every land is so well documented that it can no longer be questioned.

As religion fades, the sanctions which sustain the structure of the moral order lose their force and result in a confusion of social values. In the midst of such confusion, secular theories of morality become popular. This gives rise to an increase in moral laxity, a disregard

---

[29] For a lengthy discussion of this issue, see *The Secular City Debate,* ed. Daniel J. Callahan (New York: Macmillan Co., 1966). The book contains a series of discourses on the basic issues of secularism: how to grapple with "religionless Christianity," "sanctionless morality," "religion without God," "religion in the time of the "death of God'," etc.

for manners, a weakening of self-discipline, and the abandonment of self to excessive indulgence and pleasures, all of which are concomitants of the incapacity to assume a variety of important social responsibilities, particularly those related to marriage and the family. Yet marriages continue to be contracted and dissolved while children are conceived and born, bereft of the growth-fostering atmosphere and stability of a home life characterized by the watchful care of mature and loving parents. Personalities formed under such adverse conditions are almost certain to be unstable. The increase in crime, the expanding rate of divorce, mental illness, and alcoholism, the dependence upon tranquilizers, the escape from reality into the drug experience, the breakdown of law and order, the corruption of political institutions, and the unethical practices of modern business and industry are all symptomatic of the decomposition of the moral order.

The conflict in value systems has created many basic uncertainties, and, as the moral order has decomposed, feelings of personal anxiety and social insecurity have increased. It is therefore not surprising to find that trying to deal with insecurity has become a pervasive concern of modern society. On the personal level this concern is formally expressed in the development of the "helping professions" such as counseling and psychiatry (a development which is basically secular and replaces the support and guidance formerly available through the religious order). On the social level one of the basic reactions to insecurity has been mistrust and the consequent build-up of elaborate and costly defense systems and tenuous alliances. Rather than identify the fundamental causes of insecurity and deal with them, we have created institutions to deal with the symptoms: mental hospitals to help those who can no longer cope with anxiety; prisons for those who react to anxiety by threatening the security of others; foreign aid to help those who cannot remove social insecurities because war has ruined their means of obtaining adequate resources; armed forces to deal with those who are regarded as enemies and a threat to our own security. People who are conflict-ridden or suppressed by injustice can either withdraw (create a fantasy world to escape anxiety and finally become institutionalized) or strike out (pursue the route of crime and end up in prison or join violent political movements). Nations which are conflict-ridden internally by injustice and in conflict with other nations or externally oppressed can also withdraw or attack. Without a sharing of universal values, however, both withdrawal and attack are dysfunctional and only create further disunity and therefore more insecurity. The size of the institutions created to deal with the symptoms and the staggering amount of resources required to maintain them reflect the magnitude of the problem; their strangely contradictory nature betrays the conflicts in our value system.

One of the most effective antidotes to insecurity and anxiety is meaning. A primary source of meaning for man is the perception of sense-making relationships and an emotional acceptance of them. As history shows, traditional religion was unable to make sense out of its relationship to the emergence of science. It failed to arrive at a distinction between faith and superstition, went on to deny the truth of science, and drove a wedge between reason and faith— between science and religion. Instead of facilitating the perception of sense-making relationships by adjusting to the truths of science, religious leaders insisted upon ignorance or intellectual dishonesty and thereby increased man's insecurity. The effect was to abandon to science the responsibility of making sense out of things. Science took the responsibility seriously. During the last half-century there has been an almost frantic investment of time, energy, and material resources in all of the enterprises of science. It is no wonder that man has delivered to himself an awesome technology that has brought him on the one hand a measure of security because of the increased predictability of events in the material world, but on the other hand has provided him with a power of almost incalculable dimensions which, because he has lost his moral bearings, is a constant threat to his survival.

The crisis humanity presently faces can be simply stated: because true religion is dying out, the moral order is collapsing while science and technology, guided by a profusion of materialistic and secular philosophies, have been permitted to concentrate too many of their powers on developing more efficient ways of destroying man. In other words, the priorities in values are being reversed and are causing widespread disorder in man's relationship to his environment. He has thus entered a period of crises fraught with many dangers.

Teetering on the edge of oblivion, what can man do to face this crisis of incomprehensible proportions? If the foregoing analysis is correct, we have only one hope——a renaissance of religion based on spiritual values that do not deny the truth of science, but which can direct the awesome power of modern technology into constructive channels of service to a mankind that is unified by the power of new moral order derived from those values.

Rebirth of Religion and the Re-education of Humanity

IN THE MIDST of the accumulating wreckage of the old order, a new faith——the Bahá'í Faith——has appeared. The wellspring of this faith, the revelation of Bahá'u'lláh, bountifully showered upon humanity a little over a century ago, has demonstrated to an ever-growing circle of concerned human beings its power to prevent the crisis from extinguishing the human race. The tangible manifestation of this power is a rapidly expanding world-wide Bahá'í Community which thrives upon a new culture——a culture which educates the children born into it and re-educates the adults who join it. It is the creation and spreading of this new culture——new ways of thinking, feeling, and acting——that constitute the most powerfully constructive educational force at work on the planet today. Placing this process of enculturation in a broad but simple educational context, we can regard the whole world as the classroom, all of humanity as the class, Bahá'u'lláh as the teacher, and His revelation as the curriculum.[30]

The objective of this divine curriculum is to unify man through the creation of a universal culture, the ultimate concern of which is man's relationship to God. In this culture the religious order determines the moral order in a way that enables the technological order to be controlled and utilized for the benefit of all mankind. In other words, its purpose is to educate man to his spiritual reality, establish a world order which reflects that reality, replace materialism as the motivating force behind human conduct, and restore technology to a position of service. It makes clear the order of priority among the value systems, removes the conflicts among them, and therefore deals with the causes of social and personal insecurity.

Turning away from materialism is a prerequisite to the attainment of social unity precisely for the reason that material things taken as an ultimate concern draw out of man characteristics which work against the achievement of unity: greed, avarice, covetousness, reckless ambition to dominate, and injustice in dealing with those who are weak or belong to minority groups.[31] What the new moral order requires are the opposites of these characteristics. We cannot rely upon science and scientific values to develop such characteristics in man because they do not, by themselves, create the kind of motivation needed. Scientific inference can only confer probability

---

[30] "The prophets of God are the first educators. They bestow universal education upon man and cause him to rise from lowest levels of savagery to the highest pinnacles of spiritual development."--'Abdu'l-Bahá in *Bahá'í World Faith* (Wilmette, Ill." Bahá'í Publishing Trust, 1943), p. 249. "From the heaven of God's Will, and for the purpose of ennobling the world of being and of elevating the minds and souls of men, hath been sent down that which is the most effective instrument for the education of the whole human race."--Bahá'u'lláh, *Gleanings from the Writings of Bahá'u'lláh* (Wilmette, Ill." Bahá'í Publishing Trust, 1956), p. 95.

[31] Bahá'u'lláh and 'Abdu'l-Bahá, *The Reality of Man* (Wilmette, Ill." Bahá'í Publishing Trust, 1966), p. 51.

upon its conclusions. As important as this is, the transformation of humanity will nonetheless depend upon a power and dynamic born of certitude and affirmation rather than probability. Religion, because of the spiritual values it can generate, confers certitude upon altruistic aspirations and makes selfless action possible. These, in turn, help to create and maintain the bonds of unity on which the new moral order must depend for its structural durability. For these reasons, the reeducation––the transformation––of man is contingent upon the emergence of a culture in which universal spiritual values are dominant. In essence, this is the basic rationale underlying the Bahá'í perspective on education.

It should be noted that the Bahá'í Faith, in establishing a value system which rejects materialism as a basis for community life, does not teach that science and technology are in themselves bad. It is only when technology and science are directed by a materialistic philosophy rather than by a highly developed religious sense that they no longer serve mankind and, in fact, may destroy it. Bahá'u'lláh has stated: *"Your sciences shall not profit you in this day, nor your arts, nor your treasures, nor your glory. Cast them all behind your backs, and set your faces towards the Most Sublime Word ..."*[32] 'Abdu'l-Bahá, the son of Bahá'u'lláh, even goes so far as to say that the sciences, which are accepted and beloved when operating under the influence of the love of God, are not only fruitless without it, but are the cause of insanity.[33] He pleads for us to *"turn our hearts away from the world of matter and live in the spiritual world,"* for *"It alone can give us freedom!"*[34] and asserts that if *"the spiritual nature of the soul has been so strengthened that it holds the material side in subjection, then*

---

[32] Bahá'u'lláh, *Epistle to the Son of the Wolf* (Wilmette, Ill." Bahá'í Publishing Trust, 1953), pp. 97-8.

[33] 'Abdu'l-Bahá, *Tablets of 'Abdu'l-Bahá Abbas,* III (Chicago: Bahá'í Publishing Society, 1909-16), 687-8.

[34] *The Reality of Man,* p. 16.

does man approach the divine; his humanity becomes so glorified that the virtues of the celestial assembly are manifested in him; he radiates the mercy of God, he stimulates the spiritual progress of mankind, for he becomes a lamp to show light on their path."[35]

The Supreme Talisman—Man Spiritually Educated

BAHÁ'U'LLÁH, the Educator of the new era, characterized man as a treasury of potentialities which could be drawn out through education:

> *Man is the supreme Talisman. Lack of a proper education hath, however, deprived him of that which he doth inherently possess. Through a word proceeding out of the mouth of God he was called into being; by one word more he was guided to recognize the Source of his education; by yet another word his station and destiny were safeguarded. The Great Being saith: Regard man as a mine rich in gems of inestimable value. Education can, alone, cause it to reveal its treasures, and enable mankind to benefit therefrom. If any man were to meditate on that which the Scriptures, sent down from the heaven of God's holy Will, have revealed, he will readily recognize that their purpose is that all men shall be regarded as one soul, so that the seal bearing the words, "The Kingdom shall be God's," may be stamped on every heart, and the light of Divine bounty, of grace, and mercy may envelop all mankind.*[36]

---

[35] Ibid., pp. 13-4.
[36] *Gleanings.* pp. 259-60.

Man's only hope of becoming the supreme talisman, of developing his potentialities, is to have a *"proper education"*. The meaning of "talisman" points to the spiritual nature of those *"gems of inestimable value"*––the potentialities of man––and confirms the thesis that a proper education must therefore be based upon his spiritual realities. A talisman is an object which is cut or engraved with a sign "that attracts power from the heavens" and is thought to act as a charm which averts evil and brings good fortune. In the statement quoted above, Bahá'u'lláh specifies the nature of the seal or engraving (which signifies the spiritual quality of man's identity because of the Source of his being and his education), assures him protection from evil (safeguards his station and destiny), and brings him good fortune (envelops him with *"the light of Divine bounty, of grace, and mercy"*).

The "engraving" on the supreme talisman is a spiritual one. It is synonymous with the image of God.[37] That image represents all the attributes of God which are inherently possessed by man and can be expressed in the form of virtues.[38] It is these virtues, latent within us as potentialities, that are the *"gems of inestimable value"* which *"proper education"* can reveal.

The criterion for determining whether or not any educative experience is *"proper"* is whether or not it furthers God's purpose for man. Bahá'u'lláh affirmed knowing and loving God as the *"generating impulse and the primary purpose"* underlying man's creation.[39] Any

---

[37] In *The Hidden Words of Bahá'u'lláh* (Wilmette, Ill." Bahá'í Publishing Trust, 1963), p. 4, Bahá'u'lláh writes: *"Veiled in My immemorial being and in the ancient eternity of My essence, I knew My love for thee; therefore I created thee, have engraved on thee Mine image and revealed to thee My beauty.'*

[38] *"Upon the inmost reality of each and every created thing He hath shed the light of one of His names, and made it a recipient of the glory of one of His attributes. Upon the reality of man, however, He hath focused the radiance of all of His names and attributes, and made it a mirror of His own Self. Alone of all created things man hath been singled out for so great a favor, so enduring a bounty."*––Gleanings, p. 65.

[39] Ibid.

experience which reflects that purpose will have the power to release human potential––to reveal those gems of inestimable value which we inherently possess. It is imperative that we be aware of this verity, because it is consciousness of that purpose which keeps us in touch with our spiritual reality, inhibits self-alienation, and safeguards our destiny. Being out of touch with that purpose will always create an identity problem, for one cannot become his true self––find his true identity––if his capacities for knowing and loving are impaired or suppressed. When formal systems of education become attuned to God's purpose for man, they will function as institutionalized means of assisting every student to become his true self.[40]

Formal Means of Education in the New World Order

WHILE MOST SOCIETIES have both formal and informal means of educating the young, the formal means, represented by such institutions as schools, universities, or other training agencies, make up only a small, although important, part of the total educative force present within any given culture. The detailed specifications of educational institutions that will be produced by a Bahá'í culture cannot be made with any certainty so early in the development of the Faith. However, Bahá'u'lláh and 'Abdu'l-Bahá made numerous statements about education which provide basic guidelines for the development of educational institutions. In the new world order education will be compulsory.[41] It will consist in part of a standard curriculum for the whole world[42] and will include, at least,

---

[40] *"Through the Teachings of this Day Star of Truth every man will advance and develop until he attaineth the station at which he can manifest all the potential forces with which his inmost true self hath been endowed."*––Ibid., p. 68.

[41] Shoghi Effendi, *The World Order of Bahá'u'lláh* (Wilmette, Ill." Bahá'í Publishing Committee, 1938, p. xi.

[42] 'Abdu'l-Bahá, *Promulgation of Universal Peace* (Chicago: Executive Board of Bahá'í Temple Unity, 1921-22), I, 177.

all sciences,[43] agriculture,[44] art,[45] music,[46] literature and speech,[47] and a universal auxiliary language.[48] Training will emphasize the development of *"good manners"*, *"praiseworthy virtues and qualities"*, and spirituality.[49] Science and religion will exist as complementary areas in the curriculum, rather than as conflicting systems of thought and action.[50] Particular care will be given to promote the understanding and acceptance of the oneness of mankind as essential to world peace.[51] Special attention will be given to the education of very young children,[52] of parents,[53] of both girls and boys with a preference given to girls if the education of both cannot be managed (since mothers usually have more responsibility for training children),[54] and of members of minority groups.[55] In the new order the process of becoming educated will be in itself regarded as an act of worship[56] and will therefore be a spiritual activity motivated

---

[43] *Tablets of 'Abdu'l-Bahá Abbas*, II, 448-9.

[44] 'Abdu'l-Bahá in *Bahá'í World Faith*, p. 377.

[45] *Tablets of 'Abdu'l-Bahá Abbas*, II, 449-50.

[46] Ibid., III, p. 512.

[47] Ibid., pp. 501-2.

[48] 'Abdu'l-Bahá, *Bahá'í Peace Program* (New York: Bahá'í Publishing Committee, 1930), p. 16.

[49] *Tablets of 'Abdu'l-Bahá Abbas,* I, 87. See also II, 373. It should be noted here that Bahá'u'lláh Writings mention over 1400 virtues to be acquired by man.

[50] 'Abdu'l-Bahá, quoted in J. E. Esslemont, *Bahá'u'lláh and the New Era,* 3rd, rev. ed. (Wilmette, Ill." Bahá'í Publishing Trust, 1970), p. 202.

[51] 'Abdu'l-Bahá, *Star of the West,* IX, 9, p. 98. See also Shoghi Effendi, *The Advent of Divine Justice* (Wilmette, Ill." Bahá'í Publishing Trust, 1963), p. 30.

[52] *Tablets of 'Abdu'l-Bahá Abbas,* III, 606.

[53] Ibid., pp. 578-9.

[54] Ibid., pp. 579-80.

[55] 'Abdu'l-Bahá, *America's Spiritual Mission* (Wilmette, Ill." Bahá'í Publishing Trust, 1948), p. 10.

[56] 'Abdu'l-Bahá in *Bahá'í World Faith,* pp. 377-8.

by religious conviction rather than a secular activity motivated by purely economic considerations.

The above list is far from complete, but, whatever the specifications and functions of Bahá'í educational institutions of the future, they will fully reflect the essentials of the culture created by Bahá'u'lláh, for if culture——that ubiquitous educator of man——is to provide a *"proper"* education, it must reflect a scale of values which places spiritual values in a dominant position among all others. It is only that kind of culture which has the power to release the potentialities of man and create the supreme talisman that man is longing to become. Nothing short of a Manifestation of God——a Moses, a Christ, a Buddha, a Muhammad——has the power to generate a new culture in which spiritual values are dominant.

In this age a new culture has been generated by Bahá'u'lláh. It is based on His revelation and is promulgated by the Bahá'í institutions which He fashioned. This new culture, which is being spread from country to country and transmitted to the oncoming generation, brings to mankind the great promise of becoming spiritually re-educated and insures a quality of survival that is both purposeful and munificent.

CHAPTER 7

———◆·◆·◆———

THE MEANING OF LIFE

By **Daniel C. Jordan**
Published in *The Meaning of Deepening:* 1973

The question of the meaning of "meaning" is a very old one. It has, in fact, plagued philosophers and thinkers for centuries. Whatever unresolved arguments there are about the issue, most will agree that it is very difficult, if not impossible, to grasp the nature of meaning without considering the idea of purpose. No matter how hard we try to understand the meaning of meaning, we always somehow come back to the concept of purpose. In brief, if we are without a sense of purpose, we will find life meaningless and unfulfilled. If it is God's purpose for man that we adopt as our own, the kind of meaning infused into our lives will be spiritual. Seen in this light, deepening is synonymous with the process of having spiritual meaning infused into our lives.

Meaninglessness and Society

At the present juncture in the history of man we see a pervasive meaninglessness reflected in people around us and in current social institutions. Meaninglessness is a characteristic hallmark—perhaps the dominant symptom—of the collapsing world order. Without meaning in one's life, one lacks motivation and becomes apathetic, a condition close to spiritual or psychological death. Although breathing, one feels no vitality. Lacking motivation and vitality, one has no sense of direction, no feeling of destiny, no sense of future. Such a condition cannot be tolerated indefinitely. If there is no source of motivation arising from a sense of destiny and purpose, something else will take its place. In the absence of spiritual motivation, physical desires stand ready to fill the void. If one abandons himself to physical desires and lets them become the determinants of his behavior, he might as well be an animal. 'Abdu'l-Bahá makes a number of references to how easy it is for man, when he loses sight of his purpose, to have no spiritual meaning in his life and to become like an animal.[57] To become like an animal is to become socially irresponsible, to become unfit as a friend, spouse, parent, or citizen—in essence, to sow the seeds of destruction. Greed and violence ultimately become the

---

[57] *". . . when man does not open his mind and heart to the blessings of the spirit, . . . man is in a sorry plight! . . . All his aspirations and desires being strengthened by the lower side of the soul's nature, he becomes more and more brutal, until his whole being is in no way superior to that of the beasts that perish. Men such as this, plan to work evil, to hurt and to destroy . . . ."* 'Abdu'l-Bahá, *Paris Talks*, p. 97.
"Some men's lives are solely occupied with the things of this world; their minds are so circumscribed by exterior manners and traditional interests that they are blind to any other realm of existence, to the spiritual significance of all things! They think and dream of earthly fame, of material progress. Sensuous delights and comfortable surroundings bound their horizon, their highest ambitions centre in successes of worldly conditions and circumstances! . . . Like the animal, they have no thought beyond their own physical well-being." Ibid., pp. 98-99.

characteristics of man's behavior when physical desires are the primary sources of his motivation.

Meaninglessness and the Individual

Just as meaninglessness is the hallmark of the collapse of the old order, it is also the chief symptom of mental illness in individuals. Not only is the old world order being rolled up; each personality that is too tightly bound to that order is being rolled up too.[58] In other words, anybody who is attached to and clings to the old order will collapse as it collapses. That explains, particularly in the Western world, the alarming rates of mental breakdown. It is almost impossible for anybody who grows up in the Western world to be without attachments to the old order. Therefore, as it crumbles, we are all likely to feel that we are crumbling a little too. That is one reason why Bahá'u'lláh places such emphasis on the need for becoming detached.[59] If we are detached, we will not be so likely to collapse when we experience the old world order collapsing around us.

---

[58] . *"Soon will the present day Order be rolled up, and a new one spread out in its stead. Verily, thy Lord speaketh the truth and is the Knower of things unseen.' 'By Myself, the day is approaching when We will have rolled up the world and all that is therein, and spread out a new Order in its stead.'"* Bahá'u'lláh, quoted in Shoghi Effendi, *The World Order of Bahá'u'lláh,* pp. 161-62.

[59] . *"The world and its vanities, and its glory, and whatever delights it can offer, are all, in the sight of God, as worthless as, nay, even more contemptible than, dust and ashes. Would that the hearts of men could comprehend it! Cleanse yourselves thoroughly, O people of Bahá, from the defilement of the world, and of all that pertaineth unto it . . . Cast them away unto such as may desire them, and fasten your eyes upon this most holy and effulgent Vision."* Bahá'u'lláh, *Gleanings from the Writings of Bahá'u'lláh,* p. 304.
"It behoveth the people of Bahá to die to the world and all that is therein, to be so detached from all earthly things that the inmates of Paradise may inhale from their garment the sweet smelling savor of sanctity. . . ." Ibid., p. 100.

Persons who feel themselves beginning to fall apart frequently describe their internal, subjective states in terms of meaninglessness. Throughout the world professional counselors and therapists encounter patient after patient who describe meaninglessness as one of their greatest troubles: "I have no meaning in my life. It all seems so strange. I don't know what to do. I feel like I'm falling to pieces." Thus, on the one hand, we have masses of people held together by social institutions of the old order, institutions which are operating outside of the influence of God's purpose for man and are thus enveloped in meaninglessness. On the other hand, we have individuals who are attached to those institutions and who therefore reflect the same meaninglessness.

Anxiety

One of the concomitants of meaninglessness is stress or anxiety. Lettered or unlettered, everyone knows what anxiety is, whatever its source. For many people in the world, much anxiety comes from poverty. But for most of us in the Western world anxiety comes from being out of touch with our purpose to the extent that life loses its meaning.

If one has no sense of purpose in life, it is almost impossible to formulate long-range goals. This means that there is no central activity into which one's energy may be invested. When energy has no goal, no purpose to express, it will be subjectively experienced as anxiety. Anxiety has most of the bodily symptoms that fear produces, and it feels very much the same way. But fear is easier to deal with, for it almost always has a definite object. Anxiety is not so easily managed because it is more free-floating; it has no object. It may keep one from sleeping, or it may make one sleepy most of the time; it makes the heart beat faster and makes one feel "on edge" for long periods of time. Medical science has now created a wide variety of drugs which can remove the bodily symptoms and ease the subjective experience of anxiety. Yet no amount of drugs will eliminate the cause of anxiety. That can only be done by giving one's life meaning by knowing God's purpose for man. Of course, it is easier to visit the drugstore and invest a few dollars in a bottle of pills than it is to become deepened as a Bahá'í. But in the long run drugs will be a waste of money and a waste of time as well. As soon as the effect of the drug has worn off, the anxiety will still be there. Although in extreme cases a physician may legitimately prescribe medication to reduce tension, it can never be regarded as a permanent solution to the problem of anxiety.

The Bahá'í Solution to Anxiety

One of the best medicines for reducing anxiety is having perceptions which make sense out of all the events going on about us. This is one of the general functions of Bahá'u'lláh's Revelation. It makes sense out of things. The Bahá'í Teachings on progressive revelation, to take one example, make sense out of history. Thus, a Bahá'í child may be more advanced than his history teacher because he has a grasp of history seen in the light of God's purpose for man, whereas the history teacher is busy trying to explain the intricacies of wars and treaties without the benefit of any major integrating principle. One can memorize the dates of invasions and battles and the names of people who played a role in them. But that kind of knowledge by itself does not make sense out of man's history. The Bahá'í Teaching of progressive revelation, however, indicates that man is an ever-evolving creature and that the chief instruments of his evolution are the Manifestations of God and Their continuing revelations. The Manifestations appear from time to time, creating higher and higher levels of unity; in Their wake come new civilizations. Such cycles always involve the pain of giving up the old and obsolete and creating something new. Bahá'í know that a Manifestation has recently come and that He has explained the new cycle. Therefore they are in a position to understand the present turmoil and to know why things will probably get worse. But they also know that things will eventually get better until an unutterably glorious Most Great Peace will come. Current events thus make sense, and that is enough to keep a Bahá'í going.

It makes us wonder how those who have not heard of Bahá'u'lláh manage to live, particularly those who are willing to examine the world situation carefully. It is enough to make them want to give up. It also explains the massive tendency to escape from the present crises and pressures through alcohol, drugs, and other means. When one cannot make sense out of things which are becoming progressively worse, one becomes anxious, nervous, and upset and seeks relief, however illusory. It is true that knowing what is going to happen, particularly if things are getting worse, will make one anxious too. Knowing what principles to apply in any situation, however, and knowing that right actions will ultimately lead one out of difficulty enables one to manage that anxiety and even to convert it into courage. This is what courage is: the capacity to use the energy produced by anxiety for constructive ends. Thus the best antidote for anxiety is being able to make sense out of things and being able to take constructive action. There is no adequate source of guidance for making sense out of things except the Revelation of Bahá'u'lláh.

Bahá'u'lláh created Bahá'í institutions to serve as the legitimate instruments of His Revelation and to plan courses of action consistent with His interpretation of this critical juncture in man's history. The plans and decisions made by Bahá'í institutions enable us to take the most constructive action possible in a given crisis, and they steer us through whatever difficulties we have now and whatever difficulties may come. Thus a major source of meaning in our lives comes through our active understanding of our purpose as it is expressed in the plans of those institutions which Bahá'u'lláh has created. Therefore every Bahá'í must understand that an indispensable part of his deepening will come through his establishing enduring and life-giving bonds with all of Bahá'u'lláh institutions, through his knowing the people who function on those institutions, through his participating in the elections which place them there, through his praying for them, and through his supporting the operations and functions of those institutions with his talents and material resources.

Reality—Knowing and Loving God

There is yet another aspect of meaning which relates purpose to reality. If one is out of touch with the purpose of something, he is out of touch with the reality of that thing. Suppose, for example, that someone wins a refrigerator in a contest and, not understanding the purpose of the refrigerator, stores his boots in it and puts it on the front porch to display to the neighbors. A person who relates to a refrigerator by using it as a closet for his boots is out of touch with the reality of that refrigerator because he does not understand its purpose. Not to understand the purpose of the refrigerator means that one is not able to make use of its essential power–refrigeration.

What happens then if a human being is out of touch with his reality because he does not understand his purpose? He becomes self-alienated––a word which has become popular as a description of mental illness. One who is self-alienated does not know who he is or where he is going. If one does not know who he is and where he is going, he is going to be upset. Moreover, one's relationships to other human beings will be disturbed because he will feel impelled to cling to the people around him and to impose himself on them; and he will be unable to assume responsibility for himself or others.

Thus, it is absolutely essential for us to be in touch with our reality. Both Bahá'u'lláh and 'Abdu'l-Bahá make clear statements about reality and the importance of being in touch with it.

'Abdu'l-Bahá writes:

Praise be to God! the mediaeval ages of darkness have passed away and this century of radiance has dawned,—this century wherein the reality of things is becoming evident ... [60]

... this is clearly the century of a new life, the century of the revelation of the reality and therefore the greatest of all centuries. [61]

O Friends of God! Strive ye so that this darkness may be utterly dispelled and the Hidden Mystery may be revealed and the realities of things made evident and manifest. [62]

The primary way through which we come in contact with the reality of things is to understand their purpose. Therefore if we want to be in touch with our own reality and have the maximum amount of meaning in this life, we must gain a clearer apprehension of our purpose. Bahá'u'lláh explains man's purpose in several ways in different places. The following statement is one of His most moving explanations of our purpose. In it He relates purpose to reality and describes the magnitude of the favor bestowed on man. Ultimately, such comprehension is the essence of all Bahá'í deepening:

Having created the world and all that liveth and moveth therein, He, through the direct operation of His unconstrained and sovereign Will, chose to confer upon man the unique distinction and capacity to know Him and to love Him—a capacity that must needs be regarded as the generating impulse and the primary purpose underlying the whole of creation ... Upon

---

[60] 'Abdu'l-Bahá, in *Bahá'í World Faith*, p. 279.

[61] Ibid., p. 225.

[62] Ibid., p. 217.

*the inmost reality of each and every created thing He
hath shed the light of one of His names, and made
it a recipient of the glory of one of His attributes.
Upon the reality of man, however, He hath focused
the radiance of all of His names and attributes, and
made it a mirror of His own Self. Alone of all created
things man hath been singled out for so great a favor,
so enduring a bounty.*[63]

Thus our purpose is to know and to love God. Our reality is to
express that knowledge and love by reflecting or mirroring forth the
attributes of God, a capacity that we have been given. Bahá'u'lláh
shows the interrelationship of all creation in that each thing has
been created with the capacity to reflect one of the attributes of God
and one of His Names; at the apex of creation stands man who has
been endowed with the capacity to reflect and mirror forth all of
His attributes. It is therefore a critical part of comprehending God's
purpose for man for us to know what these attributes are and what
we have to do in order to develop them.

To deepen is to develop these attributes and to acquire meaning in
our lives by coming to know our own reality through comprehension
of God's purpose for us. Without that comprehension we can have
no sense of destiny and no power to transform the world.

---

[63] Bahá'u'lláh, *Gleanings*, p. 65.

CHAPTER 8

---◆·◆·◆---

DIVINE ATTRIBUTES

By Daniel C. Jordan
Published in *The Meaning of Deepening*: 1973

The statement of The Universal House of Justice on the nature of deepening challenges us to develop a clearer understanding of the nature of God's purpose for man. The more we understand the nature of this purpose, the more we will be in touch with reality. Continually being in touch with reality will bring meaning to our lives. In essence, then, deepening is synonymous with having meaning infused into our lives. In Bahá'u'lláh's statement about God's purpose for man. He indicates that knowing and loving God is the *"generating impulse and the primary purpose underlying the whole of creation."* He assures all of us that we have the capacity to reflect the attributes of God and that this capacity constitutes our reality. Therefore, if we want to be in touch with reality, if we want to be deepened, if we want to have meaning, we must strive to understand and reflect those attributes.

Knowing and Worshiping God

The sense of purpose is an important determinant of the quality of the life we lead. It is no wonder then that Bahá'u'lláh has us reaffirm our purpose of knowing and worshiping God in a daily obligatory prayer.[64] Without a constant awareness of this basic purpose, we will not be able to let go of our attachments to those aspects of the old order which are inconsistent with our purpose, and which inhibit our spiritual development.

While Bahá'u'lláh states that one of God's purposes for man is knowing God, He also says that God is unknowable.[65] 'Abdu'l-Bahá dispels the apparent contradiction by explaining that knowing God means the comprehension and knowledge of His attributes and not of His essence, for *"The mystery of Divinity is sanctified and purified from the comprehension of the beings ..."*[66] In another passage, 'Abdu'l-Bahá says:

> *The knowledge of the Reality of the Divinity is impossible and unattainable, but the knowledge of the Manifestations of God is the knowledge of God ...*

---

[64] *"I bear witness, O my God, that Thou hast created me to know Thee and to worship Thee. I testify, at this moment, to my powerlessness and to Thy might, to my poverty and to Thy wealth.*
"There is none other God but Thee, the Help in Peril, the Self-Subsisting." Bahá'u'lláh, in *Bahá'í Prayers*, p. 117.

[65] *"He is and hath ever been veiled in the ancient eternity of His own exalted and indivisible Essence, and will everlastingly continue to remain concealed in His inaccessible majesty and glory,"* Bahá'u'lláh, *Gleanings from the Writings of Bahá'u'lláh*, p. 318.

[66] 'Abdu'l-Bahá, in *Bahá'í World Faith*, p. 322.

Blessed are those who receive the light of the divine bounties from the enlightened Dawning-points.[67]

In yet another passage, 'Abdu'l-Bahá explains:

Therefore all that the human reality knows, discovers, and understands of the names, the attributes, and the perfections of God, refer to these Holy Manifestations. There is no access to anything else: "the way is closed, and seeking is forbidden."[68]

The Manifestations of God let us know what the attributes and names of God are. Through a comprehension of those names and attributes, we can learn how to fulfill our purpose.

Reflecting the Attributes of God

Being able *to say* what our purpose is may be comprehension on one level; being able to *act out* that purpose in our daily lives is comprehension on another level. Thus, it is important for us to gain an understanding of how knowledge of the attributes of God can be translated into the way we look at the world and the way we behave. At the present time, most of us go through the entire day reflecting many of the values of the old order. What would happen if, after praying each morning, we said to ourselves, "Our purpose and function is to reflect the names and attributes of God. Everything that we think, see, and feel in the course of the day will be done with this in our consciousness"? Would that resolve not change the way we feel and behave? Bahá'u'lláh guarantees that it will if we

---

[67] Ibid., p. 323.

[68] 'Abdu'l-Bahá, *Some Answered Questions*, p. 169.

continually strive to have that truth about our purpose foremost in our consciousness.

If we were to commit to memory 'Abdu'l-Bahá's statement that *"the Divinity of God, which is the sum of all perfections, reflects itself in the reality of man"*[69] and keep it in mind throughout our waking hours, it would be impossible for us to be grouchy, irascible, uncooperative, and unjust. Such feelings and actions are not compatible with the function of reflecting the attributes of God. That is why it is essential for our deepening to involve an ever-growing awareness or consciousness centered in the verity that *"the Divinity of God ... reflects itself in the reality of man."*

The Purpose of Life

How can we come to know all of these attributes which together constitute our reality? We are given a mind, a brain, an intellect. One of their purposes is to help us comprehend the attributes of God and therefore our own reality. 'Abdu'l-Bahá writes:

> ... *God has opened the doors of ideal virtues and attainments before the face of man. He has created in his being the mysteries of the divine kingdom. He has bestowed upon him the power of intellect so that through the attributes of reason when fortified by the Holy Spirit he may penetrate and discover ideal realities ...* [70]

Bahá'u'lláh also indicates that the function of the gift of understanding (one of the powers of the intellect) is to help us understand our purpose:

---

[69] 'Abdu'l-Bahá, in *Bahá'í World Faith*, p. 311.

[70] 'Abdu'l-Bahá, *The Promulgation of Universal Peace*, p. 297.

Know thou that, according to what thy Lord, the Lord of all men, hath decreed in His Book, the favors vouchsafed by Him unto mankind have been, and will ever remain, limitless in their range. First and foremost among these favors, which the Almighty hath conferred upon man, is the gift of understanding. His purpose in conferring such a gift is none other except to enable His creature to know and recognize the one true God——exalted be His glory. This gift giveth man the power to discern the truth in all things, leadeth him to that which is right, and helpeth him to discover the secrets of creation.[71]

Discovering our purpose and our essential reality——that is what our intellect is for. Thus, after we become Bahá'ís and have this explained to us, we no longer have an excuse for saying, "Who am I?" because then we know, or at least we are on the path to knowing. Even though it may take a whole lifetime to come to know oneself fully, Bahá'u'lláh has said that each person must know himself.[72] Such knowledge enables us to avoid self-alienation and to become progressively detached and thus protected from the meaninglessness and anxiety associated with a collapsing civilization. As the civilization falls, our detachment from it, or our spirituality, will enable us to carry on even though physically we may have pain to endure.

---

[71] Bahá'u'lláh, *Gleanings*, p. 194.

[72] "*. . . man should know his own self, and know those things which lead to loftiness or baseness, to shame or to honor, to affluence or to poverty.*" Bahá'u'lláh, in *Bahá'í World Faith*, p. 167.
"*Could ye apprehend with what wonders of My munificence and bounty I have willed to entrust your souls, ye would, of a truth, rid yourselves of attachment to all created things, and would gain a true knowledge of your own selves——a knowledge which is the same as the comprehension of Mine own Being.*" Bahá'u'lláh, *Gleanings*, pp. 326-27.

Let us now examine other statements of purpose in the Writings to see how they all fit together. When someone asked the Master what the purpose of the life of a Bahá'í was, He said it was *"To acquire virtues."*[73] These virtues are synonymous with the attributes of God, a myriad of which are mentioned in the Writings of Bahá'u'lláh. A lifetime of study and meditation is involved in attaining a deep understanding of these names and attributes. Such an understanding includes knowing how to translate them into feelings and actions so that they become a living sense of destiny and purpose within each one of us. We are exposed to many of these names and attributes each time we read a Bahá'í prayer, for most end with a listing: the All-Bountiful, the All-Knowing, the Merciful, the Healer, and so on. These are the attributes which constitute our reality; if we are going to come in touch with that reality in order to achieve our purpose, we must know what they are and how they apply to us. Thus when we come to the end of the prayer, we should listen carefully to those attributes. They are there for many purposes, one of which is to enable us to become acquainted with something of our own inner reality and self. After each prayer we should meditate on those attributes and perhaps even undertake an exercise of asking ourselves, "How do these attributes or virtues apply to me and what can I do to express them?" Eventually we may begin to get an idea of what it means to be a real Bahá'í.

Rúḥíyyih Khánum has recorded Shoghi Effendi's explanation of the purpose of life to a Bahá'í. He told her that the object of life to a Bahá'í is to promote the oneness of mankind.[74] He further indicated, in *The World Order of Bahá'u'lláh*, that the oneness of mankind is the pivot around which all of Bahá'u'lláh's Teachings revolve.[75]

---

[73] 'Abdu'l-Bahá, *Paris Talks*, p. 177.

[74] Rúḥíyyih Khánum, "To the Bahá'í Youth," p. 6

[75] "The principle of the Oneness of Mankind—the pivot round which all the teachings of Bahá'u'lláh revolve—is no mere outburst of ignorant emotionalism or an expression of vague and pious hope." Shoghi Effendi, *The World Order of Bahá'u'lláh*, pp. 42-43.

The movement of the world toward unity depends upon our ability to have the meaning and substance of oneness infused into our individual lives and our collective consciousness and actions.

Bahá'u'lláh summarized the purpose of life in yet another way:

> All men have been created to carry forward an ever-advancing civilization. The Almighty beareth Me witness: To act like the beasts of the field is unworthy of man. Those virtues that befit his dignity are forbearance, mercy, compassion and lovingkindness towards all the peoples and kindreds of the earth.[76]

Acquiring virtues is essential if we are going to promote the oneness of mankind. If we do not promote the oneness of mankind, we will never carry forward an ever-advancing civilization. The most highly developed societies are always those which can unify the largest number of human beings. The most primitive, underdeveloped societies are those which have not been able to unify large numbers of human beings. If sufficiently large numbers of people are not unified in some way, a division of labor is not possible; if there cannot be a division of labor, everyone will have to be occupied with basic activities, such as hunting for food and obtaining shelter. Under such circumstances, no one will have time to devote to the kinds of pursuits that lead to technological inventions and the development of the arts. Because of the extensive division of labor in Western society we can enjoy and benefit from thousands of goods and services made or performed by millions of people whom we do not know——millions of people who have been unified and integrated into one society. It follows that the highest level of civilization that can be reached by man will come into being when the three and a half billion people on earth are organized

---

[76] Bahá'u'lláh, *Gleanings*, p. 215.

and unified so that they can help one another. It is easy to see that without the virtues about which 'Abdu'l-Bahá spoke (those virtues which reflect the attributes of God) there is little hope of uniting all of the people of the earth into one World Order.

It is unlikely, also, that we will ever be able to maintain world unity without developing our knowing and loving capacities to the fullest––capacities which, Bahá'u'lláh says, reflect our purpose. Anything we can do which enables us to love more and to know more will be consistent with our purpose if we dedicate that love and knowledge to the service of mankind, the highest station to which we can attain. In speaking of the power of love, 'Abdu'l-Bahá says:

> *If love and agreement are manifest in a single family, that family will advance, become illumined and spiritual; but if enmity and hatred exist within it destruction and dispersion are inevitable. This is likewise true of the city. If those who dwell within it manifest a spirit of accord and fellowship it will progress steadily and human conditions become brighter whereas through enmity and strife it will be degraded and its inhabitants scattered. In the same way the people of a nation develop and advance toward civilization and enlightenment through love and accord, and are disintegrated by war and strife. Finally, this is true of humanity itself in the aggregate. When love is realized and the ideal spiritual bonds unite the hearts of men, the whole human race will be uplifted, the world will continually grow more spiritual and radiant and the happiness and tranquillity of mankind will be immeasurably increased. Warfare and strife will be uprooted, disagreement and dissension pass away and*

Universal Peace unite the nations and people of the world.[77]

All of the statements about our purpose made by 'Abdu'l-Bahá and Shoghi Effendi elaborate on that primary statement of Bahá'u'lláh that man has been created to know and to love God.[78] When we begin to feel what those words mean and to translate them into action, we will have begun the process of transformation.

Spiritualizing Our Habits

When we first become Bahá'ís, we have many habits which are motivated or sustained by values of the old order. We have a spiritual obligation to get rid of all the old order habits that do not reflect God's purpose for man and replace them with habits which do, habits which will help create the new World Order. One of the essential features of a habit is that one does not have to think about it. One's actions and reactions are automatic. But to become habitual, actions must be practiced. If we can deliberately and consciously maintain an awareness of our purpose and if we can make our judgments and decisions about how we are to behave in the context of that awareness, our actions will become spiritualized. With practice over long periods of time, they will become habitually spiritualized.

It is our spiritualized behavior that presents to the rest of the world the most tangible evidence that the Bahá'í community will indeed be able to carry forward an ever-advancing civilization. This is precisely why Bahá'u'lláh says that the best way to teach is to live the life––a life which reflects the reason for our creation. Those who manage to live the life become like a magnet that attracts everyone to the divine purpose for which they were created. When those who are attracted

---

[77] 'Abdu'l-Bahá, *Promulgation of Universal Peace*, p. 136.

[78] Bahá'u'lláh, *Gleanings*, p. 65.

come in touch with their own purpose, they become acquainted with their own reality. When they know their own reality, their lives are infused with meaning. When this takes place, they become happy and joyful beings. Although happiness is not necessarily the main object of life, The Universal House of Justice has told us that, fundamentally, Bahá'ís should be happy beings.[79] We have no hope of ever being happy if we do not know what we have been created for.

Loving and Being Loved

There is yet another dimension to the nature of our purpose in its relation to our reality. Although we inherently possess the capacity to love, there is much knowledge to be gained about love. As Bahá'ís we have to know not only how to love everyone but also how to be loved. This we can accomplish by becoming more lovable. If one of our purposes is to love others and if we are unlovable, we will constantly be frustrating other people's attempts to fulfill their purpose. Nobody likes to have his efforts to fulfill his purpose frustrated. Even though he may not understand all of this, he will feel it and react to it. Therefore, we should make it easy for others to love us. The only sure way to become lovable is to acquire virtues.

Unfortunately, we have fallen into the old world order trap of somehow believing that youthfulness, good looks, and clothes make us attractive and lovable. On this erroneous assumption cosmetics experts have built one of the largest industries in the Western world. Buttressed by market research documenting the Western world's belief that our appearance is what makes us lovable, the cosmetics

---

[79] "As humanity plunges deeper into that condition of which Bahá'u'lláh wrote, 'to disclose it now would not be meet and seemly,' so must the believers increasingly stand out as assured, orientated, and fundamentally happy beings, conforming to a standard which, in direct contrast to the ignoble and amoral attitudes of modern society, is the source of their honor, strength, and maturity." The Universal House of Justice, *Wellspring of Guidance*, p. 79.

industry is able to market an incredibly large number of cosmetics at exhorbitantly high prices. Yet no matter how much is invested in cosmetics, plastic surgery, wigs, or clothing, they are not what make us lovable. Ultimately there is only one thing that makes us lovable: the acquisition of virtues.

As Bahá'í youth begin the process of becoming informed of each other's character as a prelude to choosing a mate, they must look beyond the clothes and the cosmetics to find spiritual virtues, for it is only upon a spiritual foundation that a sound marriage and family life can be based. We must always be sensitive to the concrete expressions of these virtues because they tell us about the reality of other human beings. The old world order spends much money, time, and effort trying to seduce us away from the fundamental truth that to be lovable one must have spiritual virtues which cannot be purchased.

It is easy to love someone who is lovable. Yet Bahá'ís must also love those who are not lovable, for the one who is unlovable needs love more than anyone else. Furthermore, it is difficult to become lovable unless one is loved. Thus, Bahá'ís must love the unloved people in the world who may be unloved because they have not been able to develop virtues, or reflections of the attributes of God. Loving them will enable them to become lovable, to acquire virtues, and to come in touch with their own purpose and reality. As that process unfolds, world unity in a spiritual sense will begin to emerge.

'Abdu'l-Bahá makes it very clear that our joy in living stems from our efforts to live in an awareness of our purpose, to live in constant proximity to the Kingdom:

> A man living with his thoughts in this Kingdom knows perpetual joy. The ills all flesh is heir to do not pass him by, but they only touch the surface of his life, the depths are calm and serene.[80]

---

[80] 'Abdu'l-Bahá, *Paris Talks*, p. 110.

CHAPTER 9

---◆·◆·◆---

SPIRITUAL EDUCATION

By Daniel C. Jordan
Seek ye first the kingdom ...
Published in *The Meaning of Deepening*: 1973

*It is not astonishing that although man has been created
for the knowledge and love of God, for the virtues of the
human world, for spirituality, heavenly illumination
and life eternal, nevertheless he continues ignorant and
negligent of all this? Consider how he seeks knowledge
of everything except knowledge of God ... How much
he is attracted to the mysteries of matter and how
completely unaware he is of the mysteries of divinity!*[81]

---

[81] 'Abdu'l-Bahá, *Foundations of World Unity*, p. 64.

As 'Abdu'l-Bahá indicates, most of our energy is put into material education and practically none into a spiritual education that will enable us to apprehend God's purpose for man, allow it to transform us, and become reflected in our actions. Knowing the words that describe God's purpose for man is not enough. Bahá'u'lláh tells us, *"It is incumbent upon every man of insight and understanding to strive to translate that which hath been written into reality and action."*[82] In essence this is what spiritual education is. It means absorbing the meaning of Bahá'í Writings in ways that will transform us into spiritual beings and enable us to behave and act in accordance with Bahá'í law. Once we have begun to do that, we will be deepening, we will be pursuing our spiritual destiny, we will be happy, and we will be providing an environment in which children can grow spiritually.

Dynamics of Spiritual Education

To do all of these things takes power. Thus, one very important aspect of spiritual education is knowing how to draw on the power that is required for translating *"what hath been written into reality and action."* In addressing Himself to the question of power, Bahá'u'lláh states:

> the ... task of converting satanic strength into heavenly power is one that We have been empowered to accomplish ... The Word of God, alone, can claim the distinction of being endowed with the capacity required for so great and far-reaching a change.[83]

All of man's technological achievements, the consequences of his material education, are powerless to enable us to translate *"satanic*

---

[82] Bahá'u'lláh, *Gleanings from the Writings of Bahá'u'lláh*, p. 250.

[83] Ibid., p. 200.

strength into heavenly power." The Word of God alone can do it. Therefore, Bahá'u'lláh makes prayers obligatory and admonishes us to expose ourselves daily to His Word, to immerse ourselves in the ocean of His Writings. From the Writings, which are the Word of God, we can acquire the means for *"converting satanic strength into heavenly power"* and for using that *"heavenly power"* to translate what has been written *"into reality and action."*

The Two Natures of Man

How do we manage such a conversion of *"satanic strength into heavenly power"*? Perhaps the first thing we need to do is to understand something about the nature of ourselves. It is implicit in Bahá'u'lláh's statement concerning the translation of *"satanic strength into heavenly power"* that we have at least two natures. This 'Abdu'l-Bahá affirms:

> Since Darwin's day, we have acquired a possible record of human evolution that grows richer each year. We have also amassed evidence of our affinity with apes of which Darwin could not have conceived, and have learned so much about the behavior of apes that it has become almost impossible to define any aspect of human behavior as being truly unique."

> Science on Trial. p. 100 by Douglas T. Futyyma, Editor of Evolution

> *In man there are two natures; his spiritual or higher nature and his material or lower nature. In one he*

approaches God, in the other he lives for the world alone.[84]

In other Writings, 'Abdu'l-Bahá refers to our *"earthly nature"* and our *"heavenly nature,"* our *"animal nature"* and our *"human nature."*[85] Understanding the fact that we have two natures sheds some light on the struggle that goes on inside us. It is helpful to know that each one of us has a dual personality in which one part struggles against the other until we learn how the higher nature can exercise control over the lower nature. No matter how difficult this learning process is, man has the capacity to succeed. It is one of the capacities that distinguishes him from the animal, for 'Abdu'l-Bahá tells us:

> *... the animal is not capable of apprehending the divine teachings whereas man is worthy of them and possesses the capacity to understand. In the animal kingdom there is no such bestowal ...* [86]

Submitting to the Will of God

Given the fact that we have two natures, our job is to find a way of withdrawing power from the lower nature (*"satanic strength"*) and making it available to the higher (*"heavenly power"*). Undertaking

---

[84] 'Abdu'l-Bahá, *Paris Talks*, p. 60.

[85] *"In man there are two natures; his spiritual or higher nature and his material or lower nature. In one he approaches God, in the other he lives for the world alone. Signs of both these natures are to be found in men. In his material aspect he expresses untruth, cruelty and injustice; all these are the outcome of the lower nature. The attributes of his Divine nature are shown forth in love, mercy, kindness, truth and justice, one and all being expressions of his higher nature. Every good habit, every noble quality belongs to man's spiritual nature, whereas all his imperfections and sinful actions are born of his material nature. If a man's Divine nature dominates his human nature, we have a saint."* Ibid., p. 60.

[86] 'Abdu'l-Bahá, *The Promulgation of Universal Peace*, p. 58.

this spiritual task requires an act of will. Passively hoping for transformation to take place within us with no effort from ourselves is futile.

Two Natures	Develop Through Interaction w/ Environments	Actualized as Personal Human Character
1) Physical (genome)	a) Physical	
2) Spiritual ('Psychome' or soul)	b) Human c) Spiritual	} Phenome

We must use our own will to make ourselves submit to the will of God. The Bahá'í Writings emphasize the importance volition plays in spiritual growth and development; once one becomes a Bahá'í he no longer has an excuse for perpetually placing the blame for his present condition on someone else.[87] Having become acquainted with Bahá'u'lláh and His Revelation, he can no longer say, "I cannot do anything about my life. My mother has ruined me. My father rejected me. Society has let me down. I am in a terrible condition, and somebody else did it to me." In fact, lapsing into an abysmal cycle of introspection and self-pity will only make things worse. 'Abdu'l-Bahá explains that anyone who is self-indulgent will end in a state of despair.[88] Therefore when we are feeling despair, we must ask ourselves, "Are we permitting ourselves the kind of self-indulgence that leads to despair? Are we making excuses for our lack of will?" Chances are that we may be. What we must do is concentrate on turning our will over to Bahá'u'lláh, for He states that the purpose of the Manifestation is to summon all mankind

---

[87] "All that which ye potentially possess can . . . be manifested only as a result of your own volition." Bahá'u'lláh, *Gleanings*, p. 149.

". . . the choice of good or evil belongs to man. . . ." 'Abdu'l-Bahá, *Some Answered Questions*, p. 289.

[88] "Despair, both here and hereafter, is all you will gain from self-indulgence. . . ." 'Abdu'l-Bahá, *The Secret of Divine Civilization*, p. 105.

to resignation and submissiveness to the will of God.[89] He further states, *"The source of all good is trust in God, submission unto His command, and contentment in His holy will and pleasure."*[90]

It is submission which makes everything else come right. It can make a difference in every aspect of our lives, not the least of which is our married and home life. Consider for a moment the Bahá'í marriage vow which both bride and groom say as a part of the wedding ceremony: *"We will all, verily, abide by the Will of God."*[91] Instead of pledging obedience to each other, Bahá'ís pledge submission to the will of God. Thus if two people abide by the will of God—submit their own wills to God's will—they are guaranteed a spiritual marriage and a home atmosphere conducive to the rearing of children who love God, acquire virtues, and are dedicated to carrying forward an ever-advancing civilization. When two people initiate their married life with an awareness of their submission to the will of God, they will have a marriage that will grow and strengthen with time. Furthermore, the Bahá'í law requiring consent of parents for marriage functions as an additional means of assisting those considering marriage to become aware of the purpose of marriage and to recognize that its stability rests upon both parties' submitting their will to the will of God. The surest way for a serious couple to obtain parental consent to their marriage is for them to reflect in their behavior an understanding and awareness of the need to submit their wills to the will of God. This will be the most convincing sign to parents that the proposed union will be a good one—and a spiritual one.

---

[89] *"The purpose of the one true God in manifesting Himself is to summon all mankind to truthfulness and sincerity, to piety and trustworthiness, to resignation and submissiveness to the Will of God, to forebearance and kindliness, to uprightness and wisdom."* Bahá'u'lláh, *Gleanings,* p. 299.

[90] Bahá'u'lláh, in *Bahá'í World Faith,* p. 140.

[91] Bahá'u'lláh, in *Bahá'í Prayers,* p. 186.

Whatever aspect of our lives we may be struggling with, submitting ourselves to the will of God makes us sensitive to what we must do next in order to further our own growth and development. 'Abdu'l-Bahá explains:

> If his (man's) morals become spiritual in character, his aspirations heavenly and his actions conformable to the will of God, <u>man has attained the image and likeness of his creator</u>; otherwise he is the image and likeness of satan.[92]

Bahá'u'lláh tells us that our soul, which constitutes our reality, is capable of reflecting the attributes of God.[93] One of the primary means through which it is enabled to reflect the attributes of God is our understanding God's will for today and our submitting to it. If one can do that, he is guaranteed becoming a spiritual being. Therefore, one must become sensitive to the need for preparing his soul for the attributes or virtues 'Abdu'l-Bahá says it is one's

---

[92] 'Abdu'l-Bahá, *Promulgation of Universal Peace*, p. 330.

[93] *"Know, verily, that the soul is a sign of God, a heavenly gem whose reality the most learned of men hath failed to grasp, and whose mystery no mind, however acute, can ever hope to unravel. It is the first among all created things to declare the excellence of its Creator, the first to recognize His glory, to cleave to His truth, and to bow down in adoration before Him. If it be faithful to God, it will reflect His light, and will, eventually, return unto Him."* Bahá'u'lláh, in *Bahá'í World Faith*, p. 121.

'Abdu'l-Bahá, in many passages, elaborates on the soul's ability to reflect the qualities of God: *"Consequently the Divinity of God, which is the sum of all perfections, reflects itself in the reality of man. . . . Man then is the perfect mirror facing the Sun of Truth, and is the center of radiation: the Sun of Truth shines in this mirror. The reflection of the divine perfections appears in the reality of man. . . ."* 'Abdu'l-Bahá, in *Bahá'í World Faith*, p. 311.

"Man——the true man——is soul, not body. . . ." 'Abdu'l-Bahá, *Paris Talks*, p. 85.

"Souls are like unto mirrors, and the bounty of God is like unto the sun. When the mirrors pass beyond all coloring and attain purity and polish, and are confronted with the sun, they will reflect in full perfection its light and glory." 'Abdu'l-Bahá, in *Bahá'í World Faith*, p. 367.

purpose to acquire. For it is the soul's reflecting virtues that makes one an authentic Bahá'í and enables him to be sincere. It is that authenticity, or "realness," in turn, which one communicates when he is in touch with his own reality. People are very sensitive to authenticity. They know immediately when they are in the presence of someone whose soul is reflecting the attributes of God. Thus, the process of converting the *"satanic strength"* of one's *"lower nature"* into the *"heavenly power"* of one's *"higher nature"* involves developing spiritual characteristics. Spiritual education can therefore be seen as the process of gaining expertise in recognizing and developing spiritual characteristics.

Spiritual education can be defined as the process of gaining expertise in recognizing and developing spiritual characteristics. Such expertise reflects our spiritual competence.

Man's Two Susceptibilities

What prevents man from developing heavenly characteristics? 'Abdu'l-Bahá says:

> *Man possesses two kinds of susceptibilities; the natural emotions which are like dust upon the mirror, and spiritual susceptibilities, which are merciful and heavenly characteristics.*

> *There is a power which purifies the mirror from dust and transforms its reflections into intense brilliancy and radiance so that spiritual susceptibilities may chasten the hearts and heavenly bestowals sanctify them. What is the dust which obscures the mirror? It is attachment to the world, avarice, envy, love of luxury and comfort, haughtiness and self-desire; this*

*is the dust which prevents reflection of the rays of the
Sun of Reality in the mirror.*[94]

Unfortunately, the world, submerged in a sea of materialism,
is well organized to stimulate man's *"natural emotions."* Television,
literature, art, our institutions, our legal systems, and, most of all,
our economic system are spreading the pollution of materialism
and immorality. Therefore, in this age one has to work more
earnestly at acquiring *"spiritual susceptibilities"* than in almost any
other age. Indeed, one dare not let a day go by without a conscious
effort to acquire heavenly virtues, so pervasive are the influences of
materialism. Every time one is seduced into being envious or hateful,
into putting luxury and comfort ahead of spiritual considerations,
he is preventing his soul from reflecting spiritual characteristics.

The Importance of Tests

How does one know his soul is not reflecting spiritual qualities,
especially when he has grown up in the old order and is used to it? Tests
and difficulties, primarily, make one aware. With that awareness one
can begin to avoid situations which stimulate his *"natural emotions"*
and to seek those which develop his *"spiritual susceptibilities."* It is
true, of course, that one may have tests and difficulties that do not
come from the obscuring dust of materialism. Tests and difficulties
may also come from injustices and discrimination. Even so, if one
can respond to injustice with spirituality, the reflection of heavenly
realities from his soul will have a positive effect on the source
of injustice. Nobody can remain insensitive to the reflections of
heavenly realities forever. When one is in the presence of a soul
reflecting the attributes of God, there is no way that he can pretend
that it is evil or wrong or undesirable. To do so would be like a

---

[94] 'Abdu'l-Bahá, *Promulgation of Universal Peace*, p. 239.

flower's saying, while it is blossoming, "I don't believe the sun is good." Thus, even though one's tests and difficulties may come from injustice, his response should be a spiritual response which will enable his soul to reflect even more brilliantly the attributes of God, for it is that reflection which will have a spiritualizing effect on all those around it, including those who are being unjust. Eventually it will help them to attain spiritual virtues.

'Abdu'l-Bahá wrote that without tests there can be no spiritual development. Furthermore, when tests occur, we cannot remain passive if we genuinely want spiritual development. According to notes made by Edward C. Getsinger in 1915, 'Abdu'l-Bahá said:

> Tests are a means by which a soul is measured as to its fitness, and proven out by its own acts. God knows its fitness beforehand, and also its unpreparedness, but man, with an ego, would not believe himself unfit unless some proof were given to him. Consequently his susceptibility to evil is proven to him when he falls into tests, and the tests are continued until the soul realizes its own unfitness, then remorse and regret tend to root out the weakness.[95]

These are hard words to accept, but the truth of the matter is that life is hard at times—but for a heavenly purpose.

Facing Tests in a Spiritual Manner

It is also true that all tests are not necessarily a source of development. It is possible for tests to destroy us. The difference between a test that mediates spiritual advancement and one which destroys, 'Abdu'l-Bahá says, is this: if, when we have a test, we turn to our lower

---

[95] 'Abdu'l-Bahá, *"The worst enemies of the Cause are in the Cause,"* p. 45.

nature in response to the test, it will destroy us;[96] if we turn to God and work through the higher nature, that test will be the source of spiritual strength. The act of turning to God means, in effect, praying, meditating, and fasting. These are the three basic means by which we turn to God and through which we are given the strength to face our tests in a spiritual way and therefore use those tests and difficulties as vehicles for our spiritual transformation.

Bahá'u'lláh made it clear that our soul is the vehicle for doing this, and 'Abdu'l-Bahá explains that the soul is *an attractable body, to be drawn to the Magnet of the Kingdom of God.*[97] In other words, there is within each one of us an inherent natural tendency for the soul to lead us in the right direction. Most of us have indeed had the experience of feeling well when we are going in the right direction and actually sensing the growth that has taken place when we face a test by turning to God. We have also experienced what happens when we face a test and turn away from God. We feel self-contempt, remorse, and despair.

Prayer is one form of turning to God. 'Abdu'l-Bahá states:

> *Know thou, verily, it is becoming of a weak one to supplicate to the strong One and it behoveth a seeker of bounty to beseech the glorious, bountiful One. When one supplicates to his Lord, turns to Him and seeks bounty from His ocean this supplication is by itself a*

---

[96] *"The souls who bear the tests of God become the manifestations of great bounties; for the divine trials cause some souls to become entirely lifeless, while they cause the holy souls to ascend to the highest degree of love and solidity. They cause progress and they also cause retrogression."* 'Abdu'l-Bahá, *Tablets of 'Abdu'l-Bahá Abbas*, II, 324.

"To the sincere ones, tests are as a gift from God, the Exalted, for an heroic person hasteneth, with the utmost joy and gladness, to the tests of a violent battlefield, but the coward is afraid and trembles and utters moaning and lamentation. . . . Consequently, it is made clear that for holy souls, trials are as the gift of God, the Exalted; but for weak souls they are an unexpected calamity." 'Abdu'l-Bahá, in *Bahá'í World Faith*, p. 371.

[97] Ibid., p. 366.

light to his heart, an illumination to his sight, a life to his soul and an exaltation to his being.[98]

The prayers revealed by Bahá'u'lláh, especially for the Fast, indicate the effects of fasting on the soul. He says, in one prayer:

These are the days whereon Thou hast bidden all men to observe the fast, that through it they may purify their souls and rid themselves of all attachment to any one but Thee, and that out of their hearts may ascend that which will be worthy of the court of Thy majesty and may well beseem the seat of the revelation of Thy oneness.[99]

About meditation and its relationship to the development of the soul, 'Abdu'l-Bahá makes this extraordinary statement:

It is an axiomatic fact that while you meditate you are speaking with your own spirit. In that state of mind you put certain questions to your spirit and the spirit answers: the light breaks forth and the reality is revealed.[100]

In this Dispensation, we must all pray, fast, and meditate—we must all converse with our souls because they are the means whereby we can attract the power, the will, the energy to keep ourselves turned in the direction of God. Thus, when we make a decision about what to do in the face of a given test or difficulty and that decision turns out to be right, we will know it because it will develop the spiritual susceptibilities of our souls and will enable the attributes of God to be reflected in our actions. If we do the wrong thing, we will find

---

[98] 'Abdu'l-Bahá, in *Divine Art of Living*, p. 26.

[99] Bahá'u'lláh, in *Bahá'í Prayers*, p. 173.

[100] 'Abdu'l-Bahá, *Paris Talks*, p. 174.

ourselves reflecting the characteristics of our materialistic society. This will be a sign that we should try another approach. Nobody guarantees us that we will be able to make spiritual decisions the first time we try. Practice helps. The more we practice, the quicker and easier we will be able to make spiritual decisions in the future.

Unlike educational systems where some teachers become tired of having pupils who, time after time, cannot pass the same tests and therefore finally pass them on to the next grade to be rid of them. Bahá'u'lláh does not pass anybody just because he keeps on "failing" the same test. There is no point in hoping that one can go on and on and eventually pass the test without making an effort. The same test will keep coming back to one relentlessly until he faces it and does something about it.

It is a natural tendency for a human being to think that his problem is in the people he has to live with rather than in himself. Such a person frequently leaves the city and circumstances where he has been for a while and moves to a new locality. When he finds that his new friends cause him the same difficulties and problems, he migrates to another city. Rather than facing a test, he is running away from it. If a person has been in ten cities and in each of them the people he has become acquainted with begin to cause him a number of familiar difficulties and problems, that is a sign he needs to assess his reactions; for, very likely, he is giving way to *"natural emotions."* Blaming others for one's own spiritual weaknesses makes it increasingly easy to give in to selfish desires and delays the opportunity for developing heavenly qualities.

Power for Growth

There is a power which comes to us when we are engaged in trying to reflect the attributes of God and thus express Bahá'í virtues. 'Abdu'l-Bahá says:

There is a power in this Cause, a mysterious power,
far, far, far away from the ken of men and angels.
That invisible power is the cause of all these outward
activities. It moves the hearts. It rends the mountains.
It administers the complicated affairs of the Cause. It
inspires the friends. It dashes into a thousand pieces all
the forces of opposition. It creates new spiritual worlds.
This is a mystery of the Kingdom of Abhá.[101]

That power is available and waiting for every single Bahá'í to draw upon to help him convert his *"satanic strength"* into *"heavenly power"* and dedicate that power to the plan for a new world. 'Abdu'l-Bahá says that each creature has an individual endowment, power, and responsibility in the creative plan of God.[102] Thus as we submit to the Will of God, face our tests and difficulties through prayer and meditation, and participate in the creative plan of God by helping to build a new World Order, we cannot fail to become spiritually educated. Every single believer therefore must mobilize his endowments, his talents, his skills, his capacities, his abilities, and draw upon the power in this Cause and use it responsibly in the building of a new World Order through an active participation in all of the plans created and implemented by the institutions of the Faith. This is the greatest adventure that any human being could embark upon––finding a means of *"converting satanic strength into heavenly power,"* vigorously pursuing the reconstruction of human life on this planet and assisting in the ushering in of the Most Great Peace.

---

[101] 'Abdu'l-Bahá, *"There is a power in this Cause . . .,"* p. 34.

[102] 'Abdu'l-Bahá, *Promulgation of Universal Peace*, p. 287.

CHAPTER 10

---◆◆◆---

KNOWLEDGE, VOLITION, AND ACTION

THE STEPS TO SPIRITUAL TRANSFORMATION

By Daniel C. Jordan
Published in *Comprehensive Deepening Program*: 1973

Introduction

Bahá'u'lláh has said that religion is dying out in every land.[103] One of the most striking evidences of the truth of that statement is the abdication of responsibility for one's own life on the part of an ever-increasing number of people. To be no longer in charge of

---

[103] *"The vitality of men's belief in God is dying out in every land. . . ."* Bahá'u'lláh, *Gleanings from the Writings of Bahá'u'lláh*, p. 200.

determining one's destiny is to adopt a passive attitude towards life––an attitude devoid of self-discipline, initiative, volition, and attainment. The inevitable consequence is a yielding to the pressures of the old order and conformity to behavior patterns which hasten its downfall.

Religion dies out when man forgets God's purpose for him. Without a sense of that purpose, there can be no vision of spiritual destiny, no motivation to live in the present in ways that guarantee a spiritual life in the future, no reason to resist the corrupting temptations of a collapsing civilization. The rebirth of religion, therefore, means an infusion of God's purpose for man into the affairs of men. Fundamentally, this is what the Bahá'í Faith does as it spreads throughout the world; it provides the means through which each individual follower of Bahá'u'lláh can gain knowledge of God's purpose for man in this day and, in collaboration with all of the Bahá'ís throughout the world, translate that purpose into action which will ultimately lead us to the Most Great Peace.

A true Bahá'í cannot be passive about his Faith. Bahá'u'lláh states that *"It is incumbent upon every man of insight and understanding to strive to translate that which hath been written into reality and action."*[104] 'Abdu'l-Bahá says:

> He is a true Bahá'í who strives by day and by night
> to progress and advance along the path of human
> endeavor, whose most cherished desire is so to live and
> act as to enrich and illuminate the world, whose source
> of inspiration is the essence of Divine virtue, whose
> aim in life is so to conduct himself as to be the cause
> of infinite progress. Only when he attains unto such
> perfect gifts can it be said of him that he is a true
> Bahá'í. For in this holy Dispensation, the crowning

---

[104] Ibid., p. 250.

glory of bygone ages, and cycles, true Faith is no mere acknowledgment of the Unity of God, but the living of a life that will manifest all the perfections and virtues implied in such belief.[105]

If we are serious about becoming true Bahá'ís, if this is one of our most important objectives, then we must have knowledge of God's purpose for man, the will to plan our lives around it, and the capacity to act. Without knowledge, volition, and action, no spiritual transformation can occur, for 'Abdu'l-Bahá tells us:

The attainment of any object is conditioned upon knowledge, volition and action. Unless these three conditions are forthcoming there is no execution or accomplishment.[106]

1 | Knowledge of God's Purpose for Man

To become actively engaged in directing the spiritual transformation of our own lives, conscious knowledge of God's purpose for man is essential. The transformation process is carried forward by action and reaction based on this knowledge. Since many of our habits and natural tendencies may be more congruent with patterns of the old world order than with the new, and may directly contravene Bahá'í law, many of our actions and reactions will require deliberate and conscious effort to apply this knowledge. Conscious knowledge of God's purpose for man provides a basis for making decisions that lead to spiritual growth and for choosing courses of action which consolidate the spiritual foundations of our lives.

---

[105] 'Abdu'l-Bahá, in *The Divine Art of Living*, p. 25.

[106] 'Abdu'l-Bahá, *Foundations of World Unity*, p. 101.

We find the explanation of God's purpose for man in this Age in the words of Bahá'u'lláh, 'Abdu'l-Bahá, and Shoghi Effendi. Bahá'u'lláh declares that we were created to know and to love God and that we have been endowed with the capacity to reflect every one of the names and attributes of God.[107] He further states that we were *"created to carry forward an ever-advancing civilization."*[108] 'Abdu'l-Bahá teaches that our purpose in life is to acquire virtues[109]—the attributes of God translated into human behavior. Shoghi Effendi confirms that the object of our lives should be to promote the oneness of mankind.[110] Indeed, he says that the oneness of mankind is the pivot around which all of Bahá'u'lláh's Teachings revolve.[111]

Armed with a conscious knowledge of God's purpose for man,[112] it is possible for us to take a positive and active role in determining our own spiritual destinies. The quality and effectiveness of this role will be dependent upon the depth of our knowledge and our capacity to make the decision to act and then to act.

2 | The Role of Volition in Spiritual Transformation

Taking charge of our spiritual destinies——directing the process of becoming our true selves——cannot in the last analysis, be delegated to others. Coming to a clear realization of that fact is essential to spiritual transformation. Bahá'u'lláh has written:

> *Unto each one hath been prescribed a pre-ordained*
> *measure, as decreed in God's mighty and guarded*

---

[107] Bahá'u'lláh, *Gleanings from the Writings of Bahá'u'lláh*, p. 65.

[108] Ibid., p. 215.

[109] 'Abdu'l-Bahá, *Paris Talks*, p. 177.

[110] Shoghi Effendi, quoted by Rúḥíyyih Khánum, "To the Bahá'í Youth," p. 6.

[111] Shoghi Effendi, *The World Order of Bahá'u'lláh*, p. 42.

[112] For a fuller discussion of God's purpose for man, see Daniel C. Jordan, *The Meaning of Deepening.*

*Tablets. All that which ye potentially possess can,
however, be manifested only as a result of your own
volition. Your own acts testify to this truth.*[113]

When this realization is made and fully accepted, we will stop trying to find excuses for our lack of direction or action and cease hunting for people or conditions on which to lay the blame for dissatisfaction with our spiritual state. Energy need no longer be put into these fruitless activities.

Parents, educators, counselors, and therapists, disregarding verification in experience, find it difficult to accept that mere knowledge of what we should do will not enable us actually to do it. 'Abdu'l-Bahá emphasizes that knowledge alone does not produce appropriate action:

*Mere knowledge of principles is not sufficient. We all
know and admit that justice is good but there is need
of volition and action to carry out and manifest it.
For example, we might think it good to build a church
but simply thinking of it as a good thing will not help
its erection. The ways and means must be provided;
we must will to build it and then proceed with the
construction.*[114]

A pilgrim to 'Akká reports that 'Abdu'l-Bahá explained the relationship between knowledge and will in this way:

*Will is the centre or focus of human understanding.
We must will to know God, just as we must will in
order to possess the life He has given us. The human*

---

[113] Bahá'u'lláh, *Gleanings from the Writings of Bahá'u'lláh*, p. 149.

[114] 'Abdu'l-Bahá, *Foundations of World Unity*, p. 26.

will must be subdued and trained into the Will of
God. It is a great power to have a strong will, but
a greater power to give that will to God. The will is
what we do, the understanding is what we know. Will
and understanding must be one in the Cause of God.
Intention brings attainment.[115]

The capacity to will something——volition——is a reflection of the
"ideal and heavenly force" within man:

Nature is without volition and acts perforce whereas
man possesses a mighty will ... it is evident that man is
more noble and superior; that in him there is an ideal
power surpassing nature. He has consciousness, volition,
memory, intelligent power, divine attributes and virtues
of which nature is completely deprived, bereft ...
therefore man is higher and nobler by reason of the ideal
and heavenly force latent and manifest in him.[116]

What are some of the tangible manifestations of the will at
work? It is important for us to know what they are so that when we
are experiencing them we may have the confirmation that we are
making use of that *"ideal and heavenly force"* in accordance with
God's purpose for man.

Setting Goals

Among the most important of the tangible manifestations of volition
is setting goals for oneself——*"high resolves and noble purposes,"*
'Abdu'l-Bahá refers to them:

---

[115] 'Abdu'l-Bahá, quoted in Julia M. Grundy, *Ten Days in the Light of Acca*, pp. 30-31.
[116] 'Abdu'l-Bahá, *Foundations of World Unity,* p. 70.

… man's supreme honor and real happiness lie in self-respect, in high resolves and noble purposes, in integrity and moral quality, in immaculacy of mind.[117]

It is obvious that if no goals are set, there is nothing around which to organize our behavior. Being without goals, without resolve, betrays a totally passive orientation to our Faith. The lack of goals precludes fighting our own "spiritual battles"; it precludes spiritual transformation; ultimately, it frustrates God's purpose for man.[118]

Perseverance and Patience

Striving is another tangible manifestation of the will at work, for practicing virtues requires effort. Without practice, habits cannot be formed; and it is the formation of spiritual habits which consolidates spiritual transformation. Bahá'u'lláh tells us to:

Strive that ye may be enabled to manifest to the peoples of the earth the signs of God, and to mirror forth His commandments.[119]

Striving for the sake of striving, however, cannot establish spiritual habits; rather, we must strive for a specific goal until it is achieved. This type of striving––perseverance––is a basic manifestation of

[117] 'Abdu'l-Bahá, *The Secret of Divine Civilization*, p. 19.

[118] The Universal House of Justice, in *Wellspring of Guidance*, pp. 37-38, links fighting one's own "spiritual battles" with Shoghi Effendi's admonition that "'One thing and only one thing will unfailingly and alone secure the undoubted triumph of this sacred Cause, namely, the extent to which our own inner life and private character mirror forth in their manifold aspects the splendor of those eternal principles proclaimed by Bahá'u'lláh.'"

[119] Bahá'u'lláh, quoted in Shoghi Effendi, *The Advent of Divine Justice*, p. 26.

volition. It is one of the major characteristics required if God's purpose for man is to be reflected in our lives:

> *The companions of God are, in this day, the lump that must leaven the peoples of the world. They must show forth such trustworthiness, such truthfulness and perseverance, such deeds and character that all mankind may profit by their example.*[120]

Persevering means more than keeping at something for a certain amount of time; it means not giving up in the face of difficulties and trials that may be encountered along the way. Almost anything worthy of achievement will require perseverance through hardships. The capacity to pursue an objective even in the face of great hardships is another facet of volition:

> *Everything of importance in this world demands the close attention of its seeker. The one in pursuit of anything must undergo difficulties and hardships until the object in view is attained and the great success is obtained.*[121]

In the following passage, 'Abdu'l-Bahá particularizes the role of endeavor and perseverance in achieving world peace:

> *A few, unaware of the power latent in human endeavor, consider this matter as highly impracticable, nay even beyond the scope of man's utmost efforts. Such is not the case, however. On the contrary, thanks to the unfailing grace of God, the loving-kindness of His favored ones,*

---

[120] Bahá'u'lláh, ibid., p. 19.

[121] 'Abdu'l-Bahá, *Tablets of 'Abdul-Baha Abbas*, II, 265.

the unrivaled endeavors of wise and capable souls, and the thoughts and ideas of the peerless leaders of this age, nothing whatsoever can be regarded as unattainable. Endeavor, ceaseless endeavor, is required. Nothing short of an indomitable determination can possibly achieve it. Many a cause which past ages have regarded as purely visionary, yet in this day has become most easy and practicable. Why should this most great and lofty Cause——the day-star of the firmament of true civilization and the cause of the glory, the advancement, the well-being and the success of all humanity——be regarded as impossible of achievement? Surely the day will come when its beauteous light shall shed illumination upon the assemblage of man.[122]

Responding to hardships with patience is yet another manifestation of the will in operation:

Whosoever, O my Lord, is impatient in the tribulations befalling him in Thy path, hath not drunk of the cup of Thy love nor tasted of the sweetness of Thy remembrance.[123]

Control of Action and Resisting Temptation

Striving to do certain things is not the only action which requires volition and self-discipline. Refusal to do other things, or ceasing to do them, is a significant manifestation of volition. Indeed, man's capacity to resist temptation or to discontinue vices distinguishes

---

[122] 'Abdu'l-Bahá, *Secret of Divine Civilization*, pp. 66-67.

[123] Bahá'u'lláh, *Prayers and Meditations*, p. 136.

him from the animal. This reflection of volition marks him as a spiritual being:

Nature is without volition and acts perforce whereas man possesses a mighty will … Man can voluntarily discontinue vices, nature has no power to modify the influence of its instincts.[124]

We, verily, have commanded you to refuse the dictates of your evil passions and corrupt desires, and not to transgress the bounds which the Pen of the Most High hath fixed, for these are the breath of life unto all created things.[125]

In essence, then, volition has two fundamental manifestations or functions in spiritual transformation. One is striving and persevering to achieve specific goals that are congruent with God's purpose for man. The other is resisting temptation, discontinuing vices, and controling impulses and desires that are unspiritual. Volition––will––is needed if we are to direct our lives in ways that will enable us to acquire virtues and, simultaneously, to resist all temptations to break Bahá'í laws.

3 | The Role of Self-Disciplined Action in Spiritual Transformation

Bahá'u'lláh has stated that *"It is incumbent upon every man of insight and understanding to strive to translate that which hath been written into reality and action."*[126] This translation will depend upon *"converting*

---

[124] 'Abdu'l-Bahá, *Foundations of World Unity*, p. 70.

[125] Bahá'u'lláh, *Gleanings*, p. 331.

[126] Bahá'u'lláh, *Gleanings from the Writings of Bahá'u'lláh*, p. 250.

satanic strength" into *"heavenly power."*[127] It is deeds––action––and not words that count. Spiritual transformation is not possible without action. Thought, prayer, meditation, and study of the sacred scriptures are all very important; but if no spiritual goals are set and no action is taken to achieve them, no spiritual transformation will take place. The reality of spiritual attributes can be perceived only in action. 'Abdu'l-Bahá says:

> *Love manifests its reality in deeds, not only in words–– these alone are without effect. In order that love may manifest its power there must be an object, an instrument, a motive.*[128]

> *The wrong in the world continues to exist just because people talk only of their ideals, and do not strive to put them into practice.*[129]

Not any action will do; whatever action we decide upon must reflect God's will and facilitate achievement of His purpose for man. Hence, action must be congruent with knowledge of God's purpose and will require submission of the human will to the will of God. Only then can action result in spiritual transformation.

Once action is initiated, we can very easily become lost in the action itself, thereby becoming inattentive to whether it continues to express God's purpose for man. We therefore need to make an ongoing assessment of our actions to see whether they conform to the will of God and, if they do not, to modify them by conscious and deliberate effort:

---

[127] Ibid., p. 200.

[128] 'Abdu'l-Bahá, *Paris Talks*, p. 35.

[129] Ibid., p. 16.

O SON OF BEING!

Bring thyself to account each day ere thou art summoned to a reckoning; for death, unheralded, shall come upon thee and thou shalt be called to give account for thy deeds.[130]

Two important capacities are prerequisite to our being in charge of our spiritual destinies. One of these is the capacity to see a discrepancy between our actions and God's purpose for man. The other is the ability to modify our actions to make them reflect this purpose. This is where self-discipline, the ability to take oneself in hand and correct a situation, plays a critical role.

It is the spiritual responsibility and obligation of each Bahá'í to develop this type of self-discipline. Our fellow believers cannot provide us with it, nor can the administrative institutions of the Faith develop spiritual qualities for us, though they can guide and encourage us as individuals. If we deviate greatly from God's purpose for man in a way that affects the Bahá'í community, Bahá'í institutions will help to correct the situation. Nevertheless, only the individuals can decide to deal with the inner source of a problem in his own spiritual life.

Persevering in our efforts to act in accordance with God's purpose for man, without excessive dependence on others or on Bahá'í institutions, has important consequences for the quality of our lives. Such self-disciplined action brings with it a sense of self-worth. It also builds confidence in our capacity to fight our own "spiritual battles."

Handling our own spiritual struggles is an important way of strengthening ourselves and, at the same time, of helping the Faith. Spiritual Assemblies can counsel individuals and help to resolve serious problems. But they cannot fight our spiritual battles for us. When

---

[130] Bahá'u'lláh, *The Hidden Words of Bahá'u'lláh*, p. 11.

we ask Bahá'í institutions to do this, we are diverting their energies away from their appointed tasks. The Universal House of Justice, the supreme governing body of the Bahá'í World Community, has written that "all can pray" and "fight their own spiritual battles" and that if we do it will help us to grow.[131]

Fighting our own "spiritual battles" also increases our ability, through the dynamic force of example, to assist others to take charge of their own processes of transformation. Perhaps the most important consequence of such perseverance is the effect it has upon our relationships with others. It helps us to become less possessive, exploitative, manipulative, and dependent, and freer to love and to serve. Through loving and serving we become, in turn, more worthy of love; and the love we attract helps to confirm and reinforce all of our efforts at self-discipline. Thus, a cycle of spiritual transformation is set in motion, which, when sustained by a continual immersion in the ocean of Bahá'u'lláh's words and an active participation in the building of the new World Order, guarantees continued spiritual growth and development.

O CHILDREN OF ADAM!

Holy words and pure and goodly deeds ascend unto the heaven of celestial glory. Strive that your deeds may be cleansed from the dust of self and hypocrisy and find favor at the court of glory; for ere long the assayers of mankind shall, in the holy presence of the Adored One, accept naught but absolute virtue and deeds of stainless purity. This is the day-star of wisdom and of divine mystery that hath shone above the horizon of the divine will. Blessed are they that turn thereunto.[132]

---

[131] The Universal House of Justice, *Wellspring of Guidance*, p. 38.

[132] Bahá'u'lláh, *The Hidden Words of Bahá'u'lláh*, p. 46.

PART THREE
THE ANISA EDUCATION MODEL

"If it is true, in general, that 'ideas have consequences,' then man's ideas about man have the most far-reaching consequences of all. Upon them may depend the structure of government, the patterns of culture, the purpose of education, the design of the future and the human or inhuman uses of human beings."

Floyd W. Matson, Educator and Social Philosopher, (1921-2008)

"Philosophy begins in wonder. And, at the end, when philosophic thought has done its best, the wonder remains. ... The ultimate metaphysical ground is the creative advance into novelty."

Alfred North Whitehead, Philosopher/
Mathematician, (1861-1947)

CHAPTER 11

---◆◆◆---

APPLYING KNOWLEDGE OF HUMAN DEVELOPMENT: NEW DIMENSIONS IN PARENT AND TEACHER EDUCATION

By Daniel C. Jordan, Ph.D.
Published in *Nutrition in Human Development*: 1978

The eminent philosopher, logician, and mathematician, Alfred North Whitehead, wrote an entire book in protest against inert ideas and dead knowledge. The death of knowledge, he says, comes when it is not connected to life--when it is only talked about and written down, but never acted on. To be alive, thoughts must inform action (Whitehead, 1950).

Suppose for one moment that the information presented in the preceding chapters, and all currently available knowledge about human development from other disciplines for that matter, could be made alive for everyone by applying it systematically in every child's home and school. What would be the consequences of such an effort? There is little doubt that we would begin to see the emergence of new generations of healthy, stable, and responsible human beings whose undreamed of potentialities, when fully actualized, would stagger the imagination.

What stands in the way of such an undertaking? Among the most difficult obstacles is lack of agreement among basic institutions of society on the purpose and methods of socialization and education, on the values and priorities which determine how resources will be allocated, and above all on what institutions should assume which responsibilities. Most social institutions of the past had a working agreement was far more mobile and adaptable. But, as other scholars have shown, many traditional functions of the family were lost in the process, and this made it more vulnerable.

William Ogburn's analysis of the status of the 20th century family showed how its current dilemma is due to its loss of function (Ogburn, 1938). In former times, for instance, the family functioned as a labor unit with all members working to sustain the family economically. By and large, families were self-sufficient; they consumed only what they produced. Thus, money, banks, wholesalers, retailers, manufacturing agencies, and other commercial institutions were not needed. With the rise of market capitalism, this economic function of the family was largely usurped. Because of the economic nature of the traditional household, the home was inevitably a center for education. As children grew up, they learned from other family members as they worked together. Again, with the expansion of market capitalism and the breakdown of the home as an economic unit, the education of children began to be delegated to schools. Other important functions, such as protection against external threats and insurance against the liabilities of old age were assumed by the traditional family. Today, the function of protection has been delegated to the police, and insurance companies, retirement plans of corporations, and welfare organizations take care of the aging. Formerly, the family had an important religious function, now largely delegated to the church, parochial schools, and religious organizations. Husbands and wives used to belong to the same faith, and their children were inevitably socialized into that faith. Today, the family has become secularized, and its religious function has been greatly weakened. In former times, families organized their own recreation as a unit, often in collaboration with other families. Nowadays, there is very little recreation organized and enjoyed by the family as a unit. Different members of the family go to agencies outside of the home for their recreation.

These functions—economic, educational, protective, religious, and recreational—were like bonds that held married couples and families together. One other function, that of providing intimacy, affection, and companionship, has always been an important one, and it is perhaps the primary one still present in the modern family. When the family provided this function in combination with all of the other ones as well, the bonds were strong and the family was stable. With so many other agencies assuming responsibility for so many of the functions of the family, it cannot be expected to be as strong as it was formerly. Furthermore, the quality of the function of providing affection and intimacy has also changed and made the family more vulnerable. Over the years, the affectional basis for the husband and wife relationship has been largely romanticized. Shorter's effort concentrates largely on the assembling of evidence which shows how in the western world the romantic basis for both mate selection and the husband and wife relationship in the family emerged over the years. Romance as the basis for mate selection and marital union, with all of its ecstasy, joy, pain, and despair, is still the predominant theme of literature and the dramatic arts whether presented through the theatre, cinema, or over television. There is no doubt that it is a powerful force, and when it is not tempered by other functions, the family is in jeopardy. When romance fades—and it almost inevitably does—and no other basis for the marital union is found to replace it, the marriage collapses. When the marriage collapses, the structural foundation of the family as an institution caves in.

Extraordinary changes in the institution of the family such as those described above have continued right up to the present and have left us with a post-modern family in deep trouble. Shorter concludes his book with a prediction which is very alarming:

> The nuclear family is crumbling––to be replaced, I think, by the free-floating couple, a marital dyad subject to dramatic fissions and fusions, and without the orbiting satellites of pubertal children, close friends, or neighbors––just the relatives, hovering in the background, friendly smiles on their faces (p. 280).

This is alarming because in the light of what we know about human development, it is extremely doubtful that the "free-floating couple, a marital dyad" with its "dramatic fissions and fusions" can ever bring forth a new generation free from numerous biological and psychological pathologies.

The School.

The rise of market capitalism and the industrial revolution also had enormous effects on education and the school as an institution. During this period, there was a great number of changes in educational philosophies which had direct impact on curriculum, educational administration, and sources of support for education. In spite of great differences among the educational institutions of different countries, a number of basic and common trends are evident: (1) a shift away from religious institutions as the main source of educational sponsorship outside the family; (2) a move away from notions of fixed intelligence with an acceptance of the idea that the environment plays a greater role in producing educational outcomes; (3) the emergence of the idea of life-long education and the need for a variety of institutions to collaborate in the educational process; and, (4) a growing conviction that educational institutions cannot neglect the physical and mental health of their students— that the whole person must be dealt with. Although many of these trends resulted from efforts that were aimed at remedying situations thought to be harmful or non-productive for children, by the time they were organized and supported well enough to have an effect, social change introduced new pressures and problems that required further reform.

Contemporary educators are not unaware of such pressures and problems faced by educational institutions. While there is some agreement on the diagnosis of the problem, there is little agreement on what prescriptions are required to remedy the situation, and hence no confident prognosis about the future (Daedalus, 1974).

An analysis of the literature on contemporary educational issues reveals three basic sources of problems, aside from general political and financial troubles:

(a) a too rigid adherence to the "authoritarian, teacher-dominated, abstract curriculum" view of education; or,

(b) an uncritical acceptance of child-centered approach to education broadly conceived; and,

(c) the extreme discontinuities of experience the child faces as he moves from home to school to community and the injustices involved when no provision is made to accommodate cultural differences.

Many writers have addressed the problems of the rigid, authoritarian approach. Jacques Barzun (1959) documents how "drudgery, discipline, and conformity" constitute the basic syndrome of traditional education. George Leonard (1968) condenses a complex diagnosis into one simple statement: "The ecstacy has gone out of education." Paul Goodman (1964) describes education as a system of brainwashing which leads to "spiritual destruction." Carl Rogers (1969) views the educational system as a kind of prison where children are not free to learn; John Holt (1964) outlines the many ways in which the system programs a guaranteed failure for significant numbers of children. Kozol (1967) details how education brings psychological "death at an early age." Weinstein (1970) and those interested in humanistic education view the current system as one which often punishes an expression of feeling and renders the process of acquiring knowledge a sterile, mostly irrelevant, and even destructive experience. Silberman's efforts (1970) at diagnosis indicate that education is in a period of serious crisis. As a system, it does not address the development of the whole person; rather it fragments, compartmentalizes, and precipitates self-alienation. Herbert Kohl (1967) points to the authoritarian atmosphere of the traditional school and how it snuffs out the life of learning. Caleb Gattegno (1970) argues that learning is the life of education and in order to sustain that life, teaching must be "subordinated to learning." Yet, in many schools, learning is subordinate to everything else. William Glasser (1969) illustrates how education's ill health is directly correlated with "a philosophy of non-involvement, non-relevance, and a limited emphasis on thinking."

Other educators, particularly those directing or working in many of the alternative or free schools have gone to the other extreme. They have been criticized for taking an excessively child-centered approach to education. In these schools, children are simply encouraged to "do their own thing," presumably on the grounds that each child will work consistently at his own developmental level. Individualization of instruction is supposed to take care of itself by virtue of the child's being able to choose what he wants to do and when he wants to do it for as long as he likes. But under such circumstances, most children have not learned to read, write, or compute—skills essential for subsequent development. Instead, according to Kozol (1972:33), they "make clay vases, weave Indian head bands, play with polaroid cameras, and climb over geodesic domes." This approach has led to many undesirable consequences: the erosion of academic standards; the proliferation of courses on the upper levels to include not only such time-consuming activities as driver's education, but also courses with no more substance than can be gleaned from an exchange of uninformed opinion among class members; fragmentation and dilution of the curriculum; a disinclination to take a moral stand on several important issues on the grounds that no values should be "imposed" on any child; and a toleration of abuse of the body through poor nutrition and the use of drugs within the schools.

Since the publicly supported school reflects the dominant culture, children from minority and/or economically disadvantaged backgrounds have borne the brunt of discontinuities of experience between home and their school community. A vast literature now exists which documents the conflict a child experiences when his family has one set of values and his school and community another. Such conditions have become particularly explosive when differences become unjustifiably classified as superior and inferior, and policies are created which perpetuate injustices.

These conditions are exacerbated by two other deficiencies which are not so frequently discussed in the literature but which I have come to regard as fundamental concerns: (a) a general ignorance on the part of educators and policy makers of the role biological integrity plays in the child's ability to learn, and (b) the lack of a coherent body of theory that could organize scientific knowledge of human development and address all of the conditions cited above in a comprehensive way.

Although recent history is filled with many attempts to diagnose the problems of schools, make prescriptions, and try out new approaches, the last quarter of the 20th century has arrived and the school, like its sister institution, the family, finds itself confronting problems that are deep and complex and admit of no easy or short-term solution.

Institutional Renewal and the Use of Knowledge.

What are the major points to be gleaned from this review of the recent history of the family and the school? I believe there are at least two important insights which this retrospective glance at the family and the school affords. In the first instance, we can see that institutions based on tradition are likely to lack institutional self-awareness. Although the people who comprise them learn and apply knowledge bound up in the tradition, they remain relatively unaware of the knowledge they have and why the do what they do. Hence, such institutions tend to have things "happen" to them rather than make things happen in accordance with some intentional scheme. These institutions thus "react" rather than initiate and direct the action. The idea of intentional planned change is not a part of the life of such institutions.

Secondly, we can see that institutions based, at least in part, on science and the scientific method are more conscious of the knowledge they have and are therefore able to be intentional about its use. Such institutions can initiate action and make things happen. Since science focused initially on the accumulation of information about means-ends and cause-effect relationships among phenomena of the physical world, it was almost inevitable that institutions to make use of such knowledge would find themselves making new material things––products which people needed or wanted and making them faster and more economically. Commercial institutions thus became active; traditional ones remained reactive. The former were based in large part on the development and use of scientific knowledge while the latter were based on custom and mores.

The review shows how the application of knowledge in one area––the material world––led to the development of technology which forced many changes in tradition-based social institutions such as the family, while lack of knowledge in another area––human growth, development, and the formation of values––left people without a rational basis for planning and directing changes in their lives to counterbalance the effects of technological advancement. In the absence of scientific knowledge about human development, particularly as it relates to the basic requirements of socialization and education, reactions to pressures from the rise of capitalism were primarily on an emotional level––hence, "the "onrush of sentiment" about which Shorter speaks. Although it may have had some short-term beneficial consequences, the onrush of sentiment has gone unchecked to the point where today hundreds of thousands of families lie shattered and schools remain paralyzed––both unable to perform the basic functions of socializing and educating the new generation.

These insights compel us to reflect on one extraordinary possibility: that if commercial institutions can use scientific knowledge of the material world to direct their affairs so can a science of human development be used to recreate the family and the school, endow them with institutional self-awareness and give them the capacity to manage perpetual self-renewal intentionally, in ways that guarantee survival and continually improve the quality of life. The current costs of the failure of the family and school clearly indicate that not to consider this possibility to jeopardize survival itself.

The Cost of Institutional Failure.

Because both school and family are not being successful in solving their problems, the children they are responsible for rearing are bearing the brunt of their failure and the price they are paying is high. The following statistics tell just how high the price is (Bowen, 1976). The infant mortality rate of the United States ranks fifteenth internationally. In 1974, it was 16.5 infant deaths per 1,000 live births (U.S. Health, 1975). The rate for minorities remains about two-thirds again as high as that for whites. Some 30% of all pregnant women do not begin prenatal care before the end of the first trimester, a particularly significant issue since many studies show that high infant mortality rates are associated with inadequate prenatal care. Furthermore, it is during the early phase of pregnancy that the baby's brain begins to form, and the brain's most critical period of development takes place during the first three months. In 1974, almost 500,000 teenage girls became pregnant. Over a quarter of a million of these adolescents had abortions. Both teenage mothers and their children suffer increased incidences of mortality, toxemia, veneral disease, and other complications; the children have higher rates of mental subnormality and other kinds of neurological deficiencies.

Large numbers of pregnant women consume drugs which have a potentially deleterious effect on their children. Use of LSD or marijuana increases the child's risk of malformation and death. Since there are an estimated 4 million female alcoholics in the country, the effect of alcohol on the fetus is a significant matter.

Twelve million Americans have some form of inheritable disease, and an additional 20 million have genetically determined enzyme abnormalities. Over 100,000 mentally retarded babies are born yearly. Approximately one-fourth of the cases of mental retardation can be directly attributed to particular infections, birth traumas, or genetic causes. There is a very high probability that the remaining cases are caused by inadequate prenatal and perinatal care, inadequate nutrition, and severe social and environmental deprivation. Since mental retardation afflicts some 3 million persons under the age of 20 and around 6 million in the total population, this is obviously no small problem.

In spite of the affluence of the United States, malnutrition is still a problem. Many of the estimated 27 million persons living in poverty in the United States are not able to purchase the kinds of foods that would constitute an adequate diet, and since inadequate nutrition undermines physical health and impairs the ability to learn, this serious condition needs attention.

Nutritional problems not only stem from not having enough food of the right kinds, but also from eating too much of the wrong things, such as too much sugar and certain food additives or pollutants. Pollutants also enter the body through means other than food. For instance, 40% of community water supplies in the United States do not meet Public Health Service drinking water standards. An estimated 225,000 children each year are affected by lead poisoning which in severe cases may lead to irreversible mental retardation. High blood levels of lead occur in 10% of children ages 1-5, a condition which has been correlated with emotional, perceptual, and learning disabilities (Kline, 1974).

Accidents account for more than 40% of the deaths of the age group 1-4. Motor vehicle accidents, drowning, fires, inhalation and ingestion of food and other objects, poisoning, falling, and accidents from firearms represent the rank ordering of causes of death by accidents. Many children, of course, are not killed by the accidents but suffer serious injuries some of which may permanently disable them. Somewhere between 7-10 million children under six require medical attention due to accidents each year. Two-thirds of the non-fatal injuries occur in the home. Fifty percent of all infant deaths are caused by suffocation resulting from obstruction of air passages by liquid foods, objects such as safety pins, buttons, small toys, or smothering from bed clothes, plastic materials, or strangulation related to structural defects in cribs, playpens, and highchairs. Since most accidents are preventable, their salience as a cause of death and disability among children and the fact that they mostly occur around the home, indicates the need for parental education pertaining to making the environment safe, and providing adequate supervision. Obviously, a comprehensive approach to accident prevention is possible only through systematic educational efforts.

Children do not escape the suffering of emotional and mental illness. Approximately 30% of all children have adjustment problems. Less than half of the children needing attention are receiving it, and only an estimated 5% of the children who need psychiatric care are receiving it. Approximately 18 million adults have some form of mental disturbance needing professional treatment, and yet only 10% of this number are receiving assistance. Since a large number of these adults are both parents and teachers who are in charge of the care of children, the problem is compounded.

Such disturbances on the personality level are inevitably associated with social pathologies involving groups. The breakdown of the family is the chief case in point. Out of every five divorces in the U.S. today, three of them affect children. Given the present rates, one child in six will lose a parent through divorce by the time he is 18. As of 1974, over 7 million children were in the process of learning to live with new stepparents. Approximately 10% of all children under six are living in single-parent families with no father in the home. Nearly half of all poor children under six are living in single-parent households.

Neglecting children seems criminal enough, but the truth is that a large number of children are severely abused. A 1970 survey projects a nation wide total of around 3 million battered children. A large number of these children are permanently damaged and many of them die. Not counting accidents, homicide is the fourth leading cause of death among children under 15.

The picture is depressing enough; yet what has been presented is only the briefest of reviews, and it concerns the United States almost exclusively. Statistics on the same items reflecting conditions in all other nations would be more distressing. Any sane person can see that the cost in human terms of not dealing with these problems preventively is too high, particularly when vast resources are available and expended on hundreds of foolish and insignificant enterprises. In actual dollar amounts, it costs untold billions—enough to sustain the program we are recommending many times over. A few examples will make the point clear. The total cost of care for individuals with major disorders stemming from prenatal and perinatal damage was estimated in 1971 by the U.S. Department of Health, Education, and Welfare to be $13 billion annually. The yearly loss of income due to fetal and neonatal deaths was estimated to be an additional $15.5 billion (Wallace, 1974). At the present time, the federal government spends 50 times more money on remedial efforts as it does on preventive ones. We spend $2 billion annually treating decayed teeth and would spend $8 billion if everyone were to have his dental needs taken care of (Jacobsen, 1975). The annual cost of environmentally induced diseases in the United States (cost of health services, loss of wages, compensation, and rehabilitation) is estimated at $35 billion (Kotin, 1974). It is not difficult to see that if the annual dollar amount expended were given for every item discussed, the total would be in the hundreds of billions. Add to this the cost of juvenile delinquency and crime, and the figure reaches levels that are mind boggling.

The Case for Institutional Renewal.

As the remarkable changes leading up to all of these problems were taking place in schools and in the family, psychology, sociology, anthropology, and the biomedical sciences were just beginning to emerge. There was no body of tested knowledge about human development adequate and reliable enough to use as the basis for enlightened social policy by agencies of government or other social institutions such as the family and school. Thus, when the traditional foundations of the family began to crumble, there was no knowledge of a scientific nature to replace the folk wisdom of tradition. A void was created and sentiment rushed in to fill the vacuum.

Today, however, there is a great deal of knowledge about how human being grow, develop, and learn. We no longer have any excuse for continuing to deal with these problems with only our feelings and emotions. Our minds must now be engaged to deal with them, and the best knowledge possible must be organized and applied. It appears that if a sound knowledge base is not adopted for reconstituting the family and renewing the school, the onrush of sentiment of the 19th century will have added to it "an onrush of superstition" in the late 20th century, and the family and school will have very little hope of restoration without first going through a long period of trial and error that is almost certain to be regressive. Larger and larger numbers of people are turning to fortune-tellers, tarot cards, horoscopes, commercially motivated gurus, palmistry, phrenology, occultism, and a variety of other dubious sources of advice and guidance in making critical decisions about their lives. Because superstitions destroy the ability to "make sounder judgments for the ordering of individual and social life," the family and the school should be helping to counteract them.

It seems imperative, then, that society make a deliberate effort to create a new foundation for the family and the school as two of its basic social institutions and to provide the means for the systematic education of parents and the preparation of teachers in accordance with the new foundation. It seems equally imperative that this foundation be one that uses human development knowledge as a means of determining what of the past shall be retained and what new approaches should be tried out.

Such an idea may seem an impossible one to realize. There are, however, many evidences of trends in that direction. Over the last several decades, governments have provided more and more services to schools and families. Aid to children through a variety of welfare measures and educational reforms has increased markedly during the past quarter century. Hundreds of organizations––local, state, federal, and international[23]––have come into being to advocate assistance to children, families, and schools and to initiate programs to serve them. For example, the 1975 report of the Education Commission of the States makes this recommendation:

> A coordinated comprehensive program of services to young children and their parents should be preventive in orientation and provide services on a continuous, not solely on an emergency, basis. It should utilize to the greatest extent possible the family's own child-rearing and child caring capabilities (Education Commission of the States Early Education Project, 1975:4).

Such reports reflect a growing awareness that the family and school do need extensive, systematic help on a wide scale. Without assistance, each successive generation will become progressively less capable of assuming the responsibility for the care of itself and its offspring.

Obviously, families in a state of collapse cannot very well meet the needs of their members, particularly the children. That these needs are not currently being met is evident in the variety of grim statistics already presented. However, if the family is ruled out as the institution with the primary responsibility for socializing and taking care of the oncoming generations, what alternatives can be considered? It is not outside the realm of possibility, for example, that thousands of children's homes could be established, much like orphanages. But they would have to be fully staffed with three shifts of personnel to provide around-the-clock care––a costly prospect in itself, not even considering the expenses of room, board, clothing, supplies, and educational materials. In addition, there is a significant psychological cost as well. Paid personnel rarely develop the kinds of love, trust, and commitment required for the healthy psychological development of children. Discontinuity of experience and conflicts in values caused by the differences among shifts of supervising adults take their toll on the personality formation of the children being cared for. Furthermore, staff members tend to change jobs frequently, and children who might be able to form healthy attachments are traumatized by one separation after another.

I believe that all alternatives to the institution of the family are too costly, inefficient, and very likely even detrimental. There is hardly any reasonable choice but to set about reconstructing it.

Likewise, schools in a state of crisis can hardly succeed in meeting developmental needs of children. Yet, it is difficult to imagine modern, industrial, democratic societies surviving without schools. Alternative approaches such a Ivan Illich's proposal to "deschool"[4] society are naive and unfeasible. Again, the more reasonable course seems to be that of reconstituting the school through a new system for preparing teachers.

If the conclusion that we should remake the family and renew the school is accepted, then the next step is to create the new foundation and design the means for reformation.

In spite of their precarious state, the family and the school are still the most ubiquitous of social institutions. Almost everyone belongs to a family and nearly everyone in North America has gone or is going to a school. Thus, if there is to be any significant impact on the modern family and school, collaborative action on a very wide scale is ultimately required. However, massive collaborative action will be inefficient at best, if not impossible, unless there is a unifying framework which can be used to organize knowledge from all relevant disciplines in such a way that its application through coherent program planning, personnel training, program implementation, and evaluation can be institutionalized. Julian Huxley states the case succinctly:

I would go so far as to say that the lack of a common frame of reference, the absence of any unifying set of concepts and principles, is now, if not the world's major disease, at least its most serious symptom (Huxley, 1960:88).

We need both the unifying concepts and an institution to use them in organizing and applying the considerable knowledge of human development now available.

A Conceptual Base for Organizing Human Development Knowledge.

While the plight of the family and school is an extremely serious problem, it appears that most of the pieces to a solution of the problem are available. There just seem to be too many pieces to cope with and few parents or teachers see how to fit them all together in a way that would enable these basic institutions to be restructured so that they can "make sounder judgments" and respond successfully to the critical demands that will be placed upon them during the years ahead. Up to this time, no systematic effort has been made to pull together all of the pieces for want of the kind of unifying principle Huxley advocates––one which will enable all of the pieces to cohere in an organized whole––a Gestalt that will make sense of the parts and not only shed light on the problems, but will also enable us to establish priorities that will guide the use of resources effectively. Until such a set of unifying concepts is articulated, tried out, and justified, it is doubtful that the kind of foundation for the family and school as I am envisaging will be possible.

What are the criteria for a set of unifying concepts powerful enough to pull all of the pieces together? First, it must embody propositions about the nature of man of such ultimate generality that they may be regarded as first principles.[5] Second, the concepts must show how man's relationship to his environment and, indeed, to the cosmos, influences development and behavior, i.e., account for changes over time. Third, they must be, in Huxley's terms, "suitable for our present stage of cultural evolution," and "consonant with the structure and the trends of man's present system of knowledge (Huxley, 1960:53)." Fourth, again using Huxley's phrase, they must "help to secure a pattern and direction of cultural evolution which will most effectively enable man to perform his evolutionary role in nature (Huxley, 1960:53)."

In our efforts to formulate a set of unifying principles for all the sciences dealing with human development which would meet the four criteria stated above, my colleagues and I reviewed 2,500 years of philosophical thought about the nature of man (Radhakrishnan, 1960). We examined history and the basic themes of man's literary, religious, and aesthetic heritage. Because it is a synthesis of both Eastern and Western streams of philosophical thought, we found Alfred North Whitehead's cosmology, *Process and Reality*, the most appealing system of ideas against which to test the power, coherence, and comprehensiveness of the concepts we have adopted to unify the vast amount of knowledge about human development now available.[6]

Whitehead affirmed an ancient ontological principle, namely, that everything in the universe is connected to everything else and that nothing can be understood apart from its relationships to all things it is connected to. This means that the nature of man cannot be grasped unless we understand how he is related to everything around him. Because of consciousness, memory, and the capacity for forming and using sysbols, man connects himself to everything imaginable, including ultimate unknowables. Thus, no real progress can be made in trying to understand the nature of man without considering the universe of which he is a part. Hence the search for first principles around which human development knowledge can be organized necessarily entails metaphysical thought.

Whitehead, like so many philosophers before him, cited change as the fundamental characteristic of the universe. Change means process and process presupposes potentiality. Whitehead thus set forth the basic proposition that the reality of being inheres in the process whereby potentiality is translated into actuality––a process he identifies with creativity, the "universal of universals." We drew on these basic ideas to formulate the unifying concepts around which we can organize and apply human development knowledge. They meet the four criteria specified and have provided us with the generative base for deducing a coherent body of theory which can serve as an effective guide to practice as we set about the task of educating parents and preparing teachers to teach.

From these fundamental notions, we have generated several propositions about the nature of man: that because there is no evidence to suggest that there is a limit to his ability to learn, we may assume that man is a creature of unlimited potential; that his capacity for symbolization makes his memory limitless and renders him conscious so that he knows that he knows and knows when he doesn't know; that his capacity for love and trust makes him inevitably a social and moral being naturally equipped to assume responsibility for socializing the oncoming generations; that his awareness of knowing and not knowing and his need to love and be loved make him yearn to find his place in the cosmos and give rise to his art, religion, philosophy, and science; that the knowing and loving capacities when used to unify man in service to man are the most effective instruments of evolution; and, that he is a purposeful being able to formulate ideals, plans, hypotheses, and consciously pursue them, thereby perpetually actualizing new potentialities compatable with them. All of these qualities enable him to live at the forefront of evolutionary forces and assume some control over them.

There are those who may object that this conception of man, which reflects the noblest visions and passions that have animated philosophy, science, art, and religion throughout history, has no place in a scheme for establishing a scientific enterprise, even if its purpose is to safeguard the development of man. Yet, any set of concepts which ignores these expressions of man's highest aspirations will be out of touch with the reality of man. Certainly, nothing we know from the biological and behavioral sciences would enable us to define limits to man's capacity for knowing and loving and the full range of potentialities we associate with man evolving. The pervasiveness of this view of man in literature, art, and religion confirms it as a legitimate concern of scientific inquiry, and I submit that any science of man that ignores it or refuses to deal with it is in need of overhauling. Science will, in fact, have no integrating power in human affairs as it has had in technological matters, until it addresses the distinctive characteristics of man and his ultimate concerns: emotion, value, purpose, intention, consciousness, faith, beauty, aspiration, love, art, meaning, morality, and his cosmic yearing to find out how he fits into the universe.

From these philosophical first principles which describe the fundamental nature of man, we deductively derived a comprehensive epigenetic theory of human development which can account for every developmental need at any point in the life cycle, whether biological, psychological, sociological, technological, moral, aesthetic, religious, or philosophical. The theory is therefore capable of generating ways to understand and meet any developmental need in any setting at any time. These ways can then be tried out, evaluated for their efficacy, and perpetually refined.

The theory of development defines development as the translation of potentiality into actuality; it sets forth two basic categories of potentialities, biological and psychological; fixes nutrition as the key factor in the actualization of biological potentialities; and, identifies learning as the essential factor in the actualization of psychological potentialities. The theory establishes interaction with the environment as the means by which the translation of the organism's potentiality into actuality is sustained. Facilitating the actualization of human potential then depends on knowing how to arrange the environment and guide interactions with it in order to actualize given potentialities. The theory also accounts for the varieties of two major pathologies that come in the wake of the suppression of human potential, namely, delinquency and crime on the one hand and mental illness on the other.

We propose that such a comprehensive theory of human development, all of the empirical research that it organizes into a coherent whole, and the effective guide to practice it affords can provide the scientific basis on which deliberate efforts may be expended to reconstruct a durable foundation for the family and the school as the basic institutions of society. Since the home and the family constitute the primary matrix within which each succeeding generation is nurtured and shaped, parents who are in charge of the home and the family should have their actions fully informed by the knowledge we have about human growth, development, and learning. Likewise, since schools are a powerful force which helps to shape each generation, teachers and administrators must also be informed of the principles of human development. Of course, it is not reasonable to expect every parent or teacher to have the combined knowledge of an anthropologist, biologist, pediatrician, nutritionist, educator, recreation specialist, and moral philosopher. What is reasonable, though, is the creation of a social system in which the family and the school are fully supported by other institutions whose obligation it is (1) to further develope the knowledge we have about man, and (2) to provide means for the continuing education and support of parents and teachers in their efforts to maintain the kinds of environments and guidance children require to actualize their potentialities fully.

Since the development of children is heavily influenced by the school, it would be unreasonable for it not to operate on the same principles of human development knowledge being proposed for the family. Placing both institutions on the same foundation will have the effect of bringing coherence to the experience of growing children while avoiding the damaging conflicts among values and the deleterious effects of discontinuities of experience between home and school. If parents, teachers, families, and schools are animated by the same purpose and operate on the same principles, maximum diversity of a growth fostering nature can be maintained but within a unified system. Understanding the nature of human development makes it possible to supply whatever is required for the optimum development of children while avoiding all of those things which retard or permanently impair development. As scientific knowledge about human development increases and is systematically applied in home and school, it is not difficult to envision the possibility that placing these two fundamental institutions on the same scientific foundation would quickly make them the chief instruments of human evolution, both biological and socio-cultural.

Unfortunately, the family and the school cannot be expected to reorganize themselves. The major question, then, is who will do it––what agency will help to stabilize the family and reconstitute the school?

Proposal for an Institution to Renew the Family and the School.

What I have in mind is in essence a simple idea: assemble all of the knowledge about human development from the books and journals stored in libraries, organize it according to the general conceptual scheme just presented, and make it active in the reconstitution of the family and the school. It is unlikely that these things can happen unless some agency is created with a mandate to accomplish them. A new institution is required, one which is itself based on the same foundations and devoted to the management of institutional change by making the knowledge of human development alive through the programs it promulgates and through the actions of those it educates. We therefore propose the establishment of a Human Development Center which can be designed to serve as a prototype experiment in planned social change, the potential consequences of which could well signal a reversal in some of the most harmful trends in contemporary society.

A growing body of literature on intentional social change identifies a number of pitfalls which are avoided by this proposal (Sarason, 1974; Havelock, 1973). Most efforts at intentional change are doomed to fail for the following reasons:

(a) Insufficient or no time or budget for careful advance planning prior to implementation.
(b) No adequate time or budget to train personnel thoroughly before the operation begins. Thus, the incompetence of the staff becomes one of the primary sources of difficulty that is practically impossible to overcome once implementation has begun.
(c) No provision for institutionalizing the change in one place and for establishing the means of transporting the innovation to other localities, thereby achieving a multiplier effect. Without institutionalization, operations will revert to previous forms when budgets run out or key people leave; without means for transporting the innovation, its benefits cannot be extended to ever-increasing numbers of people.

There are many other causes of failure, but these are among the most common. The Center we are proposing would be in a position, however, to apply its knowledge of human behavior in dealing with these problems, all of which can be taken into account as part of the advance planning.

The Center would establish and maintain a model school and a parent-teacher training center both of which would exemplify human development knowledge made active. These functions are of primary importance because the exemplification of ideas in action is the most powerful means of attracting interest, support, and a willingness to participate. In short, they are the chief means of dealing, in some ultimate way, with the general problems of undercapitalization and political nonviability.

The parent training function would be integrated with the operation of the school.[7] The central idea underlying this new approach to education is to help children become competent learners so that they can take charge of the actualization of their own potentialities. In the new system, child-rearing practices, the organization of family life, teaching, curriculum development, educational administration, and program evaluation are all organized around the comprehensive theory of development, thereby ensuring that what everyone in the system does will facilitate the actualization of potentialities of the students.

It is beyond the scope of this article to present details on all aspects of such a system. Only those objectives of the proposed Center's program which primarily concern nutrition will be discussed. Although other kinds of objectives will not be examined, it is important to realize that all of the potential benefits of an applied nutrition program, whether preventive or remedial, may be minimized or lost if the program is not an integral part of a comprehensive plan such as the one presented.

One of the most important objectives of the Center is to ensure that parents and teachers grasp the necessity for maintaining the biological integrity of children through proper nutrition and understand the relationship between nutrition and the capacity to learn––the means of actualizing the categories of potentially specified by the theory of development (Raman, 1975). Learning to perceive, think, feel, attend, and act at optimum levels depends on the availability of energy sources free from toxins that impair functioning, and this can only be done through proper nutrition. Thus, the school itself will serve only the most wholesome foods, free as possible from additives and excessive amounts of sugar. Furthermore, no "junk" foods will be made available through vending machines or snack bars. Students who have particular problems such as biologically-based learning disabilities will have them diagnosed and remediation provided through prescription of individualized nutritional regimens whenever warranted. In other words, the applied nutritional program of both school and home will be based on a recognition of the biochemical individuality of human beings and will be directly evident in what is served and eaten. Diets, like instruction, need to be individualized.

A related objective, equally important, is the nutrition education of the children themselves. The program to achieve this objective has three aspects: (1) the development of the right attitudes toward nutrition; (2) the development of good eating habits including acquiring a taste for the right foods; and, (3) acquisition of factual knowledge about nutrition, the preparation of food, proper eating habits and their relationship to learning and the prevention of disease. Experience has shown time and again that acquiring factual knowledge about nutrition rarely changes eating habits. A comprehensive nutrition education program therefore has to include provisions for motivating changes in eating habits and food preferences in a direction consistent with knowledge of nutrition and human development. Without home and school collaboration, it is not possible to ensure the development of proper eating habits and food preference. If home and school do not work together, one will undermine the other and the children will pay the price for the failure.

Given the fact that changing eating habits and attitudes is so much more difficult than memorizing information about nutrition, it is essential that opportunity for change be introduced at times when success is most likely. When a child is conceived and people know they are going to become parents, great and inescapable changes on many levels are introduced into their lives, and they are predisposed to modifying their own behavior to provide the best they can for their offspring. Thus, a point of maximum leverage for remaking the family is at this time. The Center would therefore train educators of parents——persons who are well versed in all of the knowledge about good nutrition and its role in conception, gestation, birth, and post-natal development of children and who are able to work with parents and parents-to-be so that they can make use of this knowledge in caring for their own children. Since adults tend to pattern their own homes and family life after the models provided by their parents, the rearing of children in the new system is the surest way to remake the family as a social institution. This is a long-term approach, but it is the only one that will ultimately accomplish the objective.

Another kind of professional to be trained at the proposed Center is youth counselors. At the time of puberty, the identity of the maturing youngster and his value system begin to take shape. This time is therefore also propitious for introducing change and stabilizing values. Because young people entering pubescence try to establish their independence from parents, they tend, particularly in the western world, to effect their independence by rejecting parental values and guidance. This leads to more stress than is necessary and in some cases to grave mistakes which are difficult to undo. Living through this stressful period can be greatly facilitated by good nutrition. Yet, the eating habits and food preferences of adolescents are notorious. Furthermore, during the period of the growth spurt, when the rate of growth doubles, good nutrition is essential. The millions of new cells added each day during this period can only be made out of the foods consumed. Poor nutrition means less than optimum growth. Oftentimes is spells trouble——the development of skin problems such as acne, the deterioration in the quality of hair and nails, or any number of other difficulties due to unwise dieting, e.g., fatigue, lassitude, anxiety, restlessness, and inability to pay attention. For these reasons, a community needs youth counselors who can guide youth in the ways of good nutrition, and whose own lives, because they are based on human development principles, can serve as alternative models that are consistent with what most parents would want for their sons and daughters.

Another important function of the Center would be to educate the general public about the Center and its work using all available media. At the present time, there is an excessive amount of advertising of junk foods, soft drinks, tobacco, alcohol, cereals that are mostly sugar, drugs, and any number of other commodities not suitable for human consumption. This kind of information is unrelentingly piped into each home through television. The Center would be in a good position to counterbalance the effects of such advertising by providing public service programs to increase general awareness of human development knowledge and how it can be applied in the home. As parents begin to apply their knowledge of human nutrition, the demands in the market place will change and business will be stimulated to provide what consumers need rather than what industry wants to sell.

As the benevolent consequences of such applications of human development knowledge within the home and school are observed, more and more parents, teachers, and school boards will want to participate in the effort to shift both institutions on to a scientific foundation that will guarantee the perpetual self-renewal of family and school.

Families and schools made stable because they have a foundation in human development knowledge will help to make a stable community. Since a single family cannot provide all of the resources required for its own full development, it is clear that families can exist only within a larger unit——the community, and, through the creation of appropriate social institutions, make certain the collective need is served. Medical clinics, recreational centers, and other social service agencies are primary examples. Thus, families whose lives are organized in accordance with human development principles will naturally feel the necessity for participation in community life.

They can then make certain that the general services required are provided and that the moral tenor of the community is maintained in a way that will insure the unimpaired development of its children.

The community, of course, has to govern itself. If it applied human development knowledge in the formation of social policy and law, individuals as well as commercial enterprises would be prohibited from producing and selling things that impair human development, and every attempt would be made to provide whatever is needed to guarantee an opportunity for everyone in the community to develop fully. As things stand now, commercial success is given a higher priority than the promotion of human welfare. Because of this, the public tolerates poisonous food additives, the pollution of the air and water, and the general deterioration of the environment on which depend our lives. As a case in point, less than $1 million was spent during one year by the federal government on educational campaigns concerning the dangers of smoking. Yet it spent some $50 million in subsidies to tobacco growers and permitted cigarette manufacturers to spend upwards of $250 million in advertising—an amount more than one-third of the entire federal budget for cancer research (Gonzales, 1976).

It is not difficult to see how families and schools, reconstituted as suggested, could not only reverse a number of harmful trends, but could be the chief means by which an international renaissance in civilization might be brought about. While I believe that what we are proposing is ultimately attainable, I recognize that there is a great contrast between what we have now and what we could have if the family, school, and community were reconstituted on a foundation of human development knowledge. But the contrast has to be felt if the idea is to function as a lure and we are to move forward and apply the knowledge to improve the quality of our lives. Whitehead[8] makes this point:

A race preserves its vigour so long as it harbours a real contrast between what has been and what may be; and so long as it is nerved by the vigour to adventure beyond the safeties of the past. Without adventure civilization is in full decay.

The problem has been analyzed. Its history has been reviewed. A means for solving it has been proposed; the knowledge required is largely available; a scheme for organizing the knowledge and making it usable has been suggested; and, a new social institution to apply the knowledge to improve our lives has been proposed. I believe the stage is now set for the adventure Whitehead says is required to preserve civilization from full decay. In essence, it is the adventure of making human development knowledge active in homes and schools, alive in the behavior of parents and teachers, and munificent in its long-range impact on human biological, sociological, and cultural evolution.

CHAPTER 12

THE PHILOSOPHY OF
THE ANISA MODEL

By Daniel C. Jordan and Raymond P. Shepard
Published in *World Order*: Fall 1972

THE PURPOSE OF PHILOSOPHY is to disclose the nature of our experience and to make sense out of it by presenting evidence in support of basic premises from which logical thought proceeds. By revealing consistencies and inconsistencies in our experience it creates a coherence on which understanding depends. It provides perspective––a gradation of relevance––which orders experience and gives meaning to an otherwise overwhelming abundance of fragmentary details. A more specific function of philosophy is to stimulate the formulation of theory from which testable hypotheses may be deduced. As hypotheses are confirmed, theories from which they are derived become laws; and the body of knowledge expands.

Contemporary education lacks a philosophy broad enough in scope to unify the vast knowledge we have about human growth and development and produce a body of theory that would enable us to provide solutions to the difficult and complex problems facing education as a social institution. These problems are compounded by the rapidity of social change; the future spills into the present like a torrent. Adjustments to a new situation are scarcely begun before the situation changes, making the plans to deal with it obsolete. Trying to make adjustments under such conditions, in the absence of theory derived from a unifying philosophy, has brought us to a state of crisis. The profession is rent with internal conflict; diversity has degenerated into disunity. Vast resources are wasted. Several generations of students are caught in a system impotent to serve their educational needs in a complex, modern world.

The inadequacy of contemporary educational philosophy becomes apparent when we look for a set of assumptions about the nature of man. Because it has not defined the nature of man, education is in the untenable position of having to devote its energies to the development of curricula without any coherent ideas about the nature of the creature for whom they are intended. What is true about curricula is also true about teaching methods. Surely the nature of man has profound implications for both. To ignore those implications is to precipitate a crisis.

The philosophy of the ANISA Model deals with this crisis. It incorporates a view of man full enough and rich enough to account for and to illumine the concrete experience we have of our own growth and development as we interact with the environment. From the premises of this view, we are able to proceed logically to a body of theory about education which could be empirically tested over the next several decades. The philosophy we propose represents a significant departure from contemporary educational thought and practice. It is the result of a long search that combines insights from diverse disciplines into a coherent view of man—a view which can account for the knowing and loving capacities of the human being and provide a conceptual framework that is realizable as a model for education. Since it is difficult to know where we are going unless we know where we have been, understanding the ANISA philosophy depends upon having an historical perspective on the development of the human sciences and their role in shaping education as we know it today.

WHEN PSYCHOLOGY WAS WEANED from philosophy and set out on its own to become an empirical science, there was every reason to believe that the fledgling discipline would provide a firm foundation for the development of educational theory and practice. This hope was never fully realized, largely because our psychological concepts have been based on views of man's nature which were primarily derived by analogy from the current doctrines of other disciplines, disciplines whose central interest was not in the nature of man. In fact, the history of psychology can be told as a series of conceptual borrowings from the dominant physical sciences. We find, for instance, Thomas Hobbes asserting that man seeks pleasure and avoids pain with the same necessity and compulsion that causes a stone to fall downwards. In the eighteenth and early nineteenth centuries men such as J. F. Herbart drew upon the concept of physical gravity in proposing that the motion of ideas was the basic principle of mental mechanics. James Mill followed the same form of theorizing whereas his son, John Stuart Mill, substituted the more advanced ideas of chemistry for the older mechanistic outlook of his father by propounding a theory of "mental chemistry" to replace mental mechanics.

Francis Galton, whose efforts in mental testing and statistics make him an immediate predecessor of modern American psychology, held a geologically inspired model of a stratified mind consisting of lower nutritional strata and higher strata of memory and reasoning. In this view, mental testing was akin to sinking shafts into the mind at critical points to ascertain the stage of development.

Another important example of the application of externally derived explanatory models to theorizing in the human sciences is the work of Sigmund Freud. In his case the model is not derived from a purely scientific analogy but is, nonetheless, an externally derived explanatory system. A dominant Freudian metaphor is based upon a military model of mental processes. Here, thought processes become tactical military simulations of the anticipated confrontation with reality. Blocked development is compared to the resistance of hostile enemy forces; repression, to retreat in the face of an attack; and psychotherapy, to the intervention of an ally in a civil war.[133]

A central and seemingly often unconscious assumption underlying this borrowing approach is that the methods of the natural sciences are adequate to the study of man and to a description of his more complex and distinctively human aspects. In characterizing the nature of those early basic assumptions of prerelativistic scientific philosophy, we are also characterizing the materialism of the modern age. This materialism rests on the acceptance of scientific understanding as centering around the increased knowability of the character of matter and the laws by which it operates. Further, since matter could be reduced to discrete "billiard-ball-like" elements which behaved according to the immutable laws of nature, all that is real was seen as analyzable into its atomic components.

The most important implication of this materialistic thought for the developing human sciences revolves around the issues of causality, unity, and determinism. These issues form an important

---

[133] H. Nash, "Freud and Metaphor," *Archives of General Psychiatry*, 17 (1962), 25-29.

part of the fabric of our "standard" interpretation of nature. In fact, they have become so commonplace that it is almost unquestioningly assumed that all events are explicable in terms of their immediately preceding events which are ultimately describable as laws of nature acting on particles. From this perspective one can only develop a view of the unity of nature in which everything must be the result of the same laws acting on the same particles with man being but a more complex form of organization of particles and laws.

Unity, however, viewed in this way is not congruent with what we know of the type of unity applicable to the process of man's evolution and the structuring of human societies. We therefore require a definition of unity which accounts for the diversity within its essence and explains the transcendent relation of man to the lower-order physical unity of atoms and molecules. Thus we come face-to-face with the age-old philosophical problem of determinism. How is man, who is a part of nature, produced by and subject to its laws, ever to be capable of independent action? Free will is an illusion in a world where every effect must have a necessary and sufficient physical cause. Yet, the very enterprise of producing any sort of scientific description of natural phenomena rests upon the assumption that man, at least, is a self-determining organism. Whitehead indicates that the main effect of such a radical inconsistency in the basis of modern science results in an enfeebling of our thought with superficial orderings and arbitrary starting points.[134] Many of the problems created in the wake of this style of thought are interpretable under the general heading of reductionism, which is simply the uncritical acceptance of the understanding of mechanisms and processes that operate at lower levels of nature as explanations of higher-level phenomena. The assumption is that the explanation so produced leaves no remainder

---

[134] A. N. Whitehead, *Science and the Modern World* (New York: The Free Press, 1967), p. 76.

which is unexplained. This fallacious assumption is derived from the assimilationist doctrine that abstractions which illumine one aspect of reality also apply to all others. Scientific materialism of whatever variety mistakes the part for the whole by using abstractions (e.g., irreducible billiard-ball atoms) as if they were a concrete reality and then building a description of the concrete whole in terms of the abstraction from the part.

A prime example of reductionism is the development of Gestalt psychology. The Gestalt field, which was inspired by the discoveries of electromagnetic phenomena in the early twentieth century, was meant to replace the earlier atomistic-mechanistic views by interpreting mental processes in terms of physical fields in the brain. Actually, this did help to explain some mental phenomena simply because field concepts are more inclusive in their generality than the earlier atomistic notions they attempted to replace. However, the explanatory power of Gestalt psychology is still limited because its theory is derived from lower orders of existence. Our more modern attempts to reduce the explanation of human phenomena to principles derived from the study of animals, as seen in the work of B. F. Skinner and the behavioral school of psychology, suffers from the same defect.

Efforts to capture the reality of human experience through the application of the methods of sociology and anthropology reflect a similar inadequacy. Still another popular form of reducing human behavior to manageable terms is the focusing on the chronological factors of child growth and development as the major determinants of personality. However, the attempt to lay all social problems upon the doorstep of improper childrearing does not provide a fully satisfactory answer because it fails to add useful insight into the means by which adults can be changed so that their childrearing practices can be changed.

A final form of reductionism which is very influential today is the attempt to explain all forms of experience at the level of neurophysiological processes. Such pervasive determinism has so disposed us to seek causal explanations that we have produced descriptions of human life which seem to leave almost no room for the kind of individual determination that can transcend the programming of genetic endowment, culture, and tradition. The attempt to reduce the complexity of mental life to the lowest possible levels of physical phenomena signalizes the alienation of man from nature.

AT IMPORTANT MILESTONES in the development of our scientific thought, in the work of men such as Galileo, Descartes, and Kant, the stamp of philosophical approval was placed on each new scientific development that was simultaneously creating and filling the gap between man and nature. As the development has progressed, we have become more accustomed to the idea that scientific knowledge can only come from laboratory experiments where special conditions and constraints are imposed upon the subject. We do not run into serious trouble with this approach until we come to the study of man and are confronted with the curious situation of imposing our own conceptual forms upon ourselves. In other words, with the advent of modern human sciences we have come full circle––the looking glass of scientific inquiry has indeed become a mirror in which we see the image of our own conceptualizations reflected upon ourselves. In the past technical man observed nature through the glass and asked "How?"; today modern man in his increasing awareness of the reflection of his own image is inclined to ask "Why?" This is a critical question for us because the efforts to create modern science have also watered the seeds of alienation that were sown in the soil of the seventeenth-century view of the universe, richly composted by the discarded doctrines of the scholastics.

This condition of alienation is primarily an outgrowth of the world view which prevailed during the formative age of psychology. It was the era of the unquestioned supremacy of Newtonian physics, and it naturally assumed that the methods of the physical sciences could and should be applied to the study of the mind, even if the phenomena were of a different order. As a result, the entire development of the human sciences has been overshadowed by a scientific metaphysic which has exerted a continual bias toward the search for the same type of invariant and deterministic laws which characterize the physical sciences. It has been all too easy to translate the belief in physical atoms and laws into a corresponding faith that their psychological equivalents could be found in elementary sensations and conditioned responses.

Under the influence of materialistic science, the dominant impulse has been to seek a scientific understanding of the reality of man by examining levels of reality which are essentially behind him (or below, if you prefer) — that is to say, levels which are included within but not descriptive of the reality of man. The lowest levels, of course, are not characterized by life. Examining such levels can only lead to an understanding of lifeless things which achieve nothing, rely on nothing, and therefore never make a mistake. Yet, as Michael Polanyi has pointed out, the very idea of life involves the achievement of something—and making mistakes in the process.[135] How can processes that achieve something be described in terms of processes which do not incorporate achievement? Polanyi's answer to this logical impossibility is that "a principle not present in the inanimate must come into operation when it gives birth to living things."[136] In other words, a higher level of being can come into existence only as the result of a process which is not manifest at a lower level. In this view, the comprehensive understanding of any being is dependent upon understanding the operating principles which apply to its level of patterned functioning and cannot be achieved through principles which apply to inferior levels.

---

[135] Michael Polanyi, *The Tacit Dimension* (New York: Doubleday, 1966), pp. 29-52.

[136] Ibid., p. 44.

Whitehead identified four major aggregations of patterned activities hierarchically arranged, each with a specific pattern of expression.[137] The first level is the nonliving which functions according to the laws of nature with a total suppression of individual self-expression. The next is the vegetable level in which life is superimposed upon inorganic nature. Viewed differently, the latent potentiality in lifeless matter can be seen as awakened into realization in the vegetable by the operation of a higher-order principle. In the animal level of existence, the lower levels are incorporated into that of a unified and self-directed organism. Finally, the human level incorporates them all and adds the ability to respond to the influx of ideals which shape its purposes and mold its actions.

Here we can discern the beginnings of a possible reconciliation between the world as given in experience and the world as known in science. The hierarchical view suggests a type of scientific unity which focuses on the importance of patterned action. It is a unity of process and purpose rather than a unity of kind. Furthermore, it is a view which not only admits but requires diversity as a necessary element in the structure of reality and one which places man and his potentialities at the pinnacle of an evolutionary process which is seeking its meaning through man's transcendent actualization of these potentialities. Thus, it is the spiritual and not the material nature of man which is the central determinant in the future course of evolution, and the meaning of man is to be sought in that transcendent generality which is the essence of his being rather than in the operation of laws whose powers have been expressed primarily in lower-order categories of existence.

It is a bold assertion indeed that we need a new cosmology, one which suggests that the transition from mechanism to organism, from immutable laws to hierarchical processes, is indispensable to the advent of a new era in man's awareness of the nature of the reality

---

[137] A. N. Whitehead, *Modes of Thought* (New York: The Free Press, 1968), pp. 20-30.

underlying his existence and a corresponding new era in education. This is the cosmology upon which the ANISA model is founded.

As we have seen, at the base of the problems of education is a need to eliminate the philosophical distortions which afflict the human sciences. These distortions make organization of information impossible and are the basic reason education has been unable to draw upon its "mother disciplines" in the human sciences in the same way medicine, for example, has fruitfully applied the basic principles of the physical and biological sciences. In education little success has been achieved in explaining how all of the research findings and analyses fit together to make an adequate picture of man. There is no way to make them fit so long as the spiritual reality underlying man's flesh-and-blood existence remains excluded in the persistent search to understand his material being.

ANISA makes of education an adventure in the growth of the human spirit and seeks to create a new ethos that reflects the organic and spiritual wholeness of man. The intent of ANISA is therefore to move from our present limits of understanding to a more complete picture of the potentialities of man and the conditions which foster his development. The failures of the last hundred years' efforts at giving a scientific description and reaching a scientific understanding of man have convinced us of the limitations of the scientific materialist philosophy. We have therefore adopted a philosophy of organism which can illumine those features of our existence which are characteristically human, such as consciousness, will, purpose, creativity, and the capacities to know and to love.

The first and most obvious implication of adopting such a philosophy is that the goal here sought does not lie within the borders of any existing discipline. The task of forming a more complete picture of the potentialities of man thus involves an attempt to further our understanding by recognizing that newer scientific ideas can grow out of and be made harmonious with their predecessors by including them in a larger explanatory context. From this point of view, the task is not only to criticize and disregard ideas and theories of the past but also to explain and include.

One of the clearest examples of scientific progress seen in this light is the development of modern celestial mechanics. In the early seventeenth century popular opinion held that the earth stood still and that the heavens moved. Galileo, however, asserted that it was the sun which remained stationary and that the earth moved around it. His apparent heresy was subsequently given explicit shape and theoretical elegance by Newton in the formulation of a set of laws which applied to earthly and heavenly bodies alike. Newton's more encompassing view stood until Einstein, with his relativistic mechanics, asserted that everything moves and that it is simply a choice of one's vantage point which determines the "correct" view.

No one has ever suggested that it was a change in the character of the heavens which prompted these new theories. Rather, it was the same reality which had been more successfully described by models which sprang from a more inclusive, hence more general, grasp of the problem. This example simply demonstrates that the formulation of theories requires the imposition of limits upon the phenomena to be described in order to abstract them into a special explanatory context. Abstractions may thus omit part of the truth. They are nonetheless useful to the extent that the omissions do not vitiate the conclusions drawn from them.

In the same way, the assumptions which underlie the development of the ANISA model and the basic concepts of *releasing human potential* through *attainment of learning competence* are not necessarily asserted to be an exhaustive set of ideas. They are viewed as the most basic terms upon which to build a theory useful to pedagogy that can now be formulated. They are basic in the logical sense of being more fundamental terms which, even though they themselves are abstractions from the larger reality of man's existence, still contain the seeds of those very qualities we are ultimately seeking as the flower of the process of education here proposed.

The philosophy of organism sheds light on that larger reality of man's existence by distinguishing him from a mere mechanism; for man, at the highest level of creation, represents a unity of all existence in that he incorporates the diverse qualities of lower-order mechanistic phenomena while transcending them all. His transcendence depends upon his ability to know and to love and to organize these capacities in terms of purpose or aim. Thought and feeling expressed in action under the direction of purpose reflect a nonmechanistic principle which characterizes the process of his becoming—process being the reality of man which education can no longer afford to ignore and the reality which is the central concern of ANISA.[138] The unity of all existence represented in man is dynamic; it is experienced as a consciousness in which the stored accumulations of past experiences are brought to bear upon immediate circumstances in anticipation of the future—an anticipation felt in the immediate present as purpose fused with hope and aspiration. Man is thus a conscious creature capable of creating his future out of his past by virtue of the decisions he makes in the immediate present. The quality of those decisions determines the rate by which his potentialities are translated into actuality. It is that process of translating potentiality into actuality which the philosophy underlying the ANISA model illumines. *Learning, very broadly defined, is the essential dynamic of that process and gaining conscious control over the process is what is meant by learning competence.* It is for that reason that we define learning competence as the key factor in the release of human potential at an optimum rate. Such competence depends on learning, for how to learn is in itself something that has to be learned; yet it is never taught directly in traditional schools. The focal concern of the ANISA

---

[138] In *Process and Reality* (New York: Macmillan, 1960), A. N. Whitehead expands this thesis into a fully developed cosmology.

model is the provision of experiences for young children which enable them to become competent learners——effective transformers of their own potentialities into actualities.

A translation of this philosophy first into theory and then into educational practice would bring a revolution in education by itself, but the picture is more striking than that. If the process of translating potentiality into actuality is managed in accordance with pedagogical principles derived from the view of man as a spiritual being, the actualization of potentiality is accompanied by a further creation or extension of potentiality. It is such capacity to create potentiality that enables man continually to move beyond himself. It constitutes another basic feature of his transcendent nature. Furthermore, his almost unlimited capacity to store information about his experience, his ability to form an infinite number of sentences to elaborate on those experiences and communicate their meaning to others——the indwellingness of his past surfacing into consciousness as he negotiates the immediate present——make him immanent. Thus, man is both immanent and transcendent. The fusion of immanence and transcendence makes him conscious and places him in a position to shape his own destiny, to differentiate his knowing and loving capacities into an infinity of potentialities which are integrated in action as he shapes his future. Man, the highest pinnacle of creation, thus reflects an ongoing progressive unity in the diversity of all existence.

IT IS THE PURSUIT of a comprehension of the relationships among all aspects of our experiences that brings us meaning. We are creatures which require meaning in order to continue the process of creating higher levels of organization or unity within ourselves——a process synonymous with the release of potential. That we can love and be loved, know and know that we know; that we can consciously move beyond ourselves into the future on the basis of what we decide to do at any given moment, thereby making the most out of our past as we push into that future (which makes us both immanent and transcendent); that we are able to have a sense of purpose which brings meaning and directs unlimited creative powers in making decisions and carrying them out––all of these are meant by the phrase *the spiritual nature of man.*

This understanding of man and his potentialities removes the obviously "factual" and the "material" from the center of our view of the cosmos and replaces them with the sensitive reaction of the experiencing and self-actualizing subject himself as the ultimate determinant of the "grain" or "texture" of reality. A reality which is so constructed reflects a recognition that man's desire to find meaning and purpose in experience comes from deep within his being and is an expression of that same upward thrust which in past ages was responsible for mere survival of the species and is, today, urging him onward to new attainments far removed from mere physical survival.

Any educational system that hopes to facilitate the release of human potential has the prime responsibility of recognizing that meaning in life. Therefore, relevance in education is associated not only with the highest intellectual achievements of mankind but also with his most profound emotional and spiritual insights; for within the individual occurs the interaction of the breadth of his thought with the depths of his being––his ability to know and his ability to love––that reflects a higher-order purpose, establishes the relationships among things, and creates a meaning in experience.

Since mankind at large has asserted the meaning of experience in its art as well as its science, educators, in their concern for the whole individual, must recognize that both our art and our science share the common obligation to open our minds, to refine our emotions, to protect our sense of beauty, and to heighten our ability to create it.

The two main assumptions upon which the development of the ANISA model rests––the unity of mankind and the spiritual nature of man––are not only directly related to the character of the hierarchical process model which ANISA represents. They are required by it. They are required in the sense that a scientific view of education must express both the being and the becoming of man. Being and becoming require each other. Together they constitute a complete picture of man; individually they are abstractions which can only be evaluated by examining one of them in reference to the other.

In our view, the unity of mankind is determined by man's true station as the most highly evolved creature in the world we experience; and the spiritual nature of man is an expression of the operation of a higher-order principle as yet transcendent in relation to man's present condition, a principle which consciousness compels us to accept on faith.

Thus, mankind's collective evolution into a future, better described in spiritual terms rather than in material ones, requires of education the ability to impart to each individual child the knowledge that it is his nature to be within the world and yet to transcend it; that of all creation, man is the vehicle of the evolution of the universe and the highest expression of the unity in all existence. That evolution and that expression constitute the process of his becoming.

CHAPTER 13

ANISA

THE ANISA MODEL

**A NEW EDUCATIONAL SYSTEM FOR
DEVELOPING HUMAN POTENTIAL**

**By Daniel C. Jordan
Donald T. Streets
Published in *World Order*: Spring 1972**

*Anisa comes from a root word that refers to a flowering and fragrant
plant or tree. It has been used to represent the "Tree of Life," an ancient
symbol which conveys the qualities of beauty, grace, nurturance, shelter,*

and cycles of fruition. The Anisa logogram was designed to illustrate these qualities and suggests their significance for an organic conception of education.

In 1967 the American Academy of Arts and Sciences published the report of its Commission on The Year 2000. The members of the commission––biologists, psychiatrists, economists, political scientists, government officials, physical scientists, behavioral scientists, political philosophers, and futurologists––represented extraordinary talents. The purpose of the commission was to sketch hypothetical futures; to find ways of helping man to come to better decisions by anticipating problems; to identify ways and means of forestalling undesirable developments; to produce a new political theory that would enable us to approach the year 2000 with some assurance of survival; and to suggest an adequate planning process that would make it possible for us to project alternative futures and make some rational choices about them. The report itself is a fascinating compendium that brilliantly articulates problems to be faced, speculates on the issues to be resolved, and makes repeated statements to the effect that, if we are to survive, far-reaching changes in our social systems and in our view of ourselves will have to take place.

In several of the reports the importance of the role of education in shaping the future is stressed. Yet it was repeatedly pointed out that education itself must undergo a radical change if it is to help shape the future in positive ways:

> If we are to remain true to our democratic heritage, one of the most obvious implications of the predicted increase in population is that our already crowded educational system will have to be vastly expanded and overhauled ... Put together the increased number of students, the increased knowledge to be

communicated, and the increased duration of the educational experience, and then try to imagine what kind of educational system we will need by the year 2000. Can anything short of an educational revolution meet our needs.[139]

But what will be the source of the needed change? Do we know enough to bring it about? The truth of the matter is that we have an extraordinary amount of knowledge about the development of human beings, how they learn, and how they grow. Libraries are filled with books on education. In the United States alone over seven hundred journals pertinent to the problems of education are published at regular intervals. In addition, a variety of federal, state, professional, and commercial organizations disseminate information on education through thousands of news bulletins, reports, magazines, tape recordings, and films. But for lack of a unifying principle it all remains undigested and therefore not very usable. The poet Edna St. Vincent-Millay put her finger on the problem:

> Upon this gifted age,
> In its dark hour
> Reigns from the sky a meteoric shower of facts;
> They lie unquestioned, uncombined.
> Wisdom enough to leech us of our ill
> Is daily spun,
> But there exists no loom
> To weave it into fabric.[140]

---

[139] George A. Miller, "Some Psychological Perspectives on the Year 2000," *Daedalus: Journal of the American Academy of Arts and Sciences* (Summer 1967), p. 889.

[140] Edna St. Vincent-Millay, "Sonnet CXXVII," in *Collected Poems* (New York: Harper, 1956), p. 697.

The poet's pessimism notwithstanding, there exists now an educational project that gives the promise of functioning as the loom on which may be woven the fabric of a new educational system––a system that may be able to make use of that "meteoric shower of facts" by organizing them around the affirmation of the spiritual nature of man. This new educational model, or blueprint, now in the initial planning stages, is called ANISA, an Arabic word meaning "a tree in a high place that sheds a fragrance all around"–– the Tree of Life, symbolizing continual growth and fruition. The logo of the ANISA model is a contemporary version of the ancient symbol and was chosen for its power to communicate the idea of beauty in continual growth and fruition––the essence of the new model of education. The ANISA model rests on the premise that man was created to know and to love and that out of various combinations of these two capacities spring all his potentialities which it is the obligation of an educational system to develop.

ANISA also stands for American National Institute for Social Advancement, an organization devoted to the development of programs that tackle some of the critical needs of our time. It is under the auspices of this organization that the initial planning of the model took place. The ANISA educational model is now being developed at the Center for the Study of Human Potential at the School of Education of the University of Massachusetts in Amherst with the assistance of a planning grant from The New England Program in Teacher Education, Durham, New Hampshire, an affiliate of The New England Regional Commission that is devoted to the improvement of education through better teacher preparation and a wider dissemination of information on successful educational innovations.

The ANISA model is based on a redefinition of education as those processes or experiences that underlie the development or release of human potential. It promises to be an extraordinary breakthrough, with particular significance for the education of the millions of children who currently come to formal learning situations without the prerequisite experiences on which successful achievement in traditional schools is based. Starting prior to conception of the child and spanning approximately the first fifteen years of life, the ANISA model is concerned with the development of all human potentialities and not merely with the capacity to store and retrieve factual information organized along traditional curriculum lines.

Since technology has begun to solve most information storage and retrieval problems, we are compelled to redefine the role of the teacher and of the school in education. The issue becomes clear when one realizes, for instance, that because of the advancement in microphotography a youngster will in the near future be able to carry in his pocket a small card which will contain all the data now available in a standard encyclopedia. This achievement, along with the explosion of information which promises to double in amount every eight years, serves to highlight the importance of educating individuals in a way that will assist them in utilizing information rather than in merely storing it.

Any new educational system which will help humanity to survive in the future must be based on an accurate conception of the nature of man. It must enable him to grasp a noble vision of his destiny and give him the power to deal with all of the critical exigencies facing him at this perilous juncture in history. The ANISA model therefore rests on the bold assertion that man is the pinnacle of creation, endowed with unique capacities still unfathomed and for the most part unrealized. To be successful such a radically new educational system must be able to foster continual growth that is free from the kinds of developmental deficiencies which underlie both individual and social pathology. Because the ANISA model is designed to prevent such deficiencies, it will make a significant contribution to the solution of problems related to crime, mental illness, poverty, injustice, prejudice, racial strife, war, political corruption, immorality, and destructive forms of withdrawal such as alcoholism and drug abuse. Thus, it has definite implications for the bringing about of world order.

No educational system can ever hope to prevent or solve all of the problems people experience individually and collectively. But any educational system designed for the future will have to be concerned with all of these issues and with the roles educational experience can play in developing whole and healthy human beings.

Man—A Spiritual Being

PHILOSOPHICALLY, the ANISA model rests upon a clear affirmation of the spiritual nature of man and of his endowment with an infinitude of potentialities, each of which can be developed for the good of himself and the good of his fellowman.[141] By this we mean that man is far more than an animal; since he can know that he knows, know that he loves, love what he knows, and be conscious of all this, he is a creature different from other beings on the planet: the only one who can take an active part in the shaping of his own destiny. He is, in the words of Teilhard de Chardin, like the "tip of an ever-ascending arrow"—always purposeful, evolving, and growing. We hold that there is no rational way of conceptualizing an adequate educational system for the future unless it rests on an assumption of the spiritual nature of man and reflects the noblest of man's aspirations, so evident in his history, his religion, and his art.

The decision to base the development of the model upon the spiritual nature of man was not arbitrary. It has, in fact, extensive philosophical support and a growing body of scientific confirmation. Both the philosophical foundations of the model and the prominent role accorded research and theory in its detailed rationale underscore a unique feature of the model.

---

[141] *World Order* hopes to publish in subsequent issues additional articles on the ANISA model, including one elaborating the philosophical basis of the model.

In keeping with the idea of man as a spiritual being, the model is based on the premise that knowing and loving are the two basic capacities of man which reflect his purpose and constitute his characteristic powers. From the blending and differentiations of these two capacities all human potentialities are derived. While this may at first appear to be an oversimplification, closer and deeper scrutiny reveals that all the positive and creative efforts of man in some way relate to either or both of these capacities. For this reason, knowing and loving represent the bipolar axis around which the model revolves. Understanding the reciprocal interplay of these two characteristic powers, reflected on different levels, brings a new perspective on the growth and development of the potentialities of the human being.

There are many theories and philosophical perspectives which lend support to this assumption. Some, in a limited sense, have found their way into educational programs of a rather circumscribed scope. No program, however, has dared to take on as broad a definition of man as the ANISA model does. Yet without such a broad definition an educational system cannot be comprehensive. One of the current ills of education is its lack of an adequate definition of man. Thus, it is fragmentary rather than comprehensive, and it is unable to make use of the available information about human growth and development. These ailments cannot be cured without a unifying principle capable of interpreting the reality of man and organizing factual knowledge so as to inspire belief prerequisite to action. Education thus reflects a larger dilemma faced by the world—a dilemma which Julian Huxley has succinctly expressed:

> I would go so far as to say that lack of a common
> frame of reference, the absence of any unifying set

of concepts and principles, is now, if not the world's major disease, at least its most serious symptom.[142]

Learning Competence and the Development of Potential

THE ASSUMPTION of man's spiritual nature (with knowing and loving being the basic capacities out of which all potentialities are differentiated) serves as the unifying principle for the ANISA model on the philosophical level. On the functional level, the integrating principle is the definition of learning competence as the key factor in the release or development of those potentialities at an optimum rate. Therefore, the basic objective of every experience planned for the child is the development of learning competence. Any youngster who can be assisted in becoming a competent learner will have been given the main tool for negotiating his destiny, regardless of the difficulties or circumstances he may face.

How to learn is in itself something that must be learned. Yet in most traditional school settings, children are never taught how to learn because teachers are not trained to teach them how to learn. Furthermore, the need for children to become competent learners is not often emphasized or dealt with directly.

Before anything can be done about this situation, the nature of learning competence and its relationship to the development of potentialities must be understood on both the theoretical and functional levels. The education programs for ANISA teachers are organized around that objective. In essence, learning competence depends upon the ability to *differentiate* or select the significant or relevant aspects of any situation and *integrate* them or restructure them in whatever way is required to achieve a given purpose. The process of differentiation followed by integration appears as a

---

[142] Julian Huxley, *Knowledge, Morality, and Destiny* (New York: New American Library, 1960), p. 88.

central characteristic of growth for man on all levels—biological, psychological, and spiritual. Learning competence can thus be seen as an ability to manage these two complementary processes: differentiation and integration. Philosophically, differentiation reflects the knowing capacity, and integration reflects the loving capacity. Becoming fully developed depends on learning particular kinds of interactions of the two basic capacities. Some kinds of interaction pave the way for future development; others slow up, impair, or preclude further growth. On a very basic level, for instance, if one of the capacities (loving) is turned against the other (knowing), the child may hate knowing rather than loving it, or he may love not knowing. These particular interactions impair the release of potential. In fact, a good many learning disabilities can be understood in terms of these dynamics.

Each process of differentiation followed by an integration may represent a learning set that insures maximum transferability of experience to other problems or tasks. A simple example may help to make this point clear. Consider the case of a young child trying to learn what a chair is. To do this he must differentiate certain attributes of furniture which when integrated in a certain way make up a chair (that is, constitute "chairness"): four legs of certain height, seat of particular size, and back. Having made those differentiations and that particular integration, the child can then appropriately identify on sight chairs that he has never seen before and distinguish them from "non-chair" furniture or other objects which may share some but not all of the chair's attributes (tables have legs, bicycles have seats, couches have backs, etc.). This reduces the overwhelming complexity of the environment and makes the child more competent in dealing with it. In typical homes or schools, children will be taught the concept "chair" *but not the process of forming the concept.* The ANISA approach not only teaches the child what a chair is but makes him aware of how he learns the concept. That makes the learning experience maximally transferable—that is, it helps him to formulate other concepts more easily. Transferability constitutes one important characteristic of learning competence.

The ANISA model is defined by a large number of specifications which explain the primary or essential learning sets of categories of potentialities in educational terms. The more sets that correspond to reality a person has, the more competent he will become as a learner, the more power he will have for future growth and development, and the more rapidly his potential will be released.

Achieving Learning Competence in Different Categories of Potentialities

TO FACILITATE our understanding of the nature of human potential, we have divided the two characteristic powers of knowing and loving into nine fundamentally different but interrelated categories of potentialities. Each of the following sections deals briefly with the achievement of learning competence in each category.

Psycho-Motor Development. One of the first developmental tasks facing a child is gaining control over the position and movement of the voluntary muscles. Through the reciprocal process of differentiation and integration, or assimilation and accommodation in Piaget's terms, the child develops a motor-base. This motor-base is an internal structuring which develops from the experiences of undifferentiated movements that later become refined into differentiated ones and finally are integrated into a wide variety of general patterns such as walking, skipping, and running. This internal structure or schema provides the child with a reference point around which he organizes both space and time and according to which he assigns meaning to his sensory experiences.

Perceptual Development. The child comes to know his environment through his senses. Perception refers to the organization and interpretation of sensory input in terms of past experience, present needs, and future aspirations. Initially, the organization of sensory input is dependent on the motor-base. Adequate organization and interpretation also depend upon acuity––the ability to discriminate among a number of stimuli in a given dimension (visual, auditory, tactile, and so on). When the various modes of perception begin to work in a functionally integrated way, the organism increases its capabilities for receiving, sorting, storing, and utilizing information meaningfully. It is this refined capacity of perceptual acuity–– differentiating among stimuli and their integration into functionally useful patterns that contribute to learning competence. This kind of perceptual competence can be achieved through the appropriate experiences and the practice which the ANISA model provides.

Cognitive Development. Cognition refers to a variety of mental processes or operations such as equivalence, identity, closure, conjunction, disjunction, association, negation, and implication. It also deals with higher order processes such as grasping causality, managing abstractions, forming and utilizing concepts, extrapolation, interpolation, understanding correlations, mediation, reversibility, seriation, conservation, and a variety of formal operations generally involving synthesis and analysis. To teach these processes means to teach a child not just what to think but how to think. An ANISA teacher thus needs to be able to identify these processes in any learning experience in the course of a day and to provide all the feedback required so that children may recognize, master, and apply them.

Affective or Emotional Development. Affective development refers to the organization of emotions. Through development there is a progression from undifferentiated feelings to differentiation and integration of feelings into attitudes (emotional habits) and finally into values. How to feel about things, events, or ideas is learned. How to organize feeling is also learned. The resultant attitudes and values may either foster further growth or preclude it. Ultimately the mature person develops a value system which includes a high degree of cognitive structuring in which he organizes his values and attitudes in a hierarchy according to their relative importance. The most highly functional value system will predispose the human being towards a satisfying life's work and a constellation of personal habits that sustain both mental and physical health. When values, emotional habits (attitudes), and feelings are organized into a coherent whole unified by a strong sense of purpose, energies are released which would otherwise be dissipated in the maintenance of value conflicts. The purpose of the ANISA model's specifications in this area is to assist teachers in providing experiences which enable children to make the most functional organization of their emotional life. This organization must be internally consistent, relatively free from conflicts, and compatible with reason. The organization of emotion is one of the most important learning processes that occurs during a person's life. The kinds of values and attitudes a child acquires will largely determine whether or not he will seek further learning opportunities for the development and fulfillment of his capacities.

Moral Development. Whenever a person's knowing and loving capacities are directed toward other people, his actions can be classified as moral behavior. Man is a social and therefore a moral being, as well as a physical and spiritual one. He has certain inescapable responsibilities toward every other person. The acquisition of moral competence thus depends upon learning the nature of these responsibilities and acquiring attitudes, values, and behavior appropriate to them. Essential to these responsibilities is the ability of the child to relate to others in a way that facilitates the development of their potentialities so that they will reciprocate by supporting his development.

The child progresses through a number of stages beginning with an undifferentiated state characterized by lack of awareness of any rules or social relationships. He continues through the stages of establishing relationships with adults (usually parents) and then with peers; he finally arrives at a stage of autonomy when he is sensitive to the needs of others, can think abstractly about social relationships, and is capable of independent moral reasoning. Progression through these stages depends upon the child's ability to trust and to be trusted. Both abilities underlie the subsequent development of humility. Achieving moral competence involves a number of developmental patterns, such as the ability to obey adults, which evolves into the ability to abide by ground rules laid down by adults (a definite shift from people to principle); progresses through deferment of gratification, impulse control, resistance to temptation; and ultimately arrives at the mastery of self-discipline and possession of a well integrated conscience.

Perhaps the most important aspect of moral competence is the capacity to love and be loved, a capacity which begins with self-gratification, progresses through a need for adult approval and for the approval of peers, and finally develops into a need for self-approval, respect for others, altruism, and a sense of justice.

Development of Will. Volitional competence represents a kind of intrinsic motivation without which the human being cannot actively participate in the shaping of his own destiny. It includes the ability to resolve conflicting tendencies by adopting, after reflection, a subjective aim; a conscious termination of the resolving process resulting in the setting of goals and commitment to the goal set; a subphase involving elaboration of those goals into smaller, differentiated subplans; and the controlled translation of intention into action, including a self-arousal or mobilization of energy and concentration. Volitional competence also involves the process of self-correction and persistence in the face of obstacles and, finally, a reintegration of all of the subgoals into one subjective aim resulting in a consummation of action and goal achievement. The experiences many children have in school destroy, weaken, or inhibit the development of volitional competence. The ANISA model therefore contrasts sharply with traditional schooling approaches to the development of will.

Development of Creativity and Aesthetic Sensitivity. Learning competence in the area of creativity refers to the capacity to create order out of chaos (or some undifferentiated state), to identify parts and the relationships among them so that they can be integrated into a whole. This area also includes the development of a sense of humor which is dependent upon sensitivity to an unanticipated arrangement of things.

Creativity cuts across and is related to all of the other areas in a variety of ways and includes such things as divergence in thinking, intuition, fantasy, speculation, and imagination. Most important, it refers to the capacity to appreciate beauty and the inclination to organize one's own living circumstances so that they are beautiful. It includes a sensitivity to art in all its forms and an appreciation and refinement of expressive abilities that lead to aesthetic creations.

Spiritual Development. Spirituality concerns the formation of ultimate concerns and a search for one's place in the order of the cosmos.

ANISA

Achieving spirituality begins with an ability to trust and is therefore fundamentally dependent on having trustworthy parents. Out of this trust develops faith. A child's faith makes him teachable. Ultimately, spirituality rests on the formation of a belief system which may transcend reasoning but not oppose it. Spirituality involves the ability to meditate and thus assumes a conscious role in the individuation of the total personality—a personal integration around a transcendent purpose. The ANISA model provides the experiences and the means that will facilitate the emergence of a self-image that is functional in relationship to both the microcosm and the macrocosm.

Language Development. The acquisition of language is one of the most critical of all developmental tasks facing the child. Mastery of a language, its vocabulary, and its syntax and an ability to use it in both written and oral forms is critical to the achievement of general learning competence. All potentialities become human when they come under the influence of language.

Exposure to language at the appropriate time is the basic requirement for language acquisition. Good language models and a stimulating environment designed to elicit a richness of verbal expression are among the essentials for language development. In addition to these the ANISA model also provides for experiences designed to facilitate labeling or naming of things, vocabulary development, and the actual articulation of speech sounds.

The ANISA Curriculum

How does subject matter––reading, writing, arithmetic, history, social science, biology, and art––fit into the ANISA model? Since the model is primarily concerned with enabling children to master all of the processes underlying the attainment of learning competence, schools based on the ANISA model therefore will be organized to accommodate this attainment as the first priority. Such organization, however, does not necessarily mean doing away with the content of traditional curricula. It means, rather, an integration of all curricula around the processes already outlined so that learning sets which guarantee maximum transferability can be acquired. (The emphasis on processes is most characteristic of the experiences provided for the very young children.) In other words, biology, music, science, and social studies, for instance, can all be taught in ways that enable the child to remember the content of these disciplines while he is also becoming a competent learner. Because of the rapidity of social change and the speed with which the future pours into the present, competence in learning will insure survival in the future, for it is learning competence that provides maximum adaptive flexibility and the capacity not only to tolerate change but to take an active role in directing it.

Developmental Considerations

EFFECTIVE IMPLEMENTATION of the ANISA model involves, in addition to understanding the variables of learning competence and the processes on which they are based, recognition that biological maturation must be unimpaired if learning is to proceed at optimum rates. For this reason the nutritional status and health of the child are of great importance. Since the earlier stages of development have direct consequences for later ones, the model envisages beginning work with a prospective parent a year before pregnancy so that future mothers can acquire maximum health in preparation for conception and gestation. During this time the mother-to-be will have the opportunity to learn all the details of the ANISA model including how to initiate the educational program from the moment of her child's birth.

The organization of learning experiences centers on the developmental stages of the child, rather than on subject matter, with particular attention being given to critical periods in development. These periods are critical in the sense that, if certain experiences are missing at that particular time, growth and development are impaired, in some cases irreversibly. For instance, one of the important phases of language development takes place between eight months and two years. Therefore, to achieve full language development, one must guarantee that all the prerequisites for such development are present at that particular time.

Because children reach and pass through these periods at their own rate, the educational program is, therefore, completely individualized. It is not organized around specific age levels, although age will obviously have implications for the kinds of experiences which will be appropriate to any given group of children. Rather the developmental requirements of a child, whatever his age, are the basic determinants of the educational program for him.

Some Other Characteristic Features of the Model

WITH A GIFTED and well-trained staff, experiences to strengthen learning competence can be developed out of almost any situation. Thus implementation of the ANISA model will not be dependent upon extraordinary facilities or a great deal of equipment. The training program for the ANISA master-teachers is designed to equip them with all the knowledge and skill required to get the maximum amount of mileage from every learning experience.

Since teaching consolidates learning, the ANISA system will rely heavily upon the utilization of more advanced children as teachers of younger children. Five year olds will be trained to help teach three year olds, seven year olds will help teach five year olds, and so on. Thus the children themselves will function as a pool of manpower for teaching. This is not possible in most schools today because children are segregated by age level, and teachers are not trained in how to use children effectively as teachers.

The ANISA model is designed to guarantee for each child a number of successes far exceeding his failures. This requires that a child master the prerequisites of a given task before it is given to him. It also requires that teachers be able to generate a wide variety of options or alternatives in terms of instructional methodology, materials, and techniques. Failure itself is seen as a potential facilitator of learning. After all, great discoveries have most frequently been made after people have tried something, failed, and, in analyzing the reasons for failure, gained new insights into the phenomena under consideration. Taking advantage of failure in this way has to be learned, and it is in turn a very important element in the achievement of learning competence.

The model relies heavily on feedback from teachers to guide learning and change behavior rather than on traditional grading practices which usually preclude the treatment of failure in the way just discussed. The children themselves are taught self-evaluation procedures that are appropriate to any particular learning task at hand.

Traditional school systems are structured and operated in ways which tend to punish creativity in children. In the absence of a variety of alternatives and options, potentiality is suppressed and, almost inevitably, behavioral problems and learning disorders ensue. The ANISA model is designed to foster creativity by providing and encouraging the search for alternatives and the exercise of options, thereby avoiding the punishment of creativity.

The full development of the capacities for symbolic transformation is regarded as critical for future growth and development, since they are particularly germane to learning competence. This means that mastery of the fundamentals of mathematics and of a language in both written and oral forms is of paramount importance. However, instead of allocating special periods for reading and for speaking, the ANISA model provides opportunities for mastering language and mathematics throughout the activities of the entire- day. These capacities then develop organically and naturally in ways that promise to prevent many of the reading and language problems which many children experience in the present system.

If the child is to grow and develop at optimum rates, the formal educational experience, however promising it may be, cannot be discontinuous with what he experiences in his home and in his community. The ANISA model provides a means by which home, parents, and community can be involved in maintaining a total support system for the child.

Because it deals with processes of growth and development that are universal, the model is not culture-bound. It can be adopted by any cultural group, including bilingual and multiethnic groups, and still prove to be effective. With its focus on universals, the model stands as a bulwark against the transmission of racial and ethnic prejudices to the next generation. Since the ANISA model holds racism to be one of the most endemic suppressors of human potentialities known to man, staff selection and training are organized to preclude it.

Finally, the model's philosophical basis and its grounding in scientific theory and research findings make possible the eventual development of cost-effectiveness measures and accountability. Implementation plans for the model contain provisions for long range study and evaluation and a continual modification and refinement to increase its efficacy.

Staffing

WHAT KIND of staffing arrangement is most suitable for the ANISA model? We have adopted a differentiated staffing arrangement in which a master-teacher who understands both curriculum content and the processes underlying the attainment of learning competence holds a central position in the management of teaching and learning. This individual is supported by a variety of assistant teachers and aides; a diagnostician and evaluation specialist; curriculum and programming specialists; media technologists; multi-arts specialists who are competent in all the arts and know how to draw upon them to bring life and vitality into every learning experience; a family-community-school liaison worker whose job it is to reduce cultural discontinuities between family, home, and school; learning disabilities specialists; health and medical specialists; and program administrators and their staff, whose function it is to keep the model serving the purpose of releasing the potentialities of the children with efficiency.

Managing an educational program designed to release human potential at an optimum rate requires a highly skilled and experienced staff—a staff which must necessarily go through an intensive, demanding, and lengthy training. When one considers that the full development of the innumerable potentialities of the human mind and character is far more complex and challenging than placing a man on the moon, it is not difficult to appreciate the need for extensive training and preparation for staff members of this new kind of educational system.

Ultimately, the ANISA model envisages that every school will also be a teacher preparation site and that all staff members will be prepared by actively participating in all of the affairs of the school. In other words, training is based on the acquisition of knowledge about human growth and development and on learning how to apply all of the relevant theory and principles while actively engaged in working with children on a daily basis. Thus, theory is always seen in the context of practice. The model also includes the training of paraprofessionals while on the job in an open-ended system where advancement to the highest levels is possible.

Prospects

AT PRESENT, ANISA represents both a bright hope and an extraordinary promise for the emergence of a new kind of educational system based upon the affirmation of the spiritual nature of man and the limitless capacity latent in each child––a potentiality that can only be brought to life in an environment whose richness of experience is deliberately fostered and managed by an expert staff committed to the full growth and development of each child. Such a school might indeed reflect the full implications of ANISA's symbol, the Tree of Life.

CHAPTER 14

———◆•◆•◆———

BEING AND BECOMING:
THE ANISA THEORY OF
DEVELOPMENT

By Michael F. Kalinowski and Daniel C. Jordan
Published in *World Order*: Summer 1973

MAN REPRESENTS the highest expression of the organization of matter in the universe. And as part of the universe, he is describable by the same properties as other forms, but with one important exception––namely, human consciousness. Julian Huxley affirms that man is "the only repository of cosmic self-awareness in the universe," and that makes him "managing director of the biggest business of all, the business of evolution."[143]

---

[143] Julian Huxley, *Knowledge, Morality and Destiny* (New York: Mentor Books, 1960), p. 13.

In order to accommodate theoretically the mystery of life, let alone the phenomenon of consciousness as its most highly evolved attribute, most biologists have adopted "an 'organismic' position which holds that while organisms are one with nature in being composed of matter, there is 'something more' which is yet not disjunctive with matter."[144] Thus, if education is to address the problem of fostering the development of the child, it must deal with that "something more." It must impart to each child the knowledge that it is his nature to be within the world and yet to transcend it; that of all things, man is the vehicle of the evolution of the universe and the highest expression of dynamic unity in all existence—an expression which constitutes the process of his becoming.

But how can our schools be reconstituted to facilitate and support that process? To provide each child with the experience and knowledge that will ultimately enable him to direct the process of his own becoming and to cope with the tests and difficulties he must face as he strives to transcend himself and change his world, we need a *mise-en-scène*, a guide, a theory that explains the nature of becoming, a theory of development.[145] Without such a theory, there is little hope that our own advancement can be deliberately directed with any consistency and predictability.

---

[144] Dale B. Harris, "Problems in Formulating a Scientific Concept of Development," in Dale B. Harris, ed., *The Concept of Development: An Issue in the Study of Human Behavior* (Minneapolis: Univ. of Minnesota Press, 1957), p. 4.

[145] The word "mise-en'scène" comes from the theatre and refers to a production scheme through which the director breathes life into a text, thereby transforming the written word into the poetry of a total theater experience for both performer and audience.

The ANISA Model is a blueprint for a new comprehensive educational system. It is based on a philosophy that defines man as a spiritual being and a coherent body of theory concerning development, curriculum, teaching, and administration consistent with the philosophy. The New England Program in Teacher Education, Durham, New Hampshire, has provided $242,000 toward the development of the Model currently being undertaken at the Center for the Study of Human Potential, School of Education, University of Massachusetts, at Amherst.

Education today lacks that theory. Although child psychology possesses a vast body of information, the field is relatively deficient in explanatory theory. As Paul Henry Mussen, John Janeway Conger, and Jerome Kagan lament:

> There is no single comprehensive theory encompassing the vast body of accumulated data in the field of developmental psychology. A complete theory would have to include explanatory concepts accounting for the origins, as well as the mechanisms of development and change, of all aspects of psychological functioning––motor, cognitive, emotional, and social. It may be impossible to construct such an ideal theory; certainly no one has accomplished it yet.[146]

That no one has accomplished it yet is perhaps understandable; that so few have even attempted it is lamentable.

Of the few theoretical attempts that have been made, most have assumed a final state or culmination in development. Such

---

[146] Paul Henry Mussen, John Janeway Conger, and Jerome Kagan, *Child Development and Personality*, 3rd ed. (New York: Harper, 1969), p. 16.

closed-system models do not adequately explain the dynamic process of development because they give no satisfactory explanation of novelty or creativity. We believe this to be a serious weakness because it fails to account for one of the most fundamental characteristics of development, its very open-endedness. Furthermore, most of the descriptions of human life developed to date seem to leave almost no room for the kind of self-determination that can transcend the programming of family, culture, and tradition. In other words the possibility of what Whitehead calls the "creative advance into novelty" has been ignored.[147] The phenomenon of transcendence has been disregarded.

For a theory of development to be useful, it must explain the phenomenon of transcendence and be applicable to all men; it must be able to

> identify the sequential steps between two levels of maturity, to explain how one is transformed into the other, to discover the variables that effect the transformation, the factors that either facilitate or retard its occurrence, and the uniformities and differences by which it is characterized.[148]

To be comprehensive, it must arise from a philosophy that incorporates a view of man full enough and rich enough to account for and illumine the concrete experience we have of our own transformation over time as we interact with the environment. The ANISA theory of development is derived from just such a philosophy.[149]

---

[147] Alfred N. Whitehead, *Process and Reality: An Essay in Cosmology* (New York: Macmillan, 1969), pp. 41, 151.

[148] David P. Ausubel and Edmund V. Sullivan, *Theory and Problems of Child Development* (New York: Grune & Stratton, 1970), p. 3.

[149] Daniel C. Jordan and Raymond P. Shepard, "The Philosophy of the ANISA Model," *World Order*, 7, No. 1. (Fall 1972), 23-31.

ANISA Definition of Development

WE CONSIDER *"development"* synonymous with the process of becoming––the process of translating potentiality into actuality. It is comprised of any changes which have a continuous direction and which culminate in phases that are qualitatively new.

One of the main philosophical principles underlying the ANISA Model is that "existence" cannot be dissociated from "process." The notions of process and existence presuppose each other. As soon as the notion of process is admitted as basic to an understanding of existence, the idea of potentiality becomes indispensable. Alfred N. Whitehead has written that

> If the universe be interpreted in terms of static actuality, then potentiality vanishes. Everything is just what it is. Succession is mere appearance, rising from the limitation of perception. But if we start with process as fundamental, then the actualities of the present are deriving their characters from the process, and are bestowing their characters upon the future. Immediacy is the realization of the potentialities of the past, and is the storehouse of the potentialities of the future.[150]

There are two basic classes of potentiality, biological and psychological; the character of the actualities of both are derived from biological and psychological processes respectively. A *process* refers to the ordered expression of a potentiality. Much remains to be discovered about the precise nature of that ordered expression. E. S. Gollin has thus defined the primary task of developmental research as providing observations which will be useful in clarifying the

---

[150] Alfred N. Whitehead, *Modes of Thought* (New York: Free Press, 1968), pp. 99-100.

character and properties of central *processes* and in establishing their role in the determination of functional relationships throughout development.[151] (Emphasis added)

There are, no doubt, an infinite number of potentialities, each one of which may become actualized (i.e., translated into a power of the organism) through a process. We have no way of determining them all. Instead we must identify those processes which are central—those which have the greatest importance for the subsequent life of the individual. The importance of a process is defined by two criteria: (1) the degree to which it engenders effectance (i.e., the degree of control over the environment it brings to the organism), and (2) the extent to which it is fundamental to other processes (i.e., the extent to which it creates or extends potentiality).[152]

Processes themselves are initiated and maintained through interaction with the environment. This point of view is a central thesis in behavior genetics and brings a fresh perspective to the controversy over whether the underlying growth of organisms is due to external (environmental) or internal (genetic) causes. The

---

[151] E. S. Gollin, "Developmental Approach to Learning and Cognition," in Lewis P. Lipsitt and C. Spiker, *Advances in Child Development and Behavior*, II (New York: Academic Press, 1965), 161.

[152] Robert White introduced the word "effectance" in his seminal paper on competence and motivation. He wrote: "My proposal is that activity, manipulation, and exploration, which are all pretty much of a piece in the infant, be considered together as aspects of competence, and that for the present we assume that one general motivational principle lies behind it. The word I have suggested for this motive is effectance because its most characteristic feature is seen in the production of effects upon the environment. At first, these effects may consist of any changes in sensory input that follow upon activity or exertion, but before long the child becomes able to intend particular changes and to be content only with these." See Robert W. White, "Competence and the Psycho-sexual Stages of Development," in *The Nebraska Symposium on Motivation* (Lincoln: Univ. of Nebraska Press, 1960), pp. 102-03. See also White, "Motivation Reconsidered: The Concept of Competence," *Psychological Review*, 66, No. 5 (1959), 297-333.

dichotomy between heredity and environmental influences is not a useful or realistic distinction. It is more productive to understand how the expression of genetic endowment presupposes environmental influences and why the nature of environmental pressures cannot be understood apart from the genetic predisposition of the organism and the modification of the environment due to the organism's presence within it.

This reinterpretation has major implications for the study of development, shifting the focus of inquiry away from the study of innate vs. acquired characteristics as separate elements and concentrating rather upon the nature of the interaction between the organism and its environment. The quality of the interaction determines, in large part, the quality of the expression and therefore has extensive implications for the definition of teaching and a curriculum rationale. If the basic proposition in the ANISA theory of development is the definition of development as the processes of translating potentiality into actuality––processes which are sustained by interacting with the environment––the theory must define the nature of potentiality and actuality, explain the meaning of environment, and disclose the essentials of interaction. We thus proceed by classification of the phenomena under consideration and definition of the key terms used to explain relationships among them.

Classification of Potentialities

As NOTED ABOVE, we have established two basic categories of potentialities–– biological and psychological. The ANISA theory of development fixes nutrition as the primary element in actualizing biological potentialities and identifies learning as the main factor in the actualization of psychological potentialities.

The assimilation of nutrients and oxygen from the external environment is the basic form of interaction that sustains the processes underlying the release of biological potentialities. If the interaction and the environments are right and if there are no genetic deficiencies, the biological integrity of the organism will be safeguarded. Without that integrity psychological potentialities cannot be developed fully. The implications for education should be fairly obvious.[153]

The psychological potentialities of man have been organized into five categories: psychomotor, perceptual, cognitive, affective, and volitional. We have identified what we believe to be the central processes that underlie learning competence in each category and are the means through which these potentialities become actualized. The ANISA Model is functionally defined by specifications which have been written on each process. These specifications form the basis of the process aspect of the curriculum and are the foundation for the ANISA competency-based teacher preparation program.[154]

We believe the quality of any educational system of the future will be determined by the extent to which it can help children translate potentiality into actuality––a process Whitehead describes as "concrescence." Concrescence not only includes everything normally conveyed by the word development but goes beyond it to encompass man's unique ability to go beyond himself––the ability to accumulate the past and bring it to bear on the present while structuring the future, thereby moving perpetually beyond any present state of being. Learning is the means of that "moving beyond" –– the "creative advance into novelty."

Without learning competence, it will become increasingly difficult to cope with the rapidity of social change. Without learning

---

[153] See S. P. Raman, "Nutrition and Release of Human Potential: Implications and Challenges for Educational Planning," *World Order*, 7, No. 3 (Spring 1973), 27-35, for a fuller discussion.

[154] See Donald T. Streets and Daniel C. Jordan, "Guiding the Process of Becoming: The ANISA Theories of Curriculum and Teaching," on pages 29-40 of this issue of *World Order*, for a detailed explanation of how the theory of development translates into teaching practice and curriculum development.

competence "future shock" will become a more pervasive, destructive force. Without learning competence, we will not only lose control over evolution but will likely atrophy and regress ourselves.

Any educational system staffed with teachers who do not have a clear understanding of the nature of learning competence and its power in facilitating the release of potentialities is not assuming responsibility for preparing its students to shape their own destinies and manage the future wisely.

Classification of Environments

DEVELOPMENT never occurs in a vacuum. It is always the result of an organism's interaction with an environment. Since the nature of the interaction is determined not only by the organism but also by the kind of environment, it is necessary to gain some conceptual clarity about the nature of the environment. We have thus established four classifications of environments:

A. *The Physical Environment*. This includes everything except human beings. It can be broken down into three sub-categories: mineral, vegetable, and animal.

B. *The Human Environment*. This includes all human beings.

C. *The Unknowns*. The ability to know when we do not know is a natural phenomenon associated with consciousness. Ordinarily we feel compelled to find out how we are related to unknowns; we have curiosity built into us.

These three categories—the physical environment, the human environment, and the unknowns—are hierarchically conceived. The human environment contains physical matter; and both the physical and human environments have unknown aspects to them. There is, though, a fourth environment.

D. The Self. The physical, the human, and the unknown environments are all represented in the self. The body is composed of physical elements; the self we are discussing is a human self, and the unknowns in a Self include its as yet unexpressed potentialities, its future, and the phenomenon of its own personal mortality. The self is a special case of the human environment, special because for a particular person it becomes the most constant aspect of his total environment. It can never be abandoned or left behind. Though constantly present, it also is changing. Whitehead reminds us that process and a Self require each other; in separation all meaning evaporates and neither can be understood. The forms of process derive their character from the individuals involved and the environments in which they exist; the characters of the individuals can only be understood in terms of the process in which they are implicated.

As the self interacts with the environment, its potentialities (expressed through the processes) are actualized––that is, they become powers. Because development is ordered, these powers are not expressed in random fashion; they are structured. And as they are structured, factual information (which, for the most part, is the culture being transmitted to the next generation) is fused and structured with them to form the attitudes and values which constitute the character and personality of the human being. The norms of a culture appear in the values (structuring) of personalities that make up the society in which the culture inheres. Thus there is a definite, though not complete, congruence or isomorphism between personality and culture. When there is a very high degree of congruence, both personalities and the society they comprise will be very stable. There will be a low toleration for innovation and change or creativity will be practically nonexistent. When there is little congruence, both society and the personalities comprising it will be highly unstable. In extreme cases personal identities crumble, and the social system collapses. Thus, novelty by itself is devastating. Potentialities must be ordered as they are actualized, otherwise the power they represent becomes suppressive of further potential. Powers without structures are like rivers without banks; they are destructive.

The basic requirement for releasing the potentialities of individuals and societies at an optimum rate is therefore maintenance of a balance between order and change. Whitehead has explained that

> The art of progress is to preserve order amid change, and to preserve change amid order ...
>
> Order is not sufficient. What is required, is something much more complex. It is order entering upon novelty; so that the massiveness of order does not degenerate into mere repetition; and so that the novelty is always reflected upon a background of system.[155]

The optimal structuring of personality thus reflects the balance between order and change. The structuring occurs in relationship to the various environments with which the self is interacting, including its own self. Thus different value systems reflecting these environments emerge. We can therefore have an effect on the structuring and its rate by arranging the environment in particular ways.

In summary, the development of a Self—the structuring of process fused with content, the formation of values—is the fundamental expression of creativity inherent in all human beings. The quality of this integrated structuring determines personal effectance—its mastery in relating to the environment and thus the capacity for self-transcendence and continuing development.

---

[155] Whitehead, *Process and Reality*, pp. 399-400.

The Rhythm of Development

THE PROCESS of becoming presupposes movement. That movement has a rhythm. The essence of rhythm is pattern and timing. We will deal with pattern first.

Pattern. In development, pattern is reflected in sequence Because development is an orderly process and because we conceive it to be any change which has a continuous direction and which culminates in a phase that is qualitatively new, we define a *developmental sequence* as the order of those changes in an organism that yield relatively permanent but novel increments not only in its structure but in its modes of functioning as well. These changes involve passage through successive stages, each of which presupposes its antecedent and is in turn a prerequisite to its successor. A developmental sequence is said to be *invariant* if the order of passage through its successive stages is universally constant. A *stage* is a section of a developmental sequence circumscribing a basic unit of change in an organism. In the actualization of both biological and psychological potentialities, a stage––the basic unit of change––consists of differentiation and integration. In psychological expressions, a sub-stage, generalization, is added. The most obvious example of this on the biological level is the differentiation of cells and their integration into particular organs, bones, or tissues.

In our efforts to define these sub-stages on the psychological level, we reviewed the major theories of learning and development and found the processes of differentiation, integration, and generalization common to and implicit in all of them. These then became the attributes of a single stage in the expression of psychological potentialities; and the conscious ability to differentiate, integrate, and generalize aspects of experience became the criterion for judging learning competence.

Differentiation is the ability to break down experience, whether internal or external, into separate contrastable elements. *Integration* is

HARRY P. MASSOTH

the ability to combine those elements in a new way thereby providing new information, new feelings, new skills, and new perceptions which may or may not become expressed immediately in some form of overt behavior. *Generalization* is the ability to utilize that recombination in other situations. Through these processes potentiality is translated into actuality, and another stage is negotiated. Control over them constitutes learning competence.

The processes of differentiation, integration, and generalization are neither random nor haphazard. The orderly process of development is guided by conscious or unconscious intention or subjective aim, which determines what becomes abstracted, and how the abstracted or differentiated elements are then integrated and generalized. In other words, purpose inheres in subjective aim and has effects on the material world as well as on the structuring of personality.[156]

The changes that occur in the growing human being can only be comprehended in their entirety if development is regarded as a continuum, sequence being the general hierarchical pattern in which this creative advance into novelty is accomplished. The development of a human being depends on a combination of a genetically determined series of stages, which he has in common with his biological ancestors, and processes of learning that provide the means by which new stages with new properties can be developed over a single lifetime.

Completing one stage prepares the organism for the next stage in the sequence. Higher units acquire new properties in the same sense as the combination of hydrogen and oxygen under certain conditions

---

[156] The function of purpose in development has been the single most troublesome issue confronting theorists. Whitehead's organismic approach deals with both efficient and final causes and thus deals with both mechanistic (deterministic) and organismic (teleological) issues. For a further discussion of the problem see Ernest Nagel, "Determinism and Development," in Harris, ed., *The Concept of Development*, pp. 15-24, and Margaret A. Boden, *Purposive Explanation in Psychology* (Cambridge: Harvard Univ. Press, 1972).

leads to a new substance, water, with new properties that were not manifest in either of the separate constituents. It is a basic characteristic of the hierarchy that each higher level is related to the next lower level by what Michael Polanyi calls boundary conditions. The higher level can gain control over the lower level only by controlling the operations which are left open, not completely determined, by the operations at the lower level. A higher level therefore can only come into existence through a process, not manifest at a lower level. Polyani refers to the hierarchical structure of creation, rising from inanimate to the living and on to the subsequent layers of each biotic level, as the process of emergence which has culminated in the reality of man.[157] In Whitehead's terms, the already realized data of the antecedent world forms the basis of the occasion of immediate experience which, when fused with subjective aim or purpose, enables one to transcend that "boundary" and attain a higher level of organizational complexity. In other words, aspiration, ideals, hopes, or sense of purpose cannot be dismissed from a science of man and are essential to any theory of human development.

Timing. The ANISA theory of development emphasizes the importance of timing—the other major aspect of the rhythm of becoming. Though each child actualizes potential within a general pattern shared by all children, regardless of whether he lives on Lake Atitlan in the highlands of northwest Guatemala, near the Ravine of Pirre in the mountainous northeast corner of Uganda, or within walking distance of Harvard Square in Cambridge, he does so according to his own unique timetable and in his own unique style.

The dimension of time is an intrinsic property of process; it is a crucial factor in releasing potentialities at an optimum rate. The idea is not new. Plato, Quintilian, Plutarch, Pestalozzi, Huarte, Fenelon, Watts, Fordyce, Vives, Comenius, Rousseau, Montessori, and Neill,

---

[157] Michael Polanyi, *Personal Knowledge: Towards a Post-Critical Philosophy* (Chicago: Univ. of Chicago Press, 1960), pp. 393-405.

to name but a few, were aware that timing played a role; and each contributed to the understanding of the importance of that role.

Gradually evidence that there are different categories of timing in the expression of both biological and psychological potentialities has accumulated. A *sensitive period* is a limited period during which an organism is particularly amenable to certain experiences that will usually bring about significant and lasting changes in tissue growth physiological functioning, and/or psychological functioning. Maria Montessori claims to be the first to "discover the sensitive periods of infancy and make use of them from the standpoint of education," and attributes her interest to the Dutch biologist Hugo deVries.[158]

With the advent of experimental embryology, Dareste, at the turn of the century, and Stockard, some thirty years later, suggested that, if the susceptibility to a particular developmental modifier is limited only to the sensitive period and if the presence or absence of that modifier during the sensitive period results in permanent damage or change, the sensitive period should be designated a *critical period*.

The existence of sensitive and critical periods in biological development is well established. For example, the effects of the tranquilizer Thalidomide and the disease rubella on unborn children at specific times are now well known.

Another kind of sensitive period is reflected in growth spurts. The growth spurt associated with adolescence is apparent to all of us. What is not so well known is the clearly established relationship between the rhythm of growth in stature, skeletal maturation, and the development of the reproductive system. In normal girls, for instance, the menarche generally occurs during the period immediately following the year of maximum incremental growth in height. These periods are associated with a variety of psychological phenomena and therefore have many educational implications.

---

[158] Maria Montessori, *The Secret of Childhood*, trans. Barbara Barclay Carter (Bombay: Longmans, 1966), pp. 35-36.

Other forms of sensitive periods can be identified within different "biological rhythms." Such rhythms underlie most of what we assume to be constant in ourselves. We are usually unaware that our body temperature, blood pressure, pulse and respiration rates, blood sugar, hemoglobin, and amino acid levels are changing in a circadian rhythm. Adrenal hormones in our blood and concentrations of essential biochemicals throughout our nervous system fluctuate periodically. Smoothness of function seems to depend upon a high degree of integration among these "circadian production lines." Inside we know we are different from one hour of the day to the next. Our strength varies, depending upon biological time of day; our capacity to perform well on tests, for instance, varies as do many other psychological capacities. We also have various monthly, seasonal, and annual cycles.

The appearance of sensitive and critical periods in psychological development, while indicated, has not yet been fully documented. It must be kept in mind that, while these periods in biological development may appear in all children at roughly the same age, in psychological development these periods appear at times generally unique to the individual. For the most part modern researchers and theorists are very cautious about ascribing criticality in the sense of "now-or-never" to any given developmental phase or period. Clearly more research must be done.

One special kind of sensitive period occurs with the consolidation of learning at any given level. As noted earlier, with central processes there is an extension of potentiality the moment a generalization has occurred. If the process of actualizing the newly created potentialities is not initiated shortly thereafter, that sensitive period is missed, the development of the next phase is delayed, and a deceleration in the rate potentialities are released occurs. As the growing organism matures, this type of sensitive period, which we call an *acquired* or *transitional* sensitive period, becomes more important from an educational point of view.

The research of Lawrence Kohlberg and others suggests that those who have failed to develop for a period of time are more likely to become locked in or fixed at the level at which they have stopped.[159] Accordingly, one of the aims of the ANISA Model is to stimulate transition to the next stage of development before a child gets locked in at his present stage. The child can learn for himself how to identify these sensitive periods by developing an inner awareness of the state of his own consolidation of learning which enables him to prepare for the next stage. This means knowing when mere repetition of a generalization has become stifling and when it is time to introduce variation by re-differentiating, re-integrating, and generalizing on another level.

Thus timing and all of its manifestations in the organism's interaction with its environments is an important factor in the actualization of both biological and psychological potentialities.

Educational Implications

THE IMPLICATIONS for education that ANISA's theory of development portends are vast and varied. From the theory of development, we have derived two educational sub-theories: a theory of pedagogy and a theory of curriculum.[160] These theories are crucial to the ANISA Model and are not independent of the-theory of development. Indeed their coherence and efficacy depend on their congruence with the theory of development. Together they constitute the basis for extensive but orderly changes in education.

---

[159] Lawrence Kohlberg and Elliot Turiel, "Moral Development and Moral Education," in G. Lesser, ed., *Psychology and Educational Practice* (Chicago: Scott, 1971), pp. 410-65.

[160] See Streets and Jordan, "Guiding the Process of Becoming."

Development has no terminal point; one is in the words of Whitehead, "an incompletion in process of production."[161] We therefore hold that education can have no terminal point. One can continue to develop and advance from the point of conception; and once one becomes a competent learner, the world becomes a beautiful playground and an exciting laboratory for life.

Because each human being has an unlimited number of potentialities, no one can ever be regarded as uneducable. Comprehending how the actualization of potentiality creates further potentialities alters perceptions and feelings about all children and enables one to approach teaching much differently. Furthermore, it challenges the notion of "fixed intelligence" as an outmoded concept that must give away to a more dynamic and comprehensive theory of intelligence. Schools modeled on the ANISA theory of development will have teachers who can arrange environments and guide interaction with them so that children will become competent learners. And because the theory explains the ways children are similar and the ways they are unique, true individualization of instruction––the matching of particular learning experiences to a child's specific developmental level––can be accomplished. Thus, the ability to equalize educational opportunity is finally at hand.

The symbolic meaning of ANISA ––"The Tree of Life" –– with its connotation of perpetual fruition and beauty is reflected in the theory of development. Each child is a precious sapling in the process of progressively manifesting his beauty –– the fruits of his efforts at self-actualization––in association with his peers and teachers. But only those who have seen the forest and come away with a deep appreciation of the oneness of the trees, coupled with an abiding respect for the uniqueness of each tree, will be commissioned to teach in an ANISA school. For only then will they be empowered to impart that vision with a method that will ensure the creative advance of our children.

---

[161] Whitehead, *Process and Reality*, p. 248.

SELECTIVE BIBLIOGRAPHY

'Abdu'l-Bahá. *Foundations of World Unity*. Wilmette, Ill.: Bahá'í Publishing Trust, 1945.

——. *Paris Talks: Addresses Given by 'Abdu'l-Bahá in Paris in 1911-1912*. 11ᵗʰ ed. London: Bahá'í Publishing Trust, 1969.

——. *The Promulgation of Universal Peace: Discourses by 'Abdu'l-Bahá during His Visit to the United States in 1912*. Rpt. in 1 vol. Wilmette, Ill.: Bahá'í i Publishing Committee, 1943.

——. "Recent Tablets from 'Abdu'l-Bahá to American Bahá'ís: Ella Quant." *Star of the West*, 10 (November 4, 1919), 250-51.

——. "Recent Tablets from 'Abdu'l-Bahá to American Bahá'ís: Martha Root." *Star of the West*, 10 (October 16, 1919), 234-36.

——. *The Secret of Divine Civilization*. Translated by Marzieh Gail. Wilmette, Ill.: Bahá'í Publishing Trust, 1970.

——. *Some Answered Questions*. Collected and translated by Laura Clifford Barney. Wilmette, Ill.: Bahá'í Publishing Trust, 1964.

——. *Tablets of 'Abdu'l-Bahá Abbas*. Vol. 2. New York: Bahá'í Publishing Committee, 1940.

——. "There is a power in this Cause ..." *Star of the West*, 7 (June 5, 1916), 34.

—————. "The worst enemies of the Cause are in the Cause." *Star of the West*, 6 (June 24, 1915), 43-45.

Bahá'u'lláh. *Gleanings from the Writings of Bahá'u'lláh*. Translated by Shoghi Effendi. Rev. ed. Wilmette, Ill.: Bahá'í Publishing Trust, 1971.

—————. *The Hidden Words of Bahá'u'lláh*. Translated by Shoghi Effendi. Rev. ed. Wilmette, Ill.: Bahá'í Publishing Trust, 1954.

—————. *The Kitáb-i-Íqán: The Book of Certitude*. Translated by Shoghi Effendi. Wilmette, Ill.: Bahá'í Publishing Trust, 1950.

—————. *Prayers and Meditations*. Translated by Shoghi Effendi. Wilmette. Ill.: Bahá'í Publishing Trust, 1938.

—————. *The Seven Valleys and the Four Valleys*. Translated by Ali-Kuli Khan and Marzieh Gaìl. Wilmette, Ill.: Bahá'í Publishing Trust, 1970.

Bahá'u'lláh, and 'Abdu'l-Bahá. *The Divine Art of Living: Selections from Writings of Bahá'u'lláh and 'Abdu'l-Bahá*. Compiled by Mabel Hyde Paine. Rev. ed. Wilmette, Ill.: Bahá'í Publishing Trust, 1960.

Esslemont, J. E. *Bahá'u'lláh and the New Era: An Introduction to the Bahá'í Faith*. 3rd rev. ed. Wilmette, Ill.: Bahá'í Publishing Trust, 1970.

Grundy, Julia M. *Ten Days in the Light of Acca*. Chicago: Bahá'í Publishing Society, 1907.

Jordan, Daniel, C. *The Meaning of Deepening*. Wilmette, Ill.: Bahá'í Publishing Trust, 1973.

Rúḥíyyih Khánum. "To the Bahá'í Youth." *Bahá'í* News, no. 231, May 1950, pp. 6-8.

Shoghi Effendi. *The Advent of Divine Justice*. Wilmette, Ill.: Bahá'í Publishing Trust, 1969.

Shoghi Effendi. *God Passes By*. Wilmette, Ill.: Bahá'í Publishing Trust, 1944.

------(through his secretary). "Letters from the Guardian: To Individual Believers." *Bahá'í News*, no. 80 (January 1934), pp. 5-6.

------. *Messages to America: Selected Letters and Cablegrams Addressed to the Bahá'ís of North America, 1932-1946*. Wilmette, Ill.: Bahá'í Publishing Committee, 1947.

------. *The World Order of Bahá'u'lláh*. Rev. ed. Wilmette, Ill.: Bahá'í Publishing Trust, 1955.

Universal House of Justice, The, comp. *The Local Spiritual Assembly: An Institution of the Bahá'í Administrative Order*. Wilmette, Ill.: Bahá'í Publishing Trust, n.d.

------. *Wellspring of Guidance: Messages, 1963-1968*. Wilmette, Ill.: Bahá'í Publishing Trust, 1970.

BOOKS TO HELP YOU FIND OUT MORE

- Bahá'u'lláh, *Gleanings for the Writings of Bahá'u'lláh*: This is a broad selection of Bahá'u'lláh's writings, compiled and translated by Shoghi Effendi. It provides very substantive quotations on a wide range of subjects, organized into five major areas, including the Day of God, the purpose of God's Messengers and the nature of the soul.
- Bahá'u'lláh, *The Hidden Words*: This short book contains about a hundred and fifty brief meditations that are said to contain the essence of all spiritual truth.
- *Bahá'u'lláh's Teachings on Spiritual Reality*: This compilation includes writings on spiritual growth, service, God, the nature of the soul, immortality, evolution, and many practical as well as metaphysical questions.
- 'Abdu'l-Bahá, *Some Answered Questions*: These are 'Abdu'l-Bahá's answers to questions asked over dinner by a Western Bahá'í visiting the Holy Land. The topics include life after death, the nature of the soul, evolution, the Trinity, the virgin birth, free will, the return of Christ, prophecies, and dozens of other spiritual and metaphysical questions.
- Willian Sears, *Thief in the Night*: This is the most popular exploration of Christian prophecies that points to Bahá'u'lláh; it includes both spiritual prophecies and a

surprising number of prophecies that appear to have been fulfilled literally.

- William Hatcher and Douglas Martin, *The Bahá'í Faith: The Emerging Global Religion*: This is a definitive history of the Bahá'í Faith that traces its history from the mid-eighteen-hundreds to the present and discusses its teachings and principles.

- John S. Hatcher, *Close Connections: The Bridge between Spiritual and Physical Reality:* This book, written by a Bahá'í philosopher of renown, explores the questions of just what is the purpose of physical reality and how does physical reality allow us to gain insights into spiritual reality including life after death and the evolution of the soul.

- Justice St. Rain, *My Bahá'í Faith*: A personal tour of the Bahá'í teachings by a Bahá'í of long standing who writes from his own perspective on what the Bahá'í Faith has meant to him.

- Reinee Pasarow. *Answers from Heaven:* The book tells of the extraordinary near-death experiences of Reinee Pasarow and how they affected her life.

- The Universal House of Justice, *The Promise of World Peace*: A letter sent to the peoples of the world on the occasion of the International Year of Peace (1985) that provides an overview of the Bahá'í vision for world peace and a sustainable planetary system.

Where to Get Them

These books and many more can be purchased through the Bahá'í Distribution service at 1-800-999-9019 or through Special Ideas at 1-800-326-1197.

To find a Bahá'í community near you, call: 1-800-22-UNITE (228-6483).